GDP/11:

Your complete learning system. Your guide to success.

ONE SOFTWARE. ONE SYSTEM. ONE SOLUTION.

INTEGRATED SYSTEM

Together, the book and software systematically lead students through each lesson.

Cohesive system to provide an easy path to success.

ONLINE SOFTWARE

New! Online functionality. Same program, now Web-based! Partial local installation option allows typing exercises to be downloaded and completed offline.

Greater accessibility for use at home, in class, and in labs – perfect for distance learning!

Easy-to-use interface.

Seamless updates.

Automatic keyboarding and formatting error scoring.

For more information, please visit us at
www.mhhe.com/gdp11

Selected Lessons from

GREGG
College Keyboarding
AND DOCUMENT PROCESSING

Eleventh Edition
Lessons 61-120

Scot Ober
Ball State University

Jack E. Johnson
University of West Georgia

Arlene Zimmerly
Los Angeles City College

PORTLAND COMMUNITY COLLEGE
CAS 123

Boston   Burr Ridge, IL   Dubuque, IA   New York   San Francisco   St. Louis
Bangkok   Bogotá   Caracas   Lisbon   London   Madrid
Mexico City   Milan   New Delhi   Seoul   Singapore   Sydney   Taipei   Toronto

Selected Lessons from
Gregg College Keyboarding and Document Processing, Eleventh Edition Lessons 61-120
Portland Community College : CAS 123

This book is a McGraw-Hill Learning Solutions textbook and contains select material from *Gregg College Keyboarding & Document Processing, Lessons 61–120*, Eleventh Edition byScot Ober, Jack E. Johnson, and Arlene Zimmerly. Copyright © 2011, 2008, 2006, 2002, 1997, 1994, 1989, 1984, 1979, 1970, 1964, 1957 by The McGraw-Hill Companies, Inc. Reprinted with permission of the publisher. Many custom published texts are modified versions or adaptations of our best-selling textbooks. Some adaptations are printed in black and white to keep prices at a minimum, while others are in color.

2 3 4 5 6 7 8 9 0 BRP BRP 15 14

ISBN-13: 978-0-07-777159-1
ISBN-10: 0-07-777159-1
Part of
ISBN-13: 978-0-07-777160-7
ISBN-10: 0-07-777160-5

Learning Solutions Consultant: Michelle Payne
Learning Solutions Specialist: Kelly Casey
Production Editor: Carrie Brown
Printer/Binder: BR Printing

Welcome to
Gregg College Keyboarding & Document Processing   11th Edition

Your complete learning/teaching *system*
Your guide to success

Textbook

Word Manual

GDP (Gregg Document Processing)
Web-Based Software

Instructor Wraparound Edition

Online GDP Software
New! Online functionality
Same program; *now* Web-based

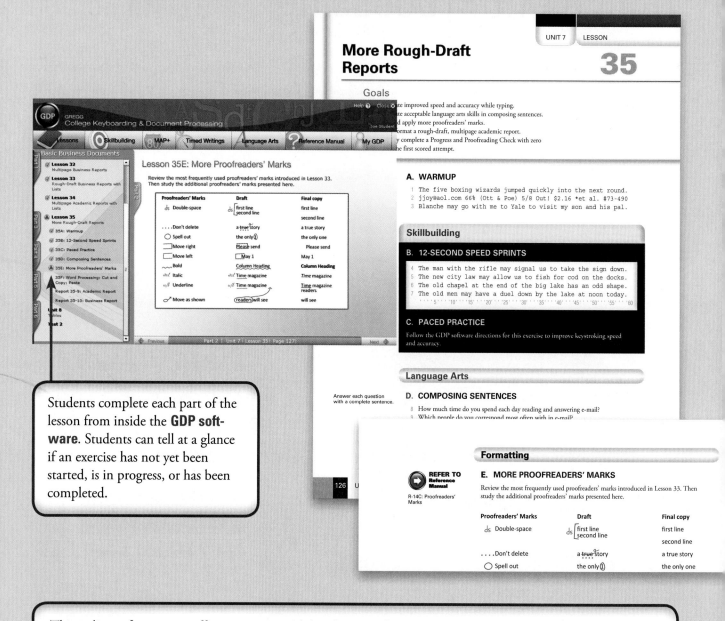

Students complete each part of the lesson from inside the **GDP software**. Students can tell at a glance if an exercise has not yet been started, is in progress, or has been completed.

This online software now offers greater accessibility for use at home, in class, and in labs—perfect for distance learning! Its easy-to-use interface makes this system simple for both you and your students . . . so that you spend more time teaching the skills you want, not learning the program. The GDP software also now allows for automatic keystroking and format scoring.

With GDP's new online functionality, updates are now seamless.

MAP+
The best just got better!

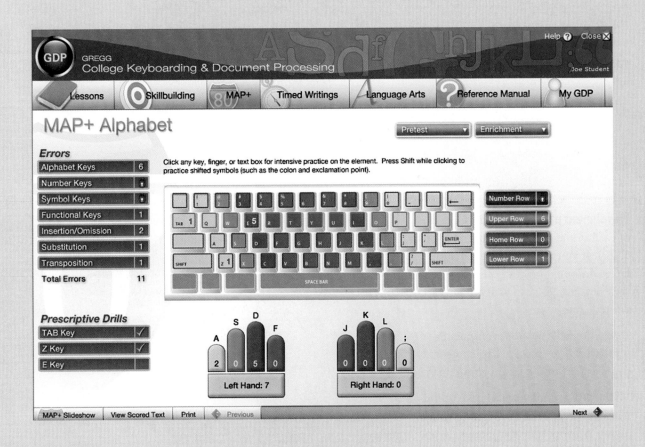

MAP+ (Misstroke Analysis and Prescription) is a *diagnostic tool* within GDP/11 that analyzes each student's pretest misstrokes and prescribes individualized remediation drills based on a powerful new scoring algorithm. MAP+ includes these features:

- **New! Unlimited drill lines**—*Now begin with Lesson 1.*

- **Interactive**—Features a streamlined interactive screen, which allows students to click anywhere for intensive practice on that key or kind of reach.

- **Continuous new drills**—Generate three *new* drill lines every time the student clicks a key or specific reach.

- **New! Deeper content**—Allows students to take a pretest and practice either alphabetic copy, numbers, or numbers and symbols.

- **Integrated**—Is a required part of each unit, although students can access MAP+ at any time from the lesson menu.

New! Enrichment Pages
More drill lines for faster touch-typing skills

Enrichment pages appear at the end of each of the new-key lessons (Lessons 1–20). If you want your students to have additional practice on each of these lessons, you can assign them as desired.

Using the GDP system, you can customize GDP to include Enrichment pages as part of the lesson requirements.

With **MAP+**, students also have unlimited new practice drills—*beginning with Lesson 1*. Every time they access MAP+ for a specific lesson, new drill lines appear that contain only those words students can type up to that point.

Enrichment • Lesson 3

Type each line 2 times.

A. NEW-KEY REINFORCEMENT

O
R
H
1 roost hotfoot solon forefoot loose offshoot odors
2 errs rater refer retro rotor harder roster resort
3 hardhats hasheesh hosanna hotshots rehashed flesh

O
R
H
4 nonfood shook forenoon stood torso onlooker hoots
5 darter terser horror roller eraser roarer errands
6 sheathed shoehorn aha thrasher handshake thrasher

O
R
H
7 shoot foothold forsooth noose stool rodeo tootles
8 narrator restorer tearjerker referral northerners
9 harshness horseshoe hotheaded shorthand threshold

O R H
O R H
O R H
10 rho ashore hoorah hero hereto shorts hoar hoarser
11 hoer holder hora horn honker forth horned shofars
12 frosh throes froth honor heron horror hoard honer

Type each line 2 times.
Do not type the colored vertical lines.

B. SHORT PHRASES

13 a loose shade|eats a short noodle|the rose thorns
14 a tattletale|she sat here|he often jostled a jerk
15 the rest of the lesson|thanks for the short looks

16 the oddest tattoos|those stolen forks|do not jerk
17 the shore floods|she flossed her teeth|jot a note
18 the earth shook hard|had a look|a tenth of a foot

Type each line 2 times.

C. CLAUSES

19 she shared her salad at the hotel near the shore;
20 three deer ran to the dark oak tree near the ark;
21 she had then also looked at the other ten horses;

22 she set all of the stolen art on that tall shelf;
23 take a seat near the dark settee and talk to her;
24 the teal sandals on her feet had soon fallen off;

25 the loose earth on the north and east had fallen;
26 ask her not to take the nonfat food to the stall;
27 the senator held a safe seat and soon left there;

Enrichment • Lesson 3   13

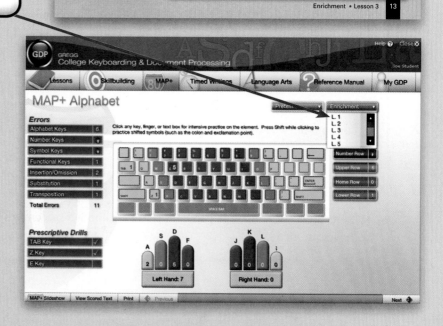

Individualized Skillbuilding
In every lesson

Warmups at the start of each lesson comprise 3 lines. Line 1 is an alphabetic sentence to review all reaches; Line 2 practices a particular type of reach; Line 3 contains easy words to help build speed.

Skillbuilding (building straight-copy speed and accuracy) is built into *every lesson*—15′–20′ of *individualized* skill-building routines.

Each student always practices on the type of drill that is appropriate for him or her and for which the **individualized** goals are challenging—but attainable.

The **timed writings** in every even-numbered lesson are controlled for difficulty, contain all letters of the alphabet, and are the exact length needed to achieve that lesson's speed goal.

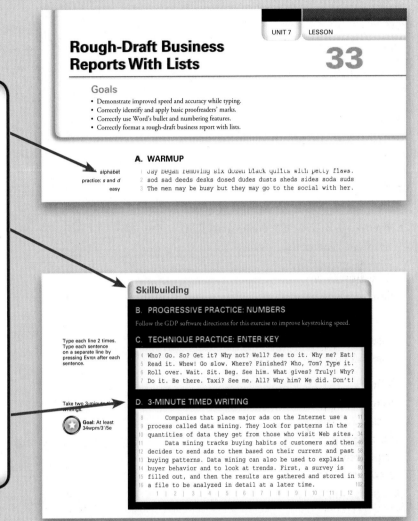

Rough-Draft Business Reports With Lists

UNIT 7   LESSON

33

Goals
- Demonstrate improved speed and accuracy while typing.
- Correctly identify and apply basic proofreaders' marks.
- Correctly use Word's bullet and numbering features.
- Correctly format a rough-draft business report with lists.

A. WARMUP

alphabet   1 Jay began removing six dozen black quilts with petty flaws.
practice: s and d   2 sod sad deeds desks dosed dudes dusts sheds sides soda suds
easy   3 The men may be busy but they may go to the social with her.

Skillbuilding

B. PROGRESSIVE PRACTICE: NUMBERS
Follow the GDP software directions for this exercise to improve keystroking speed.

C. TECHNIQUE PRACTICE: ENTER KEY

Type each line 2 times. Type each sentence on a separate line by pressing ENTER after each sentence.

4 Who? Go. So? Get it? Why not? Well? See to it. Why me? Eat!
5 Read it. Whew! Go slow. Where? Finished? Who, Tom? Type it.
6 Roll over. Wait. Sit. Beg. See him. What gives? Truly! Why?
7 Do it. Be there. Taxi? See me. All? Why him? We did. Don't!

D. 3-MINUTE TIMED WRITING

Take two 3-minute writings.

Goal: At least 34wpm/3′/5e

8   Companies that place major ads on the Internet use a   11
9 process called data mining. They look for patterns in the   22
10 quantities of data they get from those who visit Web sites.   34
11   Data mining tracks buying habits of customers and then 46
12 decides to send ads to them based on their current and past 58
13 buying patterns. Data mining can also be used to explain   69
14 buyer behavior and to look at trends. First, a survey is   80
15 filled out, and then the results are gathered and stored in 92
16 a file to be analyzed in detail at a later time.   102
   1 | 2 | 3 | 4 | 5 | 6 | 7 | 8 | 9 | 10 | 11 | 12

Language Arts
A critical document processing skill

Language arts (punctuation rules, usage, proofreading, composing, and spelling) are systematically covered. Short, easy-to-grasp exercises are incorporated throughout Lessons 21–120 with increasing difficulty.

The rules are presented, practiced, and then illustrated in the documents that students type in that lesson—for immediate reinforcement.

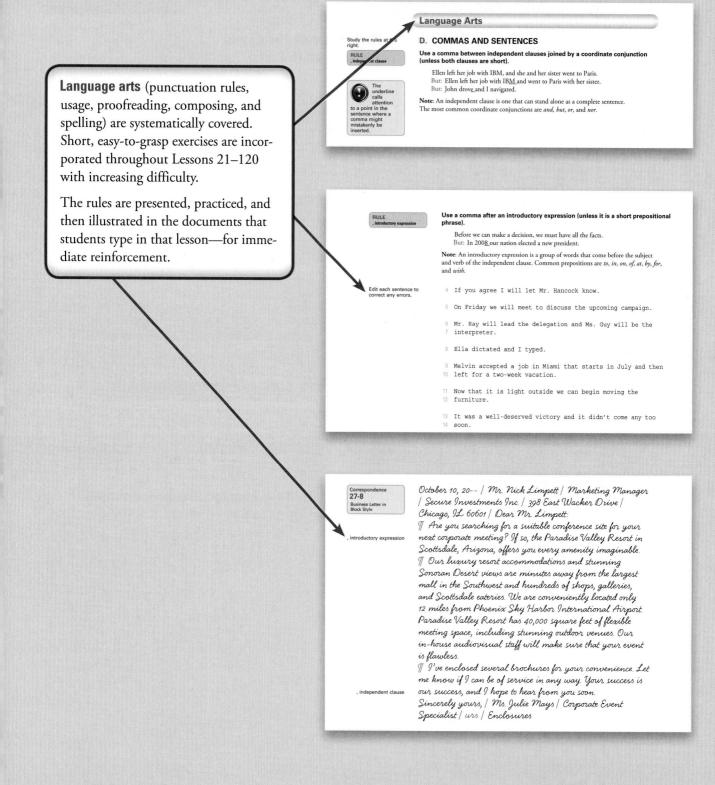

Language Arts

Study the rules at the right.

RULE
, independent clause

The underline calls attention to a point in the sentence where a comma might mistakenly be inserted.

D. COMMAS AND SENTENCES

Use a comma between independent clauses joined by a coordinate conjunction (unless both clauses are short).

Ellen left her job with IBM, and she and her sister went to Paris.
But: Ellen left her job with IBM and went to Paris with her sister.
But: John drove and I navigated.

Note: An independent clause is one that can stand alone as a complete sentence. The most common coordinate conjunctions are *and, but, or,* and *nor*.

RULE
, introductory expression

Use a comma after an introductory expression (unless it is a short prepositional phrase).

Before we can make a decision, we must have all the facts.
But: In 2008 our nation elected a new president.

Note: An introductory expression is a group of words that come before the subject and verb of the independent clause. Common prepositions are *to, in, on, of, at, by, for,* and *with*.

Edit each sentence to correct any errors.

4   If you agree I will let Mr. Hancock know.

5   On Friday we will meet to discuss the upcoming campaign.

6   Mr. Ray will lead the delegation and Ms. Guy will be the
7   interpreter.

8   Ella dictated and I typed.

9   Melvin accepted a job in Miami that starts in July and then
10 left for a two-week vacation.

11 Now that it is light outside we can begin moving the
12 furniture.

13 It was a well-deserved victory and it didn't come any too
14 soon.

Correspondence
27-8
Business Letter in Block Style

, introductory expression

, independent clause

October 10, 20-- / Mr. Nick Limpett / Marketing Manager / Secure Investments Inc. / 398 East Wacker Drive / Chicago, IL 60601 / Dear Mr. Limpett:
¶ Are you searching for a suitable conference site for your next corporate meeting? If so, the Paradise Valley Resort in Scottsdale, Arizona, offers you every amenity imaginable.
¶ Our luxury resort accommodations and stunning Sonoran Desert views are minutes away from the largest mall in the Southwest and hundreds of shops, galleries, and Scottsdale eateries. We are conveniently located only 12 miles from Phoenix Sky Harbor International Airport. Paradise Valley Resort has 40,000 square feet of flexible meeting space, including stunning outdoor venues. Our in-house audiovisual staff will make sure that your event is flawless.
¶ I've enclosed several brochures for your convenience. Let me know if I can be of service in any way. Your success is our success, and I hope to hear from you soon.
Sincerely yours, / Ms. Julie Mays / Corporate Event Specialist / urs / Enclosures

New! Expanded Ten-Key Practice

Students learn to touch-type the entire ten-key pad—a frequent job requirement. After Lesson 20, a new **Ten-Key Numeric Keypad** supplementary lesson teaches the touch typing of both the number keys *and the arithmetic operators* (+ - * and /)—for a total of 55 new lines of drills.

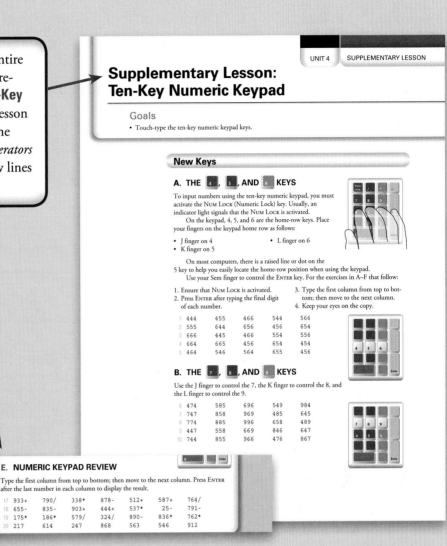

UNIT 4   SUPPLEMENTARY LESSON

Supplementary Lesson: Ten-Key Numeric Keypad

Goals
- Touch-type the ten-key numeric keypad keys.

New Keys

A. THE 4, 5, AND 6 KEYS

To input numbers using the ten-key numeric keypad, you must activate the NUM LOCK (Numeric Lock) key. Usually, an indicator light signals that the NUM LOCK is activated.

On the keypad, 4, 5, and 6 are the home-row keys. Place your fingers on the keypad home row as follows:

- J finger on 4
- K finger on 5
- L finger on 6

On most computers, there is a raised line or dot on the 5 key to help you easily locate the home-row position when using the keypad.

Use your Sem finger to control the ENTER key. For the exercises in A–F that follow:

1. Ensure that NUM LOCK is activated.
2. Press ENTER after typing the final digit of each number.
3. Type the first column from top to bottom; then move to the next column.
4. Keep your eyes on the copy.

1	444	455	466	544	566
2	555	644	656	456	654
3	666	445	466	554	556
4	664	665	456	654	454
5	464	546	564	655	456

B. THE 7, 8, AND 9 KEYS

Use the J finger to control the 7, the K finger to control the 8, and the L finger to control the 9.

6	474	585	696	549	984
7	747	858	969	485	645
8	774	885	996	658	489
9	447	558	669	846	647
10	744	855	966	476	867

E. NUMERIC KEYPAD REVIEW

Type the first column from top to bottom; then move to the next column. Press ENTER after the last number in each column to display the result.

17	933+	790/	338*	878-	512+	587+	764/
18	655-	835-	903+	444+	537*	25-	791-
19	175*	186*	579/	324/	890-	836*	762*
20	217	614	247	868	563	546	912

Word Processing Commands
Introduced on a *need-to-know* basis

Word processing commands are introduced when they are needed to format a particular job (in this lesson, students need to learn the Italic and Underline commands).

Students are referred to the corresponding lesson in the *Word Manual*, which contains step-by-step directions, with screen shots and practice exercises so that students don't get lost.

When students finish the practice exercises in the *Word Manual*, they are referred back to the text.

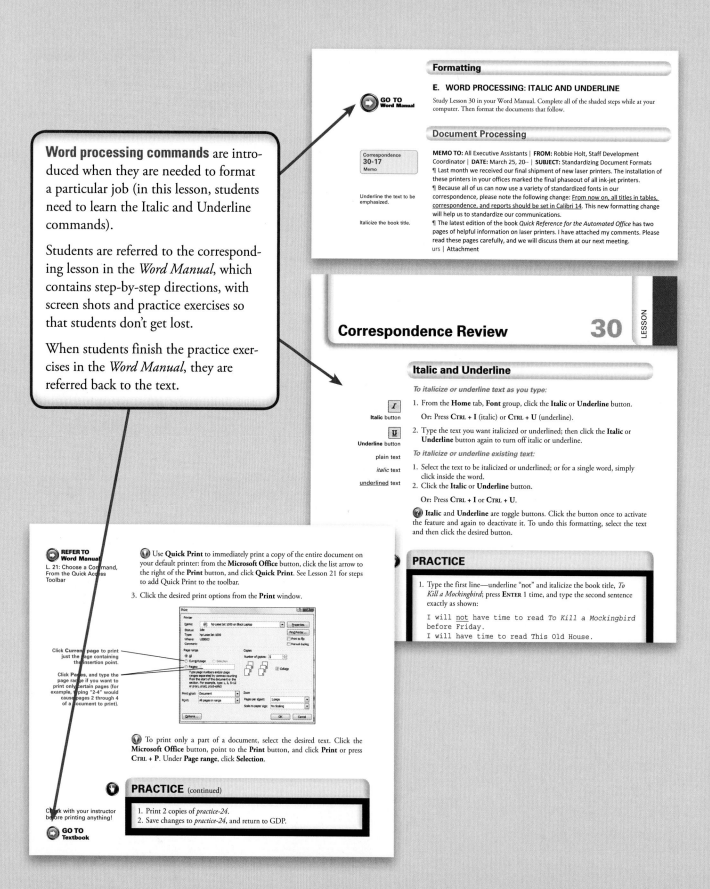

GO TO Word Manual

Formatting

E. WORD PROCESSING: ITALIC AND UNDERLINE

Study Lesson 30 in your Word Manual. Complete all of the shaded steps while at your computer. Then format the documents that follow.

Document Processing

Correspondence 30-17 Memo

Underline the text to be emphasized.

Italicize the book title.

MEMO TO: All Executive Assistants | **FROM:** Robbie Holt, Staff Development Coordinator | **DATE:** March 25, 20-- | **SUBJECT:** Standardizing Document Formats

¶ Last month we received our final shipment of new laser printers. The installation of these printers in your offices marked the final phaseout of all ink-jet printers.

¶ Because all of us can now use a variety of standardized fonts in our correspondence, please note the following change: <u>From now on, all titles in tables, correspondence, and reports should be set in Calibri 14</u>. This new formatting change will help us to standardize our communications.

¶ The latest edition of the book *Quick Reference for the Automated Office* has two pages of helpful information on laser printers. I have attached my comments. Please read these pages carefully, and we will discuss them at our next meeting.
urs | Attachment

Correspondence Review
30 LESSON

Italic and Underline

To italicize or underline text as you type:

Italic button ☐ *I*

1. From the **Home** tab, **Font** group, click the **Italic** or **Underline** button.

   Or: Press **CTRL + I** (italic) or **CTRL + U** (underline).

Underline button ☐ **U**

2. Type the text you want italicized or underlined; then click the **Italic** or **Underline** button again to turn off italic or underline.

plain text

italic text

<u>underlined</u> text

To italicize or underline existing text:

1. Select the text to be italicized or underlined; or for a single word, simply click inside the word.
2. Click the **Italic** or **Underline** button.

   Or: Press **CTRL + I** or **CTRL + U.**

❓ **Italic** and **Underline** are toggle buttons. Click the button once to activate the feature and again to deactivate it. To undo this formatting, select the text and then click the desired button.

PRACTICE

1. Type the first line—underline "not" and italicize the book title, *To Kill a Mockingbird*; press **ENTER** 1 time, and type the second sentence exactly as shown:

   ```
   I will not have time to read To Kill a Mockingbird
   before Friday.
   I will have time to read This Old House.
   ```

REFER TO Word Manual

L. 21: Choose a Command, From the Quick Access Toolbar

⬇ Use **Quick Print** to immediately print a copy of the entire document on your default printer: from the **Microsoft Office** button, click the list arrow to the right of the **Print** button, and click **Quick Print**. See Lesson 21 for steps to add Quick Print to the toolbar.

3. Click the desired print options from the **Print** window.

Click **Current page** to print just the page containing the insertion point.

Click **Pages**, and type the page range if you want to print only certain pages (for example, typing "2-4" would cause pages 2 through 4 of a document to print).

⬇ To print only a part of a document, select the desired text. Click the **Microsoft Office** button, point to the **Print** button, and click **Print** or press **CTRL + P.** Under **Page range**, click **Selection.**

⬇ **PRACTICE** (continued)

1. Print 2 copies of *practice-24.*
2. Save changes to *practice-24,* and return to GDP.

Check with your instructor before printing anything!

GO TO Textbook

GDP Instructor Help
Right where you need it!

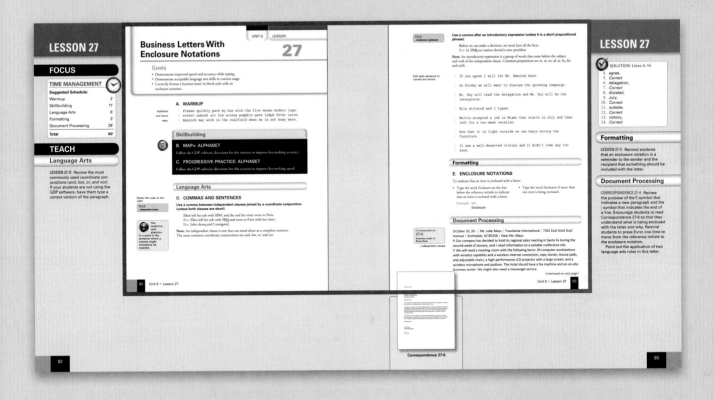

The ***Instructor Wraparound Edition (IWE)*** offers lesson plans and reduced-size student pages (shown in the red border above) to enhance classroom instruction. In addition to a mini-methods section at the front of the *IWE*, the side and bottom panels on each lesson page contain:

- Suggested times for each lesson part

- Miniature copies of the solutions for the documents students type in that lesson

- Solutions to language arts activities

- Marginal teaching notes—right where they are needed

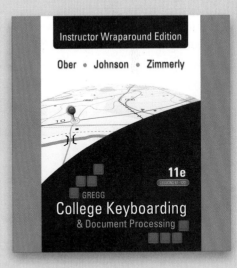

No More Grading Papers!
New! GDP now scores both keystroking and *formatting* errors

Instructors decide whether to have GDP automatically assign a grade to each document—based on parameters they choose—or to assign a grade manually.

GDP goes green. Documents don't need to be printed because they are stored and graded electronically.

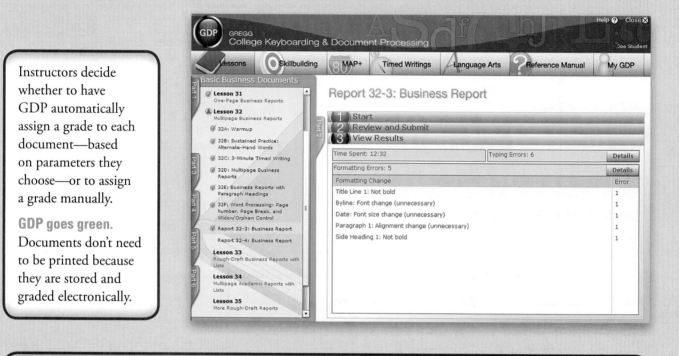

New! The customizable **GPS (Grade Posting System)** gradebook allows complete flexibility in setting up grades—with an easy-to-use, intuitive interface. Students can check their current average at any point in the school term, and instructors can save the gradebook in a comma-delimited format for uploading to Excel or to learning management systems (LMS) such as Blackboard or Angel.

Contents

PART 4
Advanced Formatting

PART 5

Specialized Applications

PART 6

Using and Designing Business Documents

Preface

Gregg College Keyboarding & Document Processing is a multicomponent instructional program designed to give the student and the instructor a high degree of flexibility and a high degree of success in meeting their respective goals. The textbook is offered in several volumes: *Lessons 1–20, Lessons 1–60, Lessons 61–120,* and *Lessons 1–120.* The GDP software is a Web-delivered, PC-compatible program providing complete lesson-by-lesson instruction for each of the 120 text lessons. The document processing *Word Manual,* used in conjunction with the textbook for Lessons 21–120, teaches the document processing skills needed to create efficient business documents using Microsoft Word.

The Kit Format

For student and instructor convenience, the core components of this instructional system—the textbook, the *Word Manual,* and the Gregg College Keyboarding & Document Processing (GDP) software—are available in a variety of kit formats.

Kit 1: Lessons 1–60 This kit, designed for the first keyboarding course, provides the Lessons 1–60 textbook, the *Word Manual,* and an access card to the GDP software. Since this kit is designed for the beginning student, its major objectives are to develop touch control of the keyboard and proper keyboarding techniques, to build basic speed and accuracy, and to provide practice in applying those basic skills to the formatting of e-mails, reports, letters, memos, tables, and other kinds of personal and business communications.

Kit 2: Lessons 61–120 This kit, designed for the second course, provides the Lessons 61–120 textbook, the *Word Manual,* and an access card to the GDP software. This course continues the development of basic keyboarding skills and emphasizes the formatting of various kinds of business correspondence, reports, tables, electronic forms, and desktop publishing projects from arranged, unarranged, handwritten, and rough-draft sources.

Kit 3: Lessons 1–120 This kit, designed for both the first and second course, provides the Lessons 1–120 textbook, the *Word Manual,* and an access card to the GDP software.

Kit 4: Lessons 1–20 This kit, designed for shorter keyboarding courses, provides the Lessons 1–20 text and an access card to the GDP software.

Supporting Materials

Gregg College Keyboarding & Document Processing offers the following instructional materials:

- The special *Instructor Wraparound Edition (IWE)* offers lesson plans and reduced-size student pages to enhance classroom instruction. Distance-learning tips, instructional methodology, adult learner strategies, and special needs features also are included in this wraparound edition. New to this edition are miniature solutions for each document the students type; they are shown in the margins of the IWE.
- The *Tests and Solutions Manual* provides solution keys for all of the formatting in Lessons 25–120 in addition to objective tests and alternative document processing tests for each part.

What's New in the 11th Edition Text?

New-Key Introduction (Lessons 1–20)

- A new Enrichment page has been added to each of the first 20 lessons—for additional practice and faster development of touch-typing skills.
- MAP+ (Misstroke Analysis and Prescription) can now be used beginning with Lesson 1, thus providing unlimited new practice drills for each of the new-key lessons.
- A new supplementary lesson, Ten-Key Numeric Keypad, follows Lesson 20; it teaches the touch typing of both the number keys and arithmetic operators (+, -, /, and *), with 55 new drill lines.
- Only 3 new keys are introduced in each lesson (instead of 4)—to provide more intensive practice on each new key; all keys are still introduced in Lessons 1–20.
- The order in which new keys are introduced has been refined to balance the workload between each hand and to take into consideration how frequently keys are used. For example, in previous editions, the hyphen key was introduced early (in Lesson 6) because students used it for manual word division. With Word's automatic hyphenation feature, students don't use this key as much anymore, and the hyphen is now introduced in Lesson 11.

Skillbuilding

- MAP+ now provides an analysis and prescription of the number and symbol keys (previously, only alphabetic reaches were included). Because of this, (a) Diagnostic Practice: Symbols and Punctuation and (b) Diagnostic Practice: Numbers have been removed.
- Every Warmup exercise has been revised. Line 1 of each Warmup is now an alphabetic sentence to review all reaches, Line 2 practices a particular type of reach, and Line 3 contains easy words to build speed.

Document Processing

- Formatting correspondence (new Unit 6) is now introduced before formatting reports (new Unit 7).
- The formatting of bulleted/numbered lists in Lesson 33 and table column headings in Lesson 38 has been simplified.
- More e-mail messages are included with added coverage of formatting, such as bulleted lists, tables, and attachments.
- Eleven new Word commands are introduced: Zoom (L. 24), Widow/Orphan Control (L. 32), Table—Align Bottom (L. 38), AutoCorrect—Hyperlink (L. 49), Bookmarks and Hyperlinks (L. 89), Cover Page—Insert (L. 90), Table—Tab (L. 92), Page Color (L. 107), Mail Merge (L. 113–115), Style Set—Word 2007 (Appendix A), and PDF Format (Appendix C).

- The electronic resume in Lesson 52 (which is not being used much anymore) has been replaced by job-interviewing documents.
- The Web project in Unit 23 has been changed from creating a company home page to (a) creating an online resume and (b) introducing Mail Merge.
- Each lesson of the *Instructor's Wraparound Edition* now displays a miniature solution for each document students type in that lesson.

Introduction to the Student

Goals

- Type at least 30wpm/3'/5e by touch.
- Correctly format a business letter in block style with standard punctuation.

Starting a Lesson

Each lesson begins with the goals for that lesson. Read the goals carefully so that you understand the purpose of your practice. In the example at the left (from Lesson 26), the goals for the lesson are to type at least 30 wpm (words per minute) on a 3-minute timed writing with no more than 5 uncorrected errors and to correctly format a business letter in block style with standard punctuation.

Building Straight-Copy Skill

Warmups. Each lesson begins with a Warmup that reinforces learned alphabet, number, and/or symbol keys; practices specific reaches; and builds speed.

Skillbuilding. The Skillbuilding portion of each lesson includes a variety of drills to individualize your keyboarding speed and accuracy development. Instructions for completing the drills are always provided beside each activity.

Additional Skillbuilding drills are included in the back of the textbook and on the GDP correlated software. These drills are intended to help you meet your individual goals.

Measuring Straight-Copy Skill

Straight-copy skill is measured in wpm. All timed writings are the exact length needed to meet the speed goal for the lesson. If you finish a timed writing before time is up, you have automatically reached your speed goal for the lesson.

Counting Errors. Specific criteria are used for counting errors. The GDP software counts an error when

1. Any stroke is incorrect.
2. Any punctuation after a word is incorrect or omitted. The word before the punctuation is counted as incorrect.
3. The spacing after a word or after its punctuation is incorrect. The word is counted as incorrect.
4. A letter or word is omitted or repeated.
5. A direction about spacing, indenting, and so on, is not followed.
6. Words are transposed.

(**Note:** Only one error is counted for each word, no matter how many errors it may contain. The GDP correlated software automatically proofreads your copy and marks any errors for you.)

Determining Speed. To compute your typing speed in wpm, the GDP software counts every 5 strokes, including spaces, as 1 "word." Horizontal word scales below an activity divide lines into 5-stroke words. Vertical word scales to the right of an activity show the number of words in each line cumulatively totaled.

For example, the illustration that follows is for a 2-minute timed writing. If you complete line 30, you have typed 11 words. If you complete line 31, you have typed 22 words. Use the bottom word scale to determine the word count of a partial line. Add that number to the cumulative total for the last complete line. The GDP correlated software automatically computes your wpm speed for you.

```
30        Zachary just paid for six seats and quit because he      11
31   could not get the views he required near the middle of the   22
32   field. In August he thinks he may go to the ticket office    34
33   to purchase tickets.                                         38
     1  |  2  |  3  |  4  |  5  |  6  |  7  |  8  |  9  |  10  |  11  |  12
```

Take two 2-minute
timed writings.

 **Goal:** At least
19wpm/2'/5e

Correcting Errors

You will make numerous errors while you are learning the keyboard; do not be overly concerned about them. Errors will decrease as you become familiar with the keyboard. Error-correction settings in the GDP software determine whether you can correct errors in timed writings and drills. Consult your instructor for error-correction guidelines.

To correct an error, press BACKSPACE (shown as ← on some keyboards) to delete the incorrect character(s). Then type the correct character(s).

If you notice an error on a different line, use the up, down, left, or right arrows to move the insertion point immediately to the left or right of the error. Press BACKSPACE to delete a character to the left of the insertion point or DELETE to delete a character to the right of the insertion point.

Typing Technique

Correct position at the keyboard enables you to type with greater speed and accuracy and with less fatigue. When typing for a long period, rest your eyes occasionally by looking away from the screen. Change position, walk around, or stretch when your muscles feel tired. Making such movements and adjustments may help prevent your body from becoming too tired. In addition, long-term bodily damage, such as carpal tunnel syndrome, can be prevented.

Follow these ergonomic principles when typing:

Workstation

1. Position your chair so that your upper and lower legs form a greater-than-90-degree angle and your lower back is supported, with your knees slightly lower than your hips.
2. Position your text on either side of the monitor as close to the monitor vertically and horizontally as possible.
3. Position the mouse on a pad next to and at the same height as your keyboard.
4. Tilt the top of the monitor slightly away from you and slightly farther than an arm's length from you.

Position at the Keyboard

5. Center your body in front of the keyboard.
6. Sit slightly reclined, with your lower back touching the back of the chair and your feet flat on the floor.
7. Keep your elbows close to your body in a relaxed position.
8. Curve your fingers naturally over the home-row position, with the back of your hands at the same angle as the keyboard.
9. Move the mouse with your whole arm—not just your wrist.

Keystroking

10. Operate all keys by touch, using the correct fingers.
11. Keep your eyes on the copy most of the time while typing.

12. Keep your forearms at a slight downward slant and raise your hands slightly when typing so that your wrists do not touch the keyboard.
13. Make quick, light strokes, returning your fingers immediately to the home-row position or moving to the next position after each stroke.

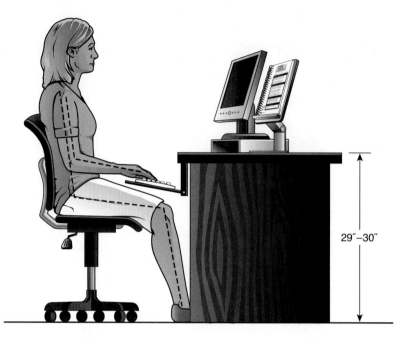

29"–30"

Tension-Reducing Exercises

A variety of government and health sources recommend the following exercises for computer users. Perform one exercise from each group, hold each position for three seconds, and repeat each exercise three times.

Neck

1. Look forward and slowly tilt your head as far to the left as possible. Then slowly tilt your head as far to the right as possible.
2. Slowly tilt your head forward until your chin rests on your chest. Then slowly tilt your head as far back as possible.

Shoulders

3. Roll your shoulders forward in a large circle. Then roll your shoulders backward in a large circle.
4. Extend both arms out to your side. Then slowly stretch them toward your back and squeeze your shoulder blades together. Finally, slowly bring your arms forward and touch the tops of your hands together in front of you.

Back

5. Place both hands behind your head, and slowly stretch your upper body backward. Then slowly bend all the way forward, stretching your arms toward the floor.
6. While seated, grab your left knee with both hands and slowly pull your leg in toward your body. Then repeat with your right knee.

Eyes

7. Close your eyes tightly. Then open them as wide as you can, blinking rapidly.
8. Follow the 20/20/20 rule: every 20 minutes, stare at an object 20 feet away for 20 seconds.

Reference Manual

COMPUTER SYSTEM
keyboard, R-2B
parts of, R-2A

CORRESPONDENCE
application letter, R-12B
attachment notation, R-4D, R-7C
blind copy notation, R-5B
block style, R-3A
body, R-3A
company name, R-5B
complimentary closing, R-3A
copy notation, R-3C, R-5B
date line, R-3A
delivery notation, R-3C, R-4A, R-5B
e-mail, R-5C–D
enclosure notation, R-3B, R-5B
envelope formatting, R-6A
executive stationery, R-4A
half-page stationery, R-4B
indented displays, R-3A
inside address, R-3A
international address, R-3D, R-5A
letter folding, R-6B
letterhead, R-3A
lists, R-3B–C, R-5B, R-12C–D
memo, R-4D, R-7C, R-9C
modified-block style, R-3B, R-3D
multiline lists, R-3B, R-5B, R-12C–D
multipage, R-5A–B, R-8A–D, R-13C
on-arrival notation, R-5A
open punctuation, R-4C
page number, R-5A–B, R-8A–D,
    R-10A–D, R-13C
personal-business, R-3D, R-12B
postscript notation, R-5B
quotation, long, R-3A
reference initials, R-3A, R-4D, R-5B
return address, R-3D, R-12B
salutation, R-3A
simplified style, R-3C
single-line lists, R-3C, R-12C–D
standard punctuation, R-3A
subject line, R-3C, R-4D, R-5A,
    R-7C
tables in, R-4D, R-5A, R-13C–D
window envelope, folding for, R-6B
window envelope, formatted for,
    R-4C
writer's identification, R-3A

EMPLOYMENT DOCUMENTS
application letter, R-12B
resume, R-12A

FORMS
R-14A

LANGUAGE ARTS
abbreviations, R-22
adjectives and adverbs, R-20
agreement, R-19
apostrophes, R-17
capitalization, R-21
colons, R-18
commas, R-15 to R-16
grammar, R-19 to R-20
hyphens, R-17
italics (or underline), R-18
mechanics, R-21 to R-22
number expression, R-21 to R-22
periods, R-18
pronouns, R-20
punctuation, R-15 to R-18
quotation marks, R-18
semicolons, R-16
sentences, R-19
underline (or italics), R-18
word usage, R-20

PROOFREADERS' MARKS
R-14C

REPORTS
academic style, R-8C–D
agenda, meeting, R-11A
APA style, R-10A–B
author/page citations, R-10C
author/year citations, R-10A
bibliography, R-9B
business, R-8A–B, R-9A
byline, R-8A, R-10A
citations, R-9D, R-10A–D
date, R-8A
endnotes, R-8C–D, R-9C
footnotes, R-8A–B, R-9A
hanging indent, R-10D
header, R-10A–B, R-10D
headings, R-9D, R-10C
headings, main, R-10A
headings, paragraph, R-8A, R-8C,
    R-9A
headings, side, R-8A–C, R-9A
indented display, R-8B, R-8D
itinerary, R-11C
left-bound, R-9A
legal document, R-11D
line numbers, R-11D
lists, R-8A, R-8C, R-9A, R-9C,
    R-11A, R-12A, R-12C–D
margins, R-9D
memo report, R-9C
minutes of a meeting, R-11B
MLA style, R-10C–D
multiline lists, R-8A, R-8C, R-11A,
    R-12A, R-12C–D

multipage academic, R-8C–D
multipage business, R-8A–B
outline, R-7A
page number, R-8B, R-8D, R-10A–B
paragraph heading, R-8A, R-9C
quotation, long, R-8B, R-8D
references page, APA style, R-10B
resume, R-12A
side heading, R-8A, R-9C
single-line lists, R-9A, R-9C, R-11A,
    R-12A, R-12C–D
spacing, R-9D
special features, R-9D
subheadings, R-10A
subject line, 2-line, R-9C
subtitle, R-8A
table of contents page, R-7D
tables in, R-8B
title, R-7A–B, R-8A–C, R-10A,
    R-10C
title, 2-line, R-8C, R-9A, R-10A,
    R-10C
title page, R-7B
transmittal memo, R-7C
works-cited page, MLA style, R-10D

TABLES
2-line column heading, R-13B
body, R-13A
bottom-aligned, R-13A–B
boxed, R-5A, R-8B, R-13A
braced column headings, R-13A
capitalization, columns, R-13D
column headings, R-4D, R-5A, R-8B,
    R-13A–D
dollar signs, R-8B, R-13A–B, R-13D
heading block, R-5, R-8B, R-13A–D
in correspondence, R-4D, R-5A,
    R-13C
in reports, R-8B
note, R-8B, R-13A
number, R-8B, R-13C
numbers in, R-4D, R-8B, R-13A–C
open, R-13B
percent signs, R-13B, R-13D
ruled, R-4D, R-13C
source, R-8B
special features, R-13D
subtitle, R-8B, R-13A–B, R-13D
table number, R-8B, R-13C
tables, R-4D, R-5A, R-8B, R-13A–C
title, R-5A, R-8B, R-13A–D
total line, R-13A, R-13C–D
vertical placement, R-13D

U.S. POSTAL SERVICE STATE ABBREVIATIONS
R-14B

A. MAJOR PARTS OF A COMPUTER SYSTEM

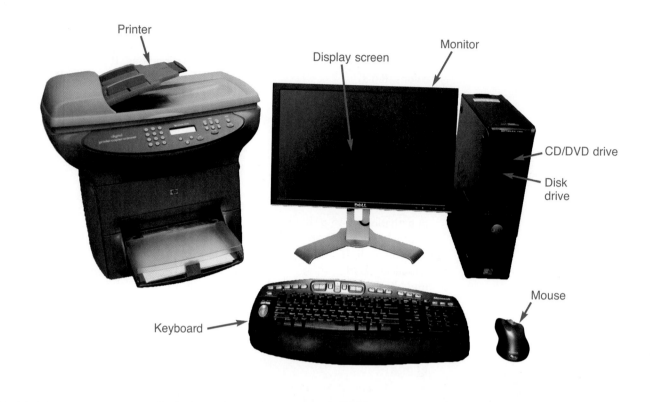

Printer

Display screen

Monitor

CD/DVD drive

Disk drive

Mouse

Keyboard

B. THE COMPUTER KEYBOARD

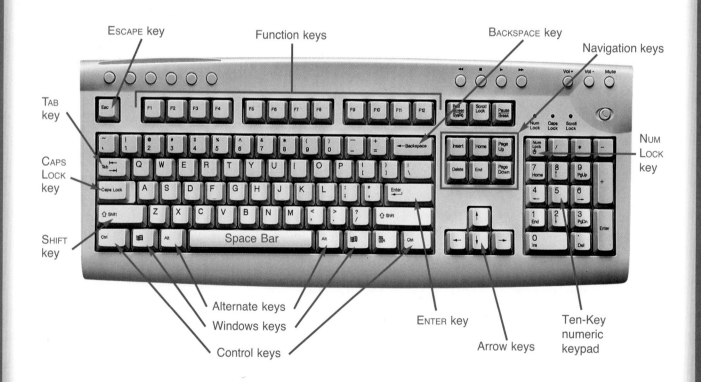

ESCAPE key

Function keys

BACKSPACE key

Navigation keys

TAB key

CAPS LOCK key

SHIFT key

NUM LOCK key

Alternate keys

Windows keys

Control keys

ENTER key

Arrow keys

Ten-Key numeric keypad

A. BUSINESS LETTER IN BLOCK STYLE

(with standard punctuation and indented display)

Date line · ↓5X · September 5, 20-- ↓4X

Inside address · Ms. Joan R. Hunter
Bolwater Associates
One Parklands Drive
Darien, CT 06820 ↓2X

Salutation · Dear Ms. Hunter: ↓2X · *Standard punctuation*

Body · You will soon receive the signed contract to have your organization conduct a one-day workshop for our employees on eliminating repetitive-motion injuries in the workplace. As we agreed, this workshop will apply to both our office and factory workers and you will conduct separate sessions for each group. ↓2X

We revised Paragraph 4-b shown below to require the instructor of this workshop to be a full-time employee of Bolwater Associates. ↓2X

→indent 0.5" · Paragraph 4-b of the Bolwater Associates agreement is hereby ←indent 0.5" amended as follows: The instructor of the one-day workshop on eliminating repetitive-motion injuries at the workplace must be a full-time employee of Bolwater Associates. ↓2X

Indented display

If this revision is satisfactory, please sign and return one copy of the contract for our files. We look forward to this opportunity to enhance the health of our employees. I know that all of us will enjoy this workshop. ↓2X

Complimentary closing · Sincerely, ↓4X · *Standard punctuation*

Signature · *Jeffrey Olszewski*

Writer's identification · Jeffrey Olszewski
Vice President for Operations

Reference initials

B. BUSINESS LETTER IN MODIFIED-BLOCK STYLE

(with multiline list and enclosure notation)

left tab: 3.25" (centerpoint)

→ tab 3.25" (centerpoint) · May 15, 20-- ↓5X ↓4X

Mr. Ichiro Xie
Bolwater Associates
One Parklands Drive
Darien, CT 06820 ↓2X

Dear Mr. Xie: ↓2X

I am returning a signed contract to have your organization conduct a one-day workshop for our employees on eliminating repetitive-motion injuries in the workplace. We have made the following changes to the contract: ↓2X

Multiline list

1. We revised Paragraph 4-b to require the instructor of this workshop to be a full-time employee of Bolwater Associates.
2. We made changes to Paragraph 10-c to require our prior approval of the agenda for the workshop. ↓2X

If these revisions are satisfactory, please sign and return one copy of the contract for our files. We look forward to this opportunity to enhance the health of our employees. I know that all of us will enjoy this workshop. ↓2X

→ tab 3.25" (centerpoint) · Sincerely, ↓4X

Jeffrey Olszewski

Jeffrey Olszewski
Vice President for Operations ↓2X

Enclosure notation · pec
Enclosure

C. BUSINESS LETTER IN SIMPLIFIED STYLE

(with subject line, single-line list; enclosure, delivery, and copy notations)

↓5X · October 5, 20-- ↓4X

Mr. Dale P. Griffin
Bolwater Associates
One Parklands Drive
Darien, CT 06820 ↓3X

Subject line · WORKSHOP CONTRACT ↓3X

I am returning the signed contract, Mr. Griffin, to have your organization conduct a one-day workshop for our employees on eliminating repetitive-motion injuries in the workplace. We have amended the following sections of the contract: ↓2X

Single-line list
- Paragraph 4-b
- Table 3
- Attachment 2 ↓2X

If these revisions are satisfactory, please sign and return one copy of the contract for our files. We look forward to this opportunity to enhance the health of our employees. I know that all of us will enjoy this workshop. ↓4X

Rogena Kyles

ROGENA KYLES, DIRECTOR ↓2X

iww

Enclosure notation · Enclosure
Delivery notation · By e-mail
Copy notation · c: Legal Department

D. PERSONAL-BUSINESS LETTER IN MODIFIED-BLOCK STYLE

(with international address and return address)

left tab: 3.25" (centerpoint)

→ tab 3.25" (centerpoint) · July 15, 20-- ↓5X ↓4X

Mr. Luis Fernandez
Vice President
Arvon Industries, Inc.
21 St. Claire Avenue East
International address · Toronto, ON M4T IL9
CANADA ↓2X

Dear Mr. Fernandez: ↓2X

As a former employee and present stockholder of Arvon Industries, I wish to protest the planned sale of the Consumer Products Division. ↓2X

According to published reports, consumer products accounted for 19 percent of last year's corporate profits, and they are expected to account for even more this year. In addition, Dun & Bradstreet predicts that consumer products nationwide will outpace the general economy for the next five years. ↓2X

I am concerned about the effect that this planned sale might have on overall corporate profits, on our cash dividends for investors, and on the economy of Melbourne, where the two consumer-products plants are located. Please ask your board of directors to reconsider this matter. ↓2X

→ tab 3.25" (centerpoint) · Sincerely, ↓4X

Jeanine Ford

Return address · Jeanine Ford
901 East Benson, Apt. 3
Fort Lauderdale, FL 33301
U.S.A.

A. BUSINESS LETTER ON EXECUTIVE STATIONERY

(7.25" × 10.5"; 1" side margins; with delivery notation)

↓5X
July 18, 20–
↓4X

Mr. Rodney Eastwood
BBL Resources
523 Northern Ridge
Fayetteville, PA 17222
↓2X

Dear Rodney:
↓2X

I see no reason why we should continue to consider the locality around Geraldton for our new plant. Even though the desirability of this site from an economic view is undeniable, there is not sufficient housing readily available for our workers.
↓2X

In trying to control urban growth, the city has been turning down the building permits for much new housing or placing so many restrictions on foreign investment as to make it too expensive.

Please continue to seek out other areas of exploration where we might form a joint partnership.
↓2X

Sincerely,
↓4X

Jennifer Gwatkin

Jennifer Gwatkin, Director
↓2X

mme
By fax

Delivery notation

B. BUSINESS LETTER ON HALF-PAGE STATIONERY

(5.5" × 8.5"; 0.75" side margins)

↓4 X
July 18, 20–
↓4X

Mr. Aristeo Olivas
BBL Resources
52A Northern Ridge
Fayetteville, PA 17222
↓2X

Dear Aristeo:
↓2X

We should discontinue considering Geraldton for our new plant. Housing is not readily available.

Please seek out other areas of exploration where we might someday form a joint partnership.
↓2X

Sincerely,
↓4X

Chimere Jones

Chimere Jones, Director
↓2X

adk

C. BUSINESS LETTER FORMATTED FOR A WINDOW ENVELOPE

(with open punctuation)

↓5X
July 18, 20–
↓3X

Ms. Reinalda Guerrero
BBL Resources
52A Northern Ridge
Fayetteville, PA 17222
↓3X

Dear Ms. Guerrero   *Open punctuation*
↓2X

I see no reason why we should even continue to consider the locality around Geraldton for our new plant. Even though the desirability of this site from an economic view is undeniable, there is insufficient housing readily available for our workers.
↓2X

In trying to control urban growth, the city has been turning down the building permits for new housing or placing so many restrictions on foreign investment as to make it too expensive.

Please continue to seek out other areas of exploration where we might form a joint partnership.
↓2X

Sincerely   *Open punctuation*
↓4X

Augustus Mays

Augustus Mays
Vice President for Operations
↓2X

woc

D. MEMO

(with ruled table, left- and right-aligned columns, and attachment notation)

↓5X →tab

MEMO TO: Nancy Price, Executive Vice President
↓2X

FROM: Arlyn J. Bunch, Operations *ajb*

DATE: July 18, 20–

SUBJECT: New Plant Site
↓2X

As you can see from the attached letter, I've informed BBL Resources that I see no reason why we should continue to consider the locality around Geraldton for our new plant. Even though the desirability of this site from an economic standpoint is undeniable, there is insufficient housing available. In fact, as of June 25, the number of appropriate single-family houses listed for sale within a 25-mile radius of Geraldton was as follows:
↓2X

Ruled table

Agent	Units
Belle Real Estate	123
Castleton Homes	11
Red Carpet	9
Geraldton Homes	5

↓1X

In addition, in trying to control urban growth, Geraldton has been either turning down building permits for new housing or placing excessive restrictions on them. Because of this deficiency of housing for our employees, we have no choice but to look elsewhere.
↓2X

woc
Attachment notation Attachment

A. MULTIPAGE BUSINESS LETTER

(page 1; with on-arrival notation, international address, subject line, and boxed table)

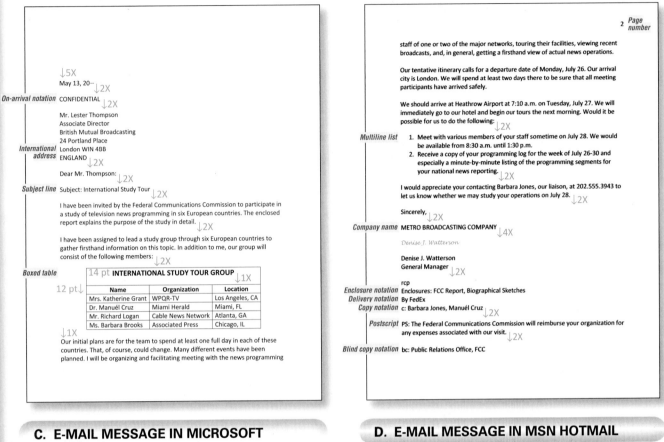

↓5X

May 13, 20-- ↓2X

On-arrival notation CONFIDENTIAL ↓2X

Mr. Lester Thompson
Associate Director
British Mutual Broadcasting
24 Portland Place
International London WIN 4BB
address ENGLAND ↓2X

Dear Mr. Thompson: ↓2X

Subject line Subject: International Study Tour ↓2X

I have been invited by the Federal Communications Commission to participate in a study of television news programming in six European countries. The enclosed report explains the purpose of the study in detail. ↓2X

I have been assigned to lead a study group through six European countries to gather firsthand information on this topic. In addition to me, our group will consist of the following members: ↓2X

Boxed table

14 pt **INTERNATIONAL STUDY TOUR GROUP** ↓1X

12 pt↓

Name	Organization	Location
Mrs. Katherine Grant	WPQR-TV	Los Angeles, CA
Dr. Manuél Cruz	Miami Herald	Miami, FL
Mr. Richard Logan	Cable News Network	Atlanta, GA
Ms. Barbara Brooks	Associated Press	Chicago, IL

↓1X

Our initial plans are for the team to spend at least one full day in each of these countries. That, of course, could change. Many different events have been planned. I will be organizing and facilitating meeting with the news programming

B. MULTIPAGE BUSINESS LETTER

(page 2; with page number; multiline list; company name; and enclosure, delivery, copy, postscript, and blind copy notations)

2 *Page number*

staff of one or two of the major networks, touring their facilities, viewing recent broadcasts, and, in general, getting a firsthand view of actual news operations.

Our tentative itinerary calls for a departure date of Monday, July 26. Our arrival city is London. We will spend at least two days there to be sure that all meeting participants have arrived safely.

We should arrive at Heathrow Airport at 7:10 a.m. on Tuesday, July 27. We will immediately go to our hotel and begin our tours the next morning. Would it be possible for us to do the following: ↓2X

Multiline list

1. Meet with various members of your staff sometime on July 28. We would be available from 8:30 a.m. until 1:30 p.m.
2. Receive a copy of your programming log for the week of July 26-30 and especially a minute-by-minute listing of the programming segments for your national news reporting. ↓2X

I would appreciate your contacting Barbara Jones, our liaison, at 202.555.3943 to let us know whether we may study your operations on July 28. ↓2X

Sincerely, ↓2X

Company name METRO BROADCASTING COMPANY ↓4X

Denise J. Watterson

Denise J. Watterson
General Manager ↓2X

rcp

Enclosure notation Enclosures: FCC Report, Biographical Sketches
Delivery notation By FedEx
Copy notation c: Barbara Jones, Manuél Cruz ↓2X

Postscript PS: The Federal Communications Commission will reimburse your organization for any expenses associated with our visit. ↓2X

Blind copy notation bc: Public Relations Office, FCC

C. E-MAIL MESSAGE IN MICROSOFT OUTLOOK

Hi, Andy and Cody:

Attached is the draft job description for the new desktop publishing position we're going to be advertising for next month. Would you please review it for accuracy and completeness.

I'd appreciate your getting back to me with any suggested changes by Thursday so that I can get the position publicized next week. Thanks.

Sandy

Sandra R. Hill
E-mail: srhill@atpi.com

D. E-MAIL MESSAGE IN MSN HOTMAIL

Hi, Andy and Cody:

Attached is the draft job description for the new desktop publishing position we're going to be advertising for next month. Would you please review it for accuracy and completeness.

I'd appreciate your getting back to me with any suggested changes by Thursday so that I can get the position publicized next week. Thanks.

Sandy

Sandra R. Hill
E-mail: srhill@atpi.com

A. FORMATTING ENVELOPES

A standard large (No. 10) envelope is 9.5 by 4.125 inches. A standard small (No. 6¾) envelope is 6.5 by 3.625 inches.

A window envelope requires no formatting, since the letter is formatted and folded so that the inside address is visible through the window.

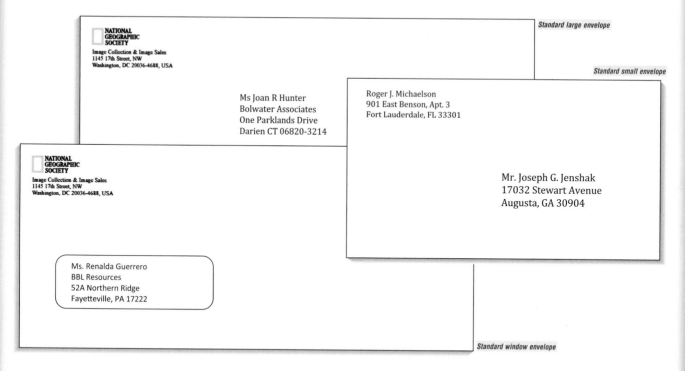

Standard large envelope

Standard small envelope

Standard window envelope

B. FOLDING LETTERS

To fold a letter for a large envelope:

1. Place the letter *face up,* and fold up the bottom third.
2. Fold the top third down to 0.5 inch from the bottom edge.
3. Insert the last crease into the envelope first, with the flap facing up.

To fold a letter for a small envelope:

1. Place the letter *face up,* and fold up the bottom half to 0.5 inch from the top.
2. Fold the right third over to the left.
3. Fold the left third over to 0.5 inch from the right edge.
4. Insert the last crease into the envelope first, with the flap facing up.

To fold a letter for a window envelope:

1. Place the letter *face down* with the letterhead at the top, and fold the bottom third of the letter up.
2. Fold the top third down so that the address shows.
3. Insert the letter into the envelope so that the address shows through the window.

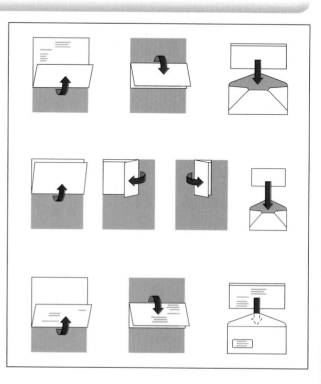

Reference Manual

A. OUTLINE

(with 2-line title)

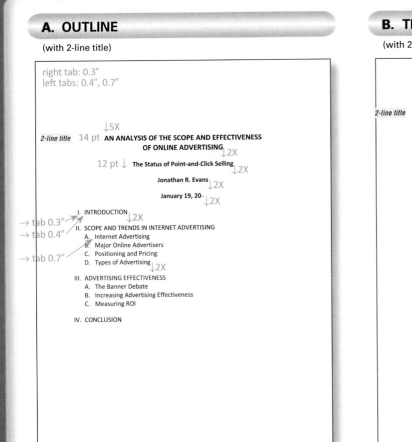

right tab: 0.3"
left tabs: 0.4", 0.7"

↓5X

2-line title 14 pt **AN ANALYSIS OF THE SCOPE AND EFFECTIVENESS OF ONLINE ADVERTISING**
↓2X

12 pt ↓ **The Status of Point-and-Click Selling**
↓2X

Jonathan R. Evans
↓2X

January 19, 20–
↓2X

I. INTRODUCTION ↓2X
→ tab 0.3"
→ tab 0.4"   II. SCOPE AND TRENDS IN INTERNET ADVERTISING
              A. Internet Advertising
              B. Major Online Advertisers
→ tab 0.7"   C. Positioning and Pricing
              D. Types of Advertising ↓2X

III. ADVERTISING EFFECTIVENESS
     A. The Banner Debate
     B. Increasing Advertising Effectiveness
     C. Measuring ROI

IV. CONCLUSION

B. TITLE PAGE

(with 2-line title)

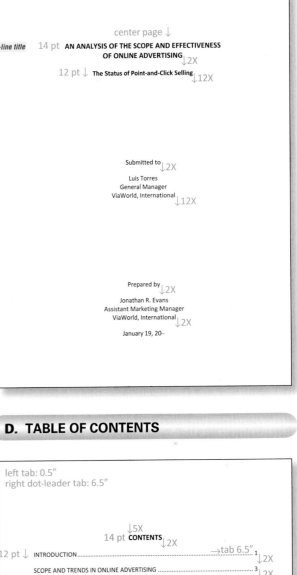

center page ↓

2-line title 14 pt **AN ANALYSIS OF THE SCOPE AND EFFECTIVENESS OF ONLINE ADVERTISING**
↓2X

12 pt ↓ **The Status of Point-and-Click Selling**
↓12X

Submitted to ↓2X

Luis Torres
General Manager
ViaWorld, International ↓12X

Prepared by ↓2X

Jonathan R. Evans
Assistant Marketing Manager
ViaWorld, International ↓2X

January 19, 20–

C. TRANSMITTAL MEMO

(with 2-line subject line and attachment notation)

↓5X →tab
MEMO TO: Luis Torres, General Manager ↓2X

FROM: Jonathan R. Evans, Assistant Marketing Manager*jre*

DATE: January 19, 20–

2-line subject line **SUBJECT:** An Analysis of the Scope and Effectiveness of Current Online
→tab Advertising in Today's Marketplace ↓2X

Here is the final report analyzing the scope and effectiveness of Internet advertising that you requested on January 5. ↓2X

The report predicts that the total value of the business-to-business e-commerce market will continue to increase by geometric proportions. New technologies aimed at increasing Internet ad interactivity and the adoption of standards for advertising response measurement and tracking will contribute to this increase. Unfortunately, as discussed in this report, the use of "rich media" and interactivity in Web advertising will create its own set of problems.

I enjoyed working on this assignment, Luis, and learned quite a bit from my analysis of the situation. Please let me know if you have any questions about the report. ↓2X

plw
Attachment notation Attachment

D. TABLE OF CONTENTS

left tab: 0.5"
right dot-leader tab: 6.5"

↓5X
14 pt **CONTENTS** ↓2X

A. MULTIPAGE BUSINESS REPORT

(page 1; with side and paragraph headings, multiline list, footnote references, and footnotes)

B. MULTIPAGE BUSINESS REPORT

(last page; with page number, indented display, side heading, boxed table with table number and note, and footnote)

C. MULTIPAGE ACADEMIC REPORT

(page 1; with 2-line title, endnote references, and multiline list)

D. MULTIPAGE ACADEMIC REPORT

(last page; with page number, indented display, and endnotes)

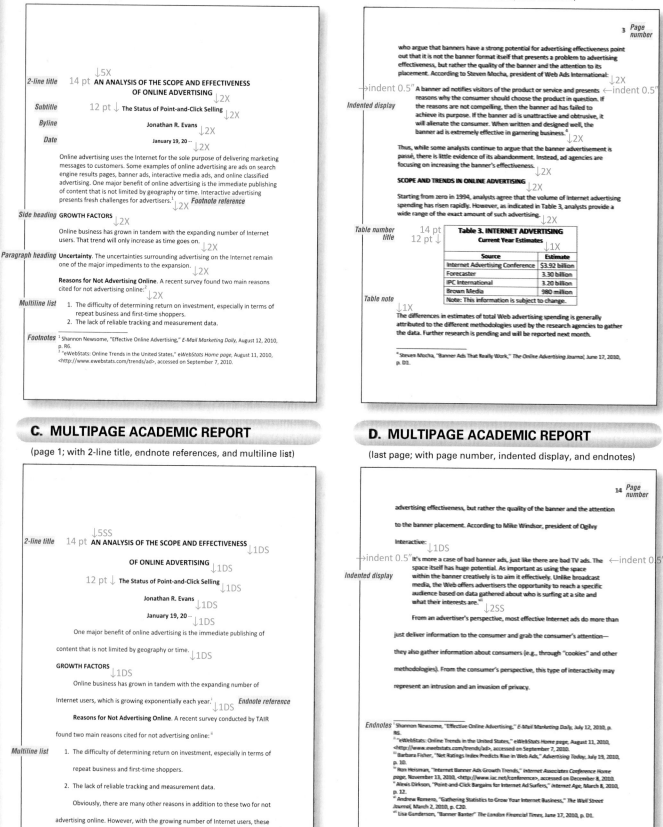

Reference Manual

A. LEFT-BOUND BUSINESS REPORT

(page 1; with 2-line title, single-line list, and footnotes)

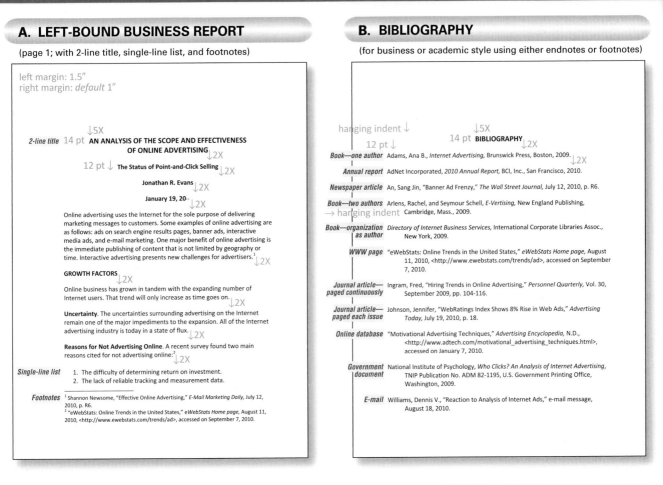

B. BIBLIOGRAPHY

(for business or academic style using either endnotes or footnotes)

C. MEMO REPORT

(page 1, with 2-line subject line, endnote references, and single-line list)

D. FORMATTING REPORTS

Margins, Spacing, and Indents. Begin the first page of each section (for example, the table of contents, first page of the body, and bibliography pages) 2 inches from the top of the page. Begin other pages 1 inch from the top. Use 1-inch default side and bottom margins for all pages. For a left-bound report, add 0.5 inch to the left margin. Single-space business reports. Double-space academic reports and indent paragraphs.

Titles and Headings. Center the title in 14-pt. font. Single-space multiline titles in a single-spaced report, and double-space multiline titles in a double-spaced report. Insert 1 blank line before and after all parts of a heading block (may include the title, subtitle, author, and/or date), and format all lines in bold. Format side headings in bold, at the left margin, with 1 blank line before and after them. Format paragraph headings at the left margin for single-spaced reports and indented for double-spaced reports in bold, followed by a period in bold and one space.

Citations. Format citations using Word's footnote (or endnote) feature.

Margins, Spacing, Headings, and Citations for APA- or MLA-Style Reports. See page R-10.

Reference Manual

A. REPORT IN APA STYLE

(page 3; with header, 2-line title, byline, main heading, subheading, and citations)

top, bottom, and side margins: *default* (1")
double-space throughout   Online Advertising 3 *Header*

2-line title   An Analysis of the Scope and Effectiveness

of Online Advertising

Byline   Jonathan R. Evans

→ tab Online advertising uses the Internet for the sole purpose of delivering

marketing messages to customers. Some examples of online advertising are ads

on search engine results pages, banner ads, interactive media ads, online

classifieds, advertising networks, and e-mail marketing (Gunderson, 2011, p. D1). *Citation*

One major benefit of online advertising is the immediate publishing of

content that is not limited by geography or time. To that end, interactive

advertising presents fresh challenges for advertisers (Newsome, 2010).

Main heading   Growth Factors

Online business has grown in tandem with the expanding number of

Internet users. That trend will only increase as time goes on (Arlens & Schell).

Subheading Uncertainty ← Italic

The uncertainties surrounding Internet advertising are impeding its

expansion. A recent survey found two main reasons cited for not advertising

online. The first is the difficulty of determining return on investment, especially in

terms of repeat business and first-time shoppers. The second is the lack of reliable

tracking and measurement data ("eWebStats," 2010).

B. REFERENCES IN APA STYLE

(page 14; with header)

top, bottom, and side margins: *default* (1")
double-space throughout   Online Advertising 14 *Header*

hanging indent ↓   References

Book—one author Adams, A. B. (2009). *Internet advertising and the upcoming electronic upheaval.*

→ *hanging indent*   Boston: Brunswick Press.

Annual report AdNet Incoporated. (2010). *2010 annual report.* San Francisco: BCI, Inc.

Newspaper article An, S. J. (2010, July 12). Banner ad frenzy. *The Wall Street Journal*, p. R6.

Book—two authors Arlens, R., & Seymour, S. (2010). *E-vertising.* Cambridge, MA: New England

Publishing.

*Book—organization
as author* Directory of business and financial services. (2009). New York: International

Corporate Libraries Association.

WWW page eWebStats: Advertising revenues and trends. (n.d.). New York: eMarketer.

Retrieved August 11, 2010, from

http://www.emarketer.com/ewebstats/2507manu.ad

*Journal article—
paged continuously* Ingram, F. (2009). Trends in online advertising. *Personnel Quarterly, 20,* 804-816.

*Journal article—
paged each issue* Johnson, J. (2010, July 19). WebRatings Index shows 4% rise in Web ads.

Advertising Today, 39, 18.

Online database Motivational advertising techniques. (2010, January). *Advertising Encyclopedia.*

Retrieved January 7, 2010, from http://www.adtech.com/ads.html

Government document National Institute of Psychology (2009). *Who clicks? An analysis of Internet*

advertising (TNIP Publication No. ADM 82-1195). Washington, DC.

C. REPORT IN MLA STYLE

(page 1; with header, heading, 2-line title, and citations)

top, bottom, and side margins: *default* (1")
double-space throughout   Evans 1 *Header*

Heading Jonathan R. Evans

Professor Inman

Management 302

19 January 20--

2-line title   An Analysis of the Scope and Effectiveness

of Online Advertising

→ tab Online advertising uses the Internet for the sole purpose of delivering

marketing messages to customers. Some examples of online advertising are ads

on search engine results pages, banner ads, interactive media ads, social network

site advertising, online classifieds, and e-mail marketing (Gunderson D1). *Citation*

One major benefit of online advertising is the immediate publishing of

information and content that is not limited by geography or time. To that end,

interactive advertising presents fresh challenges for advertisers (Newsome 59).

Online business has grown in tandem with the expanding number of

Internet users. That trend will only increase as time goes on (Arlens & Schell 376-

379). The uncertainties surrounding Internet advertising remain one of the major

impediments to the expansion. A recent survey found two main reasons cited for

not advertising online. The first is the difficulty of determining return on

investment. The second is the lack of reliable tracking and measurement data.

D. WORKS CITED IN MLA STYLE

(page 14; with header and hanging indent)

top, bottom, and side margins: *default* (1")
double-space throughout   Evans 14 *Header*

hanging indent ↓   Works Cited

Book—one author Adams, Ana. B. *Internet Advertising and the Upcoming Electronic Upheaval.*

→ *hanging indent* Boston: Brunswick Press, 2009.

Annual report AdNet Incoporated. *2010 Annual Report.* San Francisco: BCI, Inc., 2010.

Newspaper article An, Sang Jin. "Banner Ad Frenzy." *The Wall Street Journal*, 12 July 2010: R6.

Book—two authors Arlens, Rachel, and Seymour Schell. *E-vertising.* Cambridge, MA: New England

Publishing, 2009.

*Book—organization
as author* Corporate Libraries Association. *Directory of Business and Financial Services.* New

York: Corporate Libraries Association, 2009.

WWW page "eWebStats: Advertising Revenues and Trends." 11 Aug. 2009. 7 Jan. 2010

<http://www.emarketer.com/ewebstats/ad>.

*Journal article—
paged continuously* Ingram, Frank. "Trends in Online Advertising." *Personnel Quarterly* 20 (2010):

804-816.

*Journal article—
paged each issue* Johnson, June. "WRI shows 4% rise in Web ads." *WebAds Today* 19 July 2010: 18.

Online database *Motivational Advertising Techniques.* 2010. Advertising Encyclopedia. 7 Jan. 2010

<http://www.adtech.com/ads.html>.

Government document National Institute of Psychology. *Who clicks?* TNIP Publication No. ADM 82-1195.

Washington, DC. GPO: 2010.

E-mail Williams, Dan V. "Reaction to Internet Ads." E-mail to the author. 18 Aug. 2010.

Reference Manual

A. MEETING AGENDA

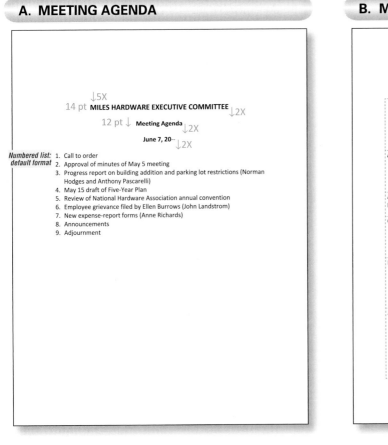

↓5X
14 pt **MILES HARDWARE EXECUTIVE COMMITTEE** ↓2X

12 pt ↓ **Meeting Agenda** ↓2X

June 7, 20-- ↓2X

Numbered list:
default format
1. Call to order
2. Approval of minutes of May 5 meeting
3. Progress report on building addition and parking lot restrictions (Norman Hodges and Anthony Pascarelli)
4. May 15 draft of Five-Year Plan
5. Review of National Hardware Association annual convention
6. Employee grievance filed by Ellen Burrows (John Landstrom)
7. New expense-report forms (Anne Richards)
8. Announcements
9. Adjournment

B. MINUTES OF A MEETING

↓5X
14 pt **RESOURCE COMMITTEE** ↓2X

12 pt ↓ **Minutes of the Meeting** ↓2X

March 13, 20-- ↓1X

ATTENDANCE	The Resource Committee met on March 13, 20--, at the Airport Sheraton in Portland, Oregon, with all members present. Michael Davis, chairperson, called the meeting to order at 2:30 p.m. ↓1X
APPROVAL OF MINUTES	The minutes of the January 27 meeting were read and approved as presented.
OLD BUSINESS	The members of the committee reviewed the sales brochure on electronic copyboards and agreed to purchase one for the conference room. Cynthia Giovanni will secure quotations from at least two suppliers.
NEW BUSINESS	The committee reviewed a request from the Purchasing Department for three new computers. After extensive discussion regarding the appropriate use of the computers and software to be purchased, the committee approved the request.
ADJOURNMENT	The meeting was adjourned at 4:45 p.m. The next meeting is scheduled for April 13 in Suite B. ↓2X Respectfully submitted, ↓4X *D. S. Madsen* D. S. Madsen, Secretary

(Note: Table shown with "View Gridlines" active.)

C. ITINERARY

↓5X
14 pt **PORTLAND SALES MEETING** ↓2X

12 pt ↓ **Itinerary for Dorothy Turner** ↓2X

March 12-15, 20-- ↓1X

THURSDAY, MARCH 12 ↓1X	
5:10 p.m.-7:06 p.m.	Flight from Detroit to Portland; Northwest 83 (800-555-1212); e-ticket; Seat 8D; nonstop. ↓2X Jack Weatherford (Home: 503-555-8029; Office: 503-555-7631) will meet your flight on Thursday, provide transportation during your visit, and return you to the airport on Saturday morning. ↓2X Airport Sheraton (503-555-4032) King-sized bed, nonsmoking room; late arrival guaranteed; Reservation No. 30ZM6-02. ↓1X
FRIDAY, MARCH 13	
9 a.m.-5:30 p.m.	Portland Sales Meeting 1931 Executive Way, Suite 10 Portland, OR 97211 (503-555-7631)
SATURDAY, MARCH 14	
7:30 a.m.-2:47 p.m.	Flight from Portland to Detroit; Northwest 360; e-ticket; Seat 9a; nonstop.

(Note: Table shown with "View Gridlines" active.)

D. LEGAL DOCUMENT

(with line numbers)

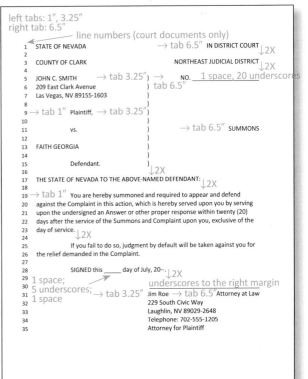

left tabs: 1", 3.25"
right tab: 6.5"

line numbers (court documents only)

1 STATE OF NEVADA   → tab 6.5" IN DISTRICT COURT ↓2X
2
3 COUNTY OF CLARK   NORTHEAST JUDICIAL DISTRICT ↓2X
4
5 JOHN C. SMITH   → tab 3.25" →   NO.   1 space, 20 underscores
6 209 East Clark Avenue   ) tab 6.5"
7 Las Vegas, NV 89155-1603   )
8   )
9 → tab 1" Plaintiff, → tab 3.25")
10   )
11   vs.   )   → tab 6.5" SUMMONS
12   )
13 FAITH GEORGIA   )
14   )
15   Defendant.   )
16   ↓2X
17 THE STATE OF NEVADA TO THE ABOVE-NAMED DEFENDANT: ↓2X
18
19 → tab 1" You are hereby summoned and required to appear and defend
20 against the Complaint in this action, which is hereby served upon you by serving
21 upon the undersigned an Answer or other proper response within twenty (20)
22 days after the service of the Summons and Complaint upon you, exclusive of the
23 day of service. ↓2X
24
25   If you fail to do so, judgment by default will be taken against you for
26 the relief demanded in the Complaint.
27
28   SIGNED this _____ day of July, 20--. ↓2X
29 1 space;
30 5 underscores; → tab 3.25" Jim Roe → tab 6.5" Attorney at Law
31 1 space   229 South Civic Way
32   underscores to the right margin
33   Laughlin, NV 89029-2648
34   Telephone: 702-555-1205
35   Attorney for Plaintiff

Reference Manual

A. RESUME

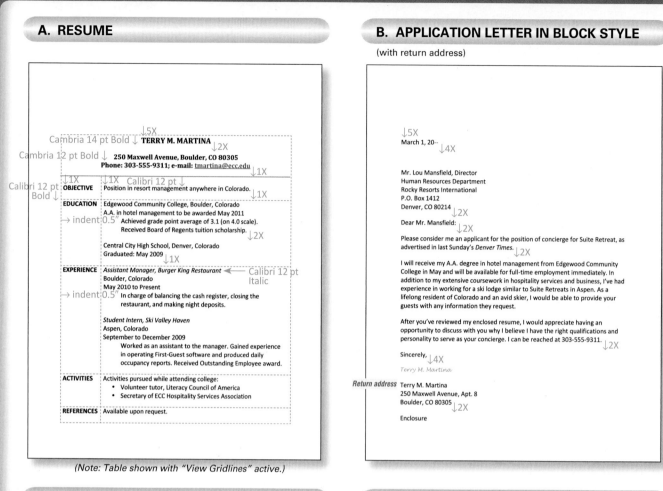

(Note: Table shown with "View Gridlines" active.)

B. APPLICATION LETTER IN BLOCK STYLE

(with return address)

C. FORMATTING LISTS

Numbers or bullets are used in documents to call attention to items in a list and to increase readability. If the sequence of the list items is important, use numbers rather than bullets.

- Insert 1 blank line before and after the list.
- Use Word's default format for all lists in either single- or double-spaced documents, including lists in documents such as a meeting agenda. Any carryover lines will be indented automatically.
- Use the same line spacing (single or double) between lines in the list as is used in the rest of the document.

The three bulleted and numbered lists shown at the right are all formatted correctly.

D. EXAMPLES OF DIFFERENT TYPES OF LISTS

According to the Internet Advertising Bureau, the following are the most common types of advertising on the Internet:

- Banner ads that feature some type of appropriate animation to attract the viewer's attention and interest.
- Sponsorship, in which an advertiser sponsors a content-based Web site.
- Interstitials, ads that flash up while a page downloads.

There is now considerable controversy about the effectiveness of banner advertising. As previously noted, a central goal of banner advertisements is to

*****

According to the Internet Advertising Bureau, the following are the most common types of advertising on the Internet, shown in order of popularity:

1. Banner ads
2. Sponsorship
3. Interstitials

There is now considerable controversy about the effectiveness of banner advertising. As previously noted, a central goal of banner advertisements is to

*****

According to the Internet Advertising Bureau, the following are the most common types of advertising on the Internet:

- Banner ads that feature some type of appropriate animation to attract the viewer's attention and interest.

- Sponsorship, in which an advertiser sponsors a Web site.

- Interstitials, ads that flash up while a page downloads.

There is now considerable controversy about the effectiveness of banner advertising. As previously noted, a central goal of banner advertisements is to

A. BOXED TABLE

(with subtitle; bottom-aligned and braced column headings; left- and right-aligned columns; total line and table note)

center page ↓
center horizontally

		Annual Sales		Quarterly Sales	
Product		**This Year**	**Last Year**	**This Quarter**	**Last Quarter**
Ink-jet: color		$ 569	$ 841	$ 120	$ 99
Ink-jet: color portable		6	24	2	6
Ink-jet: black and white		273	588	71	147
Printer/copier combination		1,622	2,054	422	509
Black-and-white laser: standard		389	507	121	129
Black-and-white laser: premium		2,368	87	592	25
Color laser		409	230	100	70
Totals		$5,636	$4,331	$1,428	$985
Note: Sales for this quarter ended at midnight, December 31.					

Title — 14 pt **AUSTIN-REEVES PRINTER DEPOT**
Subtitle — 12 pt ↓ **Sales Trends for 20--**
(000s omitted)
↓1X

align bottom ↓
Braced column headings
↓1X

Total line
Table note

B. OPEN TABLE

(with 2-line title; 2-line centered, bottom-aligned column headings; left- and right-aligned columns; column entries with dollar and percent signs)

center page ↓
center horizontally

2-line title — 14 pt **SUITE HOLIDAY RETREAT**
Row 1 — 12 pt ↓ **BOUTIQUE HOTELS**
New Lodging Rates
↓1X
Row 2
Row 3 ↓

align bottom ↓
2-line column heading

Location	Rack Rate	Discount Rate	Saving
Bozeman, Montana	$ 95.75	$ 91.50	4.4%
Chicago, Illinois	159.00	139.50	12.3%
Dallas, Texas	249.50	219.00	12.2%
Las Vegas, Nevada	98.50	89.95	8.7%
Beverly Hills, California	1,179.00	950.00	19.4%
Minneapolis, Minnesota	115.00	95.00	17.4%
New York, New York	227.50	175.00	23.1%
Orlando, Florida	105.75	98.50	6.3%
Portland, Maine	93.50	93.50	0.0%
Seattle, Washington	143.75	125.75	12.5%

Column A *Column B→*

2 spaces for each digit

3 spaces:
2 for each digit;
1 for each comma

(Note: Table shown with "View Gridlines" active.)

C. RULED TABLE

(with table number, title, centered column headings, and total line)

center page ↓
center horizontally

Table number and title — 14 pt **Table 2. RESCUE ONE COMPUTER TECHNICAL SUPPORT**
↓1X

12 pt ↓ align bottom ↓

Support Service	Fees to Date
Replacement parts	$ 9,200
Troubleshooting	12,850
Software support	5,095
Hardware support	8,032
Product literature	105
Technical documentation	150
Printer drivers	129
Total	$35,561

(Note: Table shown with "View Gridlines" active.)

D. FORMATTING TABLES

The three basic styles of tables are boxed, open, and ruled. Tables have vertical columns (Column A), horizontal rows (Row 1), and intersecting cells (Cell A1). Center a table vertically that appears alone on the page. Insert 1 blank line before and after a table that appears within a document. Automatically adjust column widths and horizontally center all tables.

Heading Block. Merge any cells in Row 1, and type the heading block. Center and bold throughout. Type the title in all-caps, 14-pt. font, and the subtitle in upper- and lowercase, 12-pt. font. If a table has a number, type *Table* in upper- and lowercase. Follow the table number with a period and 1 space. Insert 1 blank line below the heading block.

Column Headings. Center column headings. Type in upper- and lowercase and bold. Bottom-align all column headings if a row includes a 2-line column heading. Merge desired cells for braced headings.

Column Entries. Left-align text columns, and right-align number columns. Capitalize only the first word and proper nouns in column entries.

Column Entry Dollar and Percent Signs. Insert the dollar sign only before the amount in the first entry and before a total amount entry. Align the dollar sign with the longest amount in the column, inserting spaces after the dollar sign as needed (allowing for 2 spaces for each digit and 1 space for each comma). Repeat the percent sign for each number in each column entry (unless the column heading identifies the data as percentages).

Table Note and Total Line. For a note line, merge the cells of the last row and use "Note" followed by a colon. For a total line, add a top and bottom border, use "Total" or "Totals" as appropriate, and add a percent or dollar sign if needed.

A. FORMATTING BUSINESS FORMS

Many business forms can be created and filled in by using templates that are provided within commercial word processing software. Template forms can be used "as is" or they can be edited. Templates can also be used to create customized forms for any business.

When a template is opened, the form is displayed on screen. The user can then fill in the necessary information, including personalized company information. Data are entered into cells or fields, and you can move quickly from field to field with a single keystroke—usually by pressing TAB or ENTER.

Masco Shipping

PURCHASE ORDER

1335 Dublin Road
Columbus, OH 43215
Phone 614-555-3971 Fax 614-555-3980

The following number must appear on all related
correspondence, shipping papers, and invoices:
P.O. NUMBER: 1074

TO:
Reliable Office Supply
Great Lakes Distribution Center
1001 West Van Buren Street
Chicago, IL 60607

SHIP TO:

P.O. DATE	REQUISITIONER	SHIPPED VIA	F.O.B. POINT	TERMS
10/22/--	DV	Fed Ex		

QTY	UNIT	DESCRIPTION	UNIT PRICE	TOTAL
120	HO2048	Perforated ruled pads	$ 0.48	$ 57.60
36	564LQ4	Recyclable storage boxes, legal size	3.69	132.84
2	222398	Paper punch	58.67	117.34
1	B48560	Hi-style tackboard, 24" x 36", burgundy frame, blue fabric	31.98	31.98
1	J22502	Kraft catalog envelopes, 10" x 13", clasp with gummed flap, box of 500	104.86	104.86
		SUBTOTAL		444.62
		SALES TAX		26.77
		SHIPPING & HANDLING		
		OTHER		
		TOTAL		$471.39

1. Please send two copies of your invoice.
2. Enter this order in accordance with the prices, terms, delivery method, and specifications listed above.
3. Please notify us immediately if you are unable to ship as specified.
4. Send all correspondence to:
   Masco Shipping Lines
   1335 Dublin Road
   Columbus, OH 43215
   Phone 614-555-3971 Fax 614-555-3980

Authorized by _____ Date _____

B. U.S. POSTAL SERVICE ABBREVIATIONS

(for States, Territories, and Canadian Provinces)

States and Territories

Alabama	AL
Alaska	AK
Arizona	AZ
Arkansas	AR
California	CA
Colorado	CO
Connecticut	CT
Delaware	DE
District of Columbia	DC
Florida	FL
Georgia	GA
Guam	GU
Hawaii	HI
Idaho	ID
Illinois	IL
Indiana	IN
Iowa	IA
Kansas	KS
Kentucky	KY
Louisiana	LA
Maine	ME
Maryland	MD
Massachusetts	MA
Michigan	MI
Minnesota	MN
Mississippi	MS
Missouri	MO
Montana	MT
Nebraska	NE
Nevada	NV
New Hampshire	NH
New Jersey	NJ
New Mexico	NM
New York	NY
North Carolina	NC
North Dakota	ND
Ohio	OH
Oklahoma	OK
Oregon	OR
Pennsylvania	PA
Puerto Rico	PR
Rhode Island	RI
South Carolina	SC
South Dakota	SD
Tennessee	TN
Texas	TX
Utah	UT
Vermont	VT
Virgin Islands	VI
Virginia	VA
Washington	WA
West Virginia	WV
Wisconsin	WI
Wyoming	WY

Canadian Provinces

Alberta	AB
British Columbia	BC
Labrador	LB
Manitoba	MB
New Brunswick	NB
Newfoundland	NF
Northwest Territories	NT
Nova Scotia	NS
Ontario	ON
Prince Edward Island	PE
Quebec	PQ
Saskatchewan	SK
Yukon Territory	YT

C. PROOFREADERS' MARKS

Proofreaders' Marks		Draft	Final Copy
‿	Omit space	data base	database
∨ or ∧	Insert	if hes going	if he's not going,
≡	Capitalize	Maple street	Maple Street
✗	Delete	a final draft	a draft
#	Insert space	allready to	all ready to
when/if	Change word	and if you	and when you
/	Use lowercase letter	our President	our president
¶	Paragraph	… to use it.¶We can	… to use it. We can
•••	Don't delete	a true story	a true story
○	Spell out	the only①	the only one
∽	Transpose	they all see	they see all

Proofreaders' Marks		Draft	Final Copy
SS	Single-space	first line / second line	first line / second line
ds	Double-space	first line / second line	first line / second line
⌐	Move right	Please send	Please send
⌐	Move left	May I	May I
∿	Bold	Column Heading	**Column Heading**
ital	Italic	*Time* magazine	*Time* magazine
u/l	Underline	Time magazine	Time magazine readers
♂	Move as shown	readers will see	will see

Language Arts For Business

(50 "must-know" rules)

PUNCTUATION

Commas

RULE 1
, direct address
(L. 21)

Use commas before and after a name used in direct address.

Thank you, John, for responding to my e-mail so quickly.
Ladies and gentlemen, the program has been canceled.

RULE 2
, independent clause
(L. 27)

Use a comma between independent clauses joined by a coordinate conjunction (unless both clauses are short).

Ellen left her job with IBM, and she and her sister went to Paris.
But: Ellen left her job with IBM and went to Paris with her sister.
But: John drove and I navigated.

Note: An independent clause is one that can stand alone as a complete sentence.
The most common coordinate conjunctions are *and, but, or,* and *nor*.

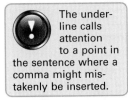

The under-
line calls
attention
to a point in
the sentence where a
comma might mis-
takenly be inserted.

RULE 3
, introductory expression
(L. 27)

Use a comma after an introductory expression (unless it is a short prepositional phrase).

Before we can make a decision, we must have all the facts.
But: In 2004 our nation elected a new president.

Note: An introductory expression is a group of words that come before the subject and verb of the independent clause. Common prepositions are *to, in, on, of, at, by, for,* and *with*.

RULE 4
, direct quotation
(L. 41)

Use a comma before and after a direct quotation.

James said, "I shall return," and then left.

RULE 5
, date
(L. 51)

Use a comma before and after the year in a complete date.

We will arrive on June 2, 2006, for the conference.
But: We will arrive on June 2 for the conference.

RULE 6
, place
(L. 51)

Use a comma before and after a state or country that follows a city (but not before a ZIP Code).

Joan moved to Vancouver, British Columbia, in May.
Send the package to Douglasville, GA 30135, by Express Mail.
But: Send the package to Georgia by Express Mail.

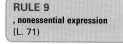

RULE 7
, series
(L. 61)

Use a comma between each item in a series of three or more.

We need to order paper, toner, and font cartridges for the printer.

They saved their work, exited their program, and turned off their computers when they finished.

Note: Do not use a comma after the last item in a series.

RULE 8
, transitional expression
(L. 61)

Use a comma before and after a transitional expression or independent comment.

It is critical, therefore, that we finish the project on time.

Our present projections, you must admit, are inadequate.

But: You must admit our present projections are inadequate.

Note: Examples of transitional expressions and independent comments are *in addition to, therefore, however, on the other hand, as a matter of fact,* and *unfortunately.*

RULE 9
, nonessential expression
(L. 71)

Use a comma before and after a nonessential expression.

Andre, who was there, can verify the statement.

But: Anyone who was there can verify the statement.

Van's first book, *Crisis of Management,* was not discussed.

Van's book *Crisis of Management* was not discussed.

Note: A nonessential expression is a group of words that may be omitted without changing the basic meaning of the sentence. Always examine the noun or pronoun that comes before the expression to determine whether the noun needs the expression to complete its meaning. If it does, the expression is *essential* and does *not* take a comma.

RULE 10
, adjacent adjectives
(L. 71)

Use a comma between two adjacent adjectives that modify the same noun.

We need an intelligent, enthusiastic individual for this job.

But: Please order a new bulletin board for our main conference room.

Note: Do not use a comma after the second adjective. Also, do not use a comma if the first adjective modifies the combined idea of the second adjective and the noun (for example, *bulletin board* and *conference room* in the second example above).

Semicolons

RULE 11
; no conjunction
(L. 97)

Use a semicolon to separate two closely related independent clauses that are not joined by a conjunction (such as *and, but, or,* or *nor*).

Management favored the vote; stockholders did not.

But: Management favored the vote, but stockholders did not.

RULE 12
; series
(L. 97)

Use a semicolon to separate three or more items in a series if any of the items already contain commas.

Staff meetings were held on Thursday, May 7; Monday, June 7; and Friday, June 12.

Note: Be sure to insert the semicolon *between* (not within) the items in a series.

Hyphens

RULE 13
- number
(L. 57)

Hyphenate compound numbers between twenty-one and ninety-nine and fractions that are expressed as words.

> Twenty-nine recommendations were approved by at least three-fourths of the members.

RULE 14
- compound adjective
(L. 67)

Hyphenate compound adjectives that come before a noun (unless the first word is an adverb ending in -ly).

> We reviewed an up-to-date report on Wednesday.
> But: The report was up to date.
> But: We reviewed the highly rated report.

Note: A compound adjective is two or more words that function as a unit to describe a noun.

Apostrophes

RULE 15
' singular noun
(L. 37)

Use 's to form the possessive of singular nouns.

> The hurricane's force caused major damage to North Carolina's coastline.

RULE 16
' plural noun
(L. 37)

Use only an apostrophe to form the possessive of plural nouns that end in s.

> The investors' goals were outlined in the stockholders' report.
> But: The investors outlined their goals in the report to the stockholders.
> But: The women's and children's clothing was on sale.

RULE 17
' pronoun
(L. 37)

Use 's to form the possessive of indefinite pronouns (such as someone's or anybody's); do not use an apostrophe with personal pronouns (such as hers, his, its, ours, theirs, and yours).

> She could select anybody's paper for a sample.
> It's time to put the file back into its cabinet.

Colons

RULE 18
: explanatory material
(L. 91)

Use a colon to introduce explanatory material that follows an independent clause.

> The computer satisfies three criteria: speed, cost, and power.
>
> But: The computer satisfies the three criteria of speed, cost, and power.
>
> Remember this: only one coupon is allowed per customer.

Note: An independent clause can stand alone as a complete sentence. Do not capitalize the word following the colon.

Periods

RULE 19
. polite request
(L. 91)

Use a period to end a sentence that is a polite request.

> Will you please call me if I can be of further assistance.

Note: Consider a sentence a polite request if you expect the reader to respond by doing as you ask rather than by giving a yes-or-no answer.

Quotation Marks

RULE 20
" direct quotation
(L. 41)

Use quotation marks around a direct quotation.

> Harrison responded by saying, "Their decision does not affect us."
>
> But: Harrison responded by saying that their decision does not affect us.

RULE 21
" title
(L. 41)

Use quotation marks around the title of a newspaper or magazine article, chapter in a book, report, and similar terms.

> The most helpful article I found was "Multimedia for All."

Italics (or Underline)

RULE 22
title or title
(L. 41)

Italicize (or underline) the titles of books, magazines, newspapers, and other complete published works.

> Grisham's *The Brethren* was reviewed in a recent *USA Today* article.

GRAMMAR

Sentences

<table>
<tr><td>

RULE 23
fragment
(L. 21)

</td></tr>
</table>

Avoid sentence fragments.

> Not: She had always wanted to be a financial manager. But had not had the needed education.
>
> But: She had always wanted to be a financial manager but had not had the needed education.

Note: A fragment is a part of a sentence that is incorrectly punctuated as a complete sentence. In the first example above, "but had not had the needed education" is not a complete sentence because it does not contain a subject.

<table>
<tr><td>

RULE 24
run-on
(L. 21)

</td></tr>
</table>

Avoid run-on sentences.

> Not: Mohamed is a competent worker he has even passed the MOS exam.
> Not: Mohamed is a competent worker, he has even passed the MOS exam.
> But: Mohamed is a competent worker; he has even passed the MOS exam.
> Or: Mohamed is a competent worker. He has even passed the MOS exam.

Note: A run-on sentence is two independent clauses that run together without any punctuation between them or with only a comma between them.

Agreement

<table>
<tr><td>

RULE 25
agreement singular
agreement plural
(L. 67)

</td></tr>
</table>

Use singular verbs and pronouns with singular subjects; use plural verbs and pronouns with plural subjects.

> I <u>was</u> happy with <u>my</u> performance.
> <u>Janet and Phoenix</u> <u>were</u> happy with <u>their</u> performance.
> Among the items discussed <u>were</u> our <u>raises and benefits</u>.

<table>
<tr><td>

RULE 26
agreement pronoun
(L. 81)

</td></tr>
</table>

Some pronouns (*anybody, each, either, everybody, everyone, much, neither, no one, nobody,* and *one*) are always singular and take a singular verb. Other pronouns (*all, any, more, most, none,* and *some*) may be singular or plural, depending on the noun to which they refer.

> <u>Each</u> of the employees has finished <u>his or her</u> task.
> <u>Much</u> <u>remains</u> to be done.
> <u>Most</u> of the pie <u>was</u> eaten, but <u>most</u> of the cookies <u>were</u> left.

<table>
<tr><td>

RULE 27
agreement intervening words
(L. 81)

</td></tr>
</table>

Disregard any intervening words that come between the subject and verb when establishing agreement.

> That <u>box</u>, containing the books and pencils, <u>has</u> not been found.
> <u>Alex</u>, accompanied by Tricia and Roxy, <u>is</u> attending the conference and taking <u>his</u> computer.

<table>
<tr><td>

RULE 28
agreement nearer noun
(L. 101)

</td></tr>
</table>

If two subjects are joined by *or, either/or, neither/nor,* or *not only/but also,* make the verb agree with the subject nearer to the verb.

> Neither the coach nor the <u>players</u> <u>are</u> at home.
> Not only the coach but also the <u>referee</u> <u>is</u> at home.
> But: <u>Both</u> the coach and the referee <u>are</u> at home.

Pronouns

RULE 29
nominative pronoun
(L. 107)

Use nominative pronouns (such as *I, he, she, we, they,* and *who*) as subjects of a sentence or clause.

> The programmer and <u>he</u> are reviewing the code.
> Barb is a person <u>who</u> can do the job.

RULE 30
objective pronoun
(L. 107)

Use objective pronouns (such as *me, him, her, us, them,* and *whom*) as objects of a verb, preposition, or infinitive.

> The code was reviewed by the programmer and <u>him</u>.
> Barb is the type of person <u>whom</u> we can trust.

Adjectives and Adverbs

RULE 31
adjective/adverb
(L. 101)

Use comparative adjectives and adverbs (*-er, more,* and *less*) when referring to two nouns or pronouns; use superlative adjectives and adverbs (*-est, most,* and *least*) when referring to more than two.

> The <u>shorter</u> of the <u>two</u> training sessions is the <u>more</u> helpful one.
> The <u>longest</u> of the <u>three</u> training sessions is the <u>least</u> helpful one.

Word Usage

RULE 32
accept/except
(L. 117)

Accept **means "to agree to";** ***except*** **means "to leave out."**

> All employees <u>except</u> the maintenance staff should <u>accept</u> the agreement.

RULE 33
affect/effect
(L. 117)

Affect **is most often used as a verb meaning "to influence";** ***effect*** **is most often used as a noun meaning "result."**

> The ruling will <u>affect</u> our domestic operations but will have no <u>effect</u> on our Asian operations.

RULE 34
farther/further
(L. 117)

Farther **refers to distance;** ***further*** **refers to extent or degree.**

> The <u>farther</u> we drove, the <u>further</u> agitated he became.

RULE 35
personal/personnel
(L. 117)

Personal **means "private";** ***personnel*** **means "employees."**

> All <u>personnel</u> agreed not to use e-mail for <u>personal</u> business.

RULE 36
principal/principle
(L. 117)

Principal **means "primary";** ***principle*** **means "rule."**

> The <u>principle</u> of fairness is our <u>principal</u> means of dealing with customers.

MECHANICS

Capitalization

RULE 37
≡ sentence
(L. 31)

Capitalize the first word of a sentence.

> Please prepare a summary of your activities.

RULE 38
≡ proper noun
(L. 31)

Capitalize proper nouns and adjectives derived from proper nouns.

> Judy Hendrix drove to Albuquerque in her new Pontiac convertible.

Note: A proper noun is the official name of a particular person, place, or thing.

RULE 39
≡ time
(L. 31)

Capitalize the names of the days of the week, months, holidays, and religious days (but do not capitalize the names of the seasons).

> On Thursday, November 25, we will celebrate Thanksgiving, the most popular holiday in the fall.

RULE 40
≡ noun #
(L. 77)

Capitalize nouns followed by a number or letter (except for the nouns *line, note, page, paragraph,* and *size*).

> Please read Chapter 5, which begins on page 94.

RULE 41
≡ compass point
(L. 77)

Capitalize compass points (such as *north, south,* or *northeast*) only when they designate definite regions.

> From Montana we drove south to reach the Southwest.

RULE 42
≡ organization
(L. 111)

Capitalize common organizational terms (such as *advertising department* and *finance committee*) only when they are the actual names of the units in the writer's own organization and when they are preceded by the word *the*.

> The report from the Advertising Department is due today.
> But: Our advertising department will submit its report today.

RULE 43
≡ course
(L. 111)

Capitalize the names of specific course titles but not the names of subjects or areas of study.

> I have enrolled in Accounting 201 and will also take a marketing course.

Number Expression

RULE 44
general
(L. 47)

In general, spell out numbers zero through ten, and use figures for numbers above ten.

> We rented two movies for tonight.
> The decision was reached after 27 precincts sent in their results.

<table>
<tr><td>

RULE 45
figure
(L. 47)

</td><td>

Use figures for

- **Dates. (Use *st, d,* or *th* only if the day comes before the month.)**

  The tax report is due on April 15 (not *April 15th*).

  We will drive to the camp on the 23d (or *23rd* or *23ʳᵈ*) of May.

- **All numbers if two or more *related* numbers both above and below ten are used in the same sentence.**

  Mr. Carter sent in 7 receipts, and Ms. Cantrell sent in 22.

  But: The 13 accountants owned three computers each.

- **Measurements (time, money, distance, weight, and percent).**

  The $500 statue we delivered at 7 a.m. weighed 6 pounds.

- **Mixed numbers.**

  Our sales are up 9½ (or *9.5*) percent over last year.

</td></tr>
<tr><td>

RULE 46
word
(L. 57)

</td><td>

Spell out

- **A number used as the first word of a sentence.**

  Seventy-five people attended the conference in San Diego.

- **The shorter of two adjacent numbers.**

  We have ordered 3 two-pound cakes and one 5-pound cake for the reception.

- **The words *million* and *billion* in round numbers (do not use decimals with round numbers).**

  Not: A $5.00 ticket can win $28,000,000 in this month's lottery.

  But: A $5 ticket can win $28 million in this month's lottery.

- **Fractions.**

  Almost one-half of the audience responded to the question.

</td></tr>
</table>

Abbreviations

<table>
<tr><td>

RULE 47
abbreviate none
(L. 67)

</td><td>

In general business writing, do not abbreviate common words (such as *dept.* or *pkg.*), compass points, units of measure, or the names of months, days of the week, cities, or states (except in addresses).

Almost one-half of the audience indicated they were at least 5 <u>feet</u> 8 inches tall.

Note: Do not insert a comma between the parts of a single measurement.

</td></tr>
<tr><td>

RULE 48
abbreviate measure
(L. 87)

</td><td>

In technical writing, on forms, and in tables, abbreviate units of measure when they occur frequently. Do not use periods.

14 oz   5 ft 10 in   50 mph   2 yrs 10 mo

</td></tr>
<tr><td>

RULE 49
abbreviate lowercase
(L. 87)

</td><td>

In most lowercase abbreviations made up of single initials, use a period after each initial but no internal spaces.

a.m.   p.m.   i.e.   e.g.   e.o.m.

Exceptions: mph   mpg   wpm

</td></tr>
<tr><td>

RULE 50
abbreviate ≡
(L. 87)

</td><td>

In most all-capital abbreviations made up of single initials, do not use periods or internal spaces.

OSHA   PBS   NBEA   WWW   VCR   MBA

Exceptions: U.S.A.   A.A.   B.S.   Ph.D.   P.O.   B.C.   A.D.

</td></tr>
</table>

PART 4

Advanced Formatting

Keyboarding in Health Services

Within the health services job cluster, there is an enormous range of opportunities in the medical and health care job market. Hundreds of different occupations exist in health care practice, including business-oriented positions. In fact, career opportunities within this cluster are among the fastest growing in the national marketplace.

The current job outlook is quite positive because the growth in managed care has significantly increased opportunities for doctors and other health professionals, particularly in the area of preventive care. In addition, the aging population requires more highly skilled medical workers.

Consider health care jobs, medical careers, health care management, and medical management. Various job possibilities exist in positions such as a medical assistant, clinical technician, nurse, medical analyst, surgical technician or surgeon, physical therapist, orderly, pharmacist, or medical researcher. Keyboarding skill is important for all of these positions.

Goals

Keyboarding

- Demonstrate improved speed and accuracy when operating the keyboard by touch.
- Type at least 43 words per minute on a 5-minute timed writing with no more than 5 errors.

Language Arts

- Demonstrate acceptable proofreading skills, including using proofreaders' marks correctly.
- Demonstrate acceptable language arts skills in punctuation, grammar, and mechanics.
- Demonstrate acceptable language arts skills in composing and spelling.

Word Processing

- Use appropriate word processing commands necessary to complete document processing activities successfully.

Document Processing

- Correctly format e-mail, multipage correspondence, multipage reports, and tables.

Objective Test

- Answer questions with acceptable accuracy on an objective test.

13

Skill Refinement

Skillbuilding and Letter Review

Goals

- Demonstrate improved speed and accuracy while typing by touch.
- Demonstrate acceptable language arts skills in comma usage.
- Correctly format a rough-draft document and apply proofreaders' marks.
- Correctly format a business letter and personal-business letter in block style and in modified-block style.

A. WARMUP

alphabet   1   Six women quietly got the prizes back from the five judges.

concentration   2   electromagnetically pseudointellectuals overdiversification

easy   3   Di may work as a tutor for the six girls who asked for one.

Skillbuilding

B. MAP+: ALPHABET

Follow the GDP software directions for this exercise to improve keystroking accuracy.

C. PROGRESSIVE PRACTICE: ALPHABET

Follow the GDP software directions for this exercise to improve keystroking speed.

Language Arts

Study the rules at the right.

D. COMMAS

Note: The callout signals in the left margin indicate which language arts rule from this lesson has been applied.

Use a comma between each item in a series of three or more.

RULE
, series

> We need to order paper, toner, and font cartridges for the printer.
> They saved their work, exited their program, and turned off their computers when they finished.

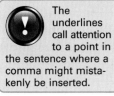

The underlines call attention to a point in the sentence where a comma might mistakenly be inserted.

Note: Do not use a comma after the last item in a series.

Use a comma before and after a transitional expression or independent comment.

It is critical, therefore, that we finish the project on time.
Our present projections, you must admit, are inadequate.
But: You must admit our present projections are inadequate.

Note: Examples of transitional expressions and independent comments are *in addition to, therefore, however, on the other hand, as a matter of fact,* and *unfortunately.*

Edit each sentence to correct any errors.

4 The lawyer the bank and the courthouse received copies.

5 The closing was delayed therefore for more than an hour.

6 The contract power of attorney and deed were in order.

7 Ms. Sperry's flight was delayed however for two hours.

8 Happily the drinks snacks and napkins arrived on time.

9 This offer I think will be unacceptable to the board.

10 Please read their report make whatever comments you feel
11 are appropriate and then route it to the others.

Formatting

E. ADVANCED FORMATTING

The document processing jobs in this unit review basic formatting for correspondence, reports, tables, and employment documents. Before beginning these jobs, review the introductory lessons in the Word Manual and the pages in the Reference Manual listed next. The fundamental information in these pages will prepare you to format and type the jobs in this unit and those that follow.

In the Word Manual, review Getting Started, Lessons 21–25, and Lesson 28. In the Reference Manual, review R-5C–D, R-14C, R-9D, R-13D, and R-12C–D.

As you format document processing jobs, note the following:

- Whenever you see "20--," type the current year in black.
- The | symbol indicates the end of a line. Press ENTER whenever you see it.
- The ¶ symbol indicates a new, blocked paragraph.
- In Word, lines wrap automatically as you approach the right margin. Your line endings in Word may not match those in the book.
- Type your own reference initials in lowercase (no periods or spaces) in

black whenever you see urs in letters or memos.
- Lines are shown with extra spacing for proofreaders' marks. Use standard spacing in all jobs.
- Center tables that appear alone on a page horizontally and vertically, and automatically adjust the column widths.
- Tables with borders removed are shown with "View Gridlines" active.

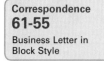

REFER TO
Word Manual
L. 45

Correspondence
61-55
Business Letter in
Block Style

REFER TO
Reference Manual

R-3A: Business Letter in
Block Style

, series

, transitional expression

June 3, 20-- | Mr. Andres Macias | Director of Product Development | Hampton Associates Inc. | 830 Market Street | San Francisco, CA 94102-1925 | Dear Mr. Macias:

¶ Have you had customer groups assist you or provide you with advice related to pending business decisions regarding computer design? Such design standards would include industrywide interfaces and computer hardware and software.

¶ I recently read an article discussing the influence consumer opinion can have on the design of various computer components. This very interesting article concluded that if customers demand standardization in computer hardware, participate in focus groups, and band together with other customers, they will see results reflected in the marketplace.

¶ I am considering organizing several focus groups and, therefore, would appreciate any advice you might have. I know your expertise will prove to be invaluable, and I thank you in advance for your time and consideration.

Sincerely yours, | Alice Karns | Product Development Manager | urs

Correspondence
61-56
Personal-Business Letter
in Block Style

REFER TO
Reference Manual

R-3D: Personal-Business
Letter in Modified-Block
Style
R-14C: Proofreaders'
Marks

, series

, transitional expression

september 1, 20--

Dr. David L. Grant | 3329 Market Street | Salem, OR 97301| Dear Dr. Grant:

¶ Thank you for your letter of August 27 (25) inquiring about my trip to New York city. Your letter brought back a lot of memories of those days when I was your student at Portland State University. We spent many weekends discussing all matters of importance and I'm sure we must have solved the worlds problems many times over. ¶ I will leave on Oct. 15th for a 2-week business trip where I will be conducting a workshop at Columbia University on the utilization of voice-activated hardware *equipment*. When I complete my work on October 22, I would love to have you and your wife join me in New York City. I plan to attend *a number of* plays, visit the Metropolitan Museum of Art and take one of the sightseeing tours. I would be happy to make hotel reservations and purchase theatre tickets.

¶ I hope you'll consider joining me in the "Big Apple"! It would be great to see you and your wife again. However, I do need to know soon so that I can proceed with our plans. I look forward to hearing from you.

Sincerely, | Rodney Dorey | 1329 Broadway # Street | Eureka, California *CA* 95501

Correspondence
61-57
Business Letter in
Modified-Block Style

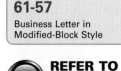

REFER TO
Reference Manual

R-3B: Business Letter in
Modified-Block Style

Open the file for Correspondence 61-55 and make the following changes:

1. Change the letter format to modified-block style.
2. Change the addressee name to this:
   Mr. Peng Lim
3. Change the salutation to this:
   Dear Mr. Lim:
4. Delete the last paragraph and replace it with this:

```
I would certainly appreciate
meeting you and discussing
this in person. Your advice
is very valuable, and your
reputation in this industry
is stellar. I will contact
you soon.
```

Skillbuilding, Memo, and E-Mail Review

Goals

- Type at least 40wpm/5'/5e.
- Correctly format a memo and an e-mail message.
- Correctly format a rough-draft document and apply proofreaders' marks.

A. WARMUP

alphabet	1	Very few phlox grew or bloomed just back of my zinc quarry.
one hand	2	tracer uplink tax lip regard plumply date phony waste polio
easy	3	The goal of their amendment is to make the city proficient.

Skillbuilding

B. SUSTAINED PRACTICE: ALTERNATE-HAND WORDS

Take a 1-minute timed writing on the boxed paragraph to establish your base speed. Then take a 1-minute timed writing on the following paragraph. As soon as you equal or exceed your base speed on this paragraph, move to the next, more difficult paragraph.

4	The town council decided to shape its destiny when a	11
5	rich landowner lent a hand by proposing to chair the audit	23
6	committee. He will be a good chairman, and eight civic	34
7	club members will work to amend some troublesome policies.	46

8	One problem relates to the change in profit for many	11
9	of the firms in the city. As giant property taxes do not	22
10	relate to income, they wish to make those taxes go down.	33
11	The result means increases in their sales or income taxes.	45

12	All eight members of the town council now agree that	11
13	it is time to join with other cities throughout the state	12
14	in lobbying with the state legislature to bring about the	35
15	needed change. The right balance in taxes is the goal.	46

16	The mayor pointed out that it is not only business	10
17	property owners who would be affected. Homeowners should	22
18	see a decrease in property taxes, and renters might see	33
19	lower rents, as taxes on rental property would be lowered.	45

1 | 2 | 3 | 4 | 5 | 6 | 7 | 8 | 9 | 10 | 11 | 12

C. 5-MINUTE TIMED WRITING

20	Digital photography has revolutionized the way we take	11
21	pictures. A digital camera puts our photos in a format that	23
22	makes them easy to print and share with others. Using a	34
23	digital camera also has the advantage that we can quickly	46
24	print out our photos and see the result of our efforts.	57
25	We can also insert our photos into word processing	68
26	documents, send them by e-mail to our friends, or post them	80
27	on the Web where they can be viewed by all. We can even	91
28	connect our camera to a television set and have our images	103
29	displayed in a slide show presentation.	111
30	Another advantage of digital photography is that the	121
31	expense of developing your own photos is much less because	133
32	you do not have to purchase rolls of film, nor do you have	145
33	to have your photos developed by others. Also, your photos	157
34	can be edited if you do not like what you see. You can crop	169
35	the photo, adjust its color or contrast, take out red-eye	180
36	imperfections, and even add or delete elements from the	192
37	photo or from other photos you have taken.	200

1 | 2 | 3 | 4 | 5 | 6 | 7 | 8 | 9 | 10 | 11 | 12

REFER TO Word Manual

L. 23 & L. 25

Correspondence 62-58
Memo

REFER TO Reference Manual

R-4D: Memo

Document Processing

MEMO TO: Min-Hong Dai, Theater Manager | **FROM:** Barbara Cornell, Executive Director | **DATE:** March 1, 20-- | **SUBJECT:** Season Ticket Price Schedule for Orchestra Hall

¶ We have tentatively scheduled 114 concerts for Orchestra Hall for the calendar year beginning September 1. The attached list shows the new season ticket prices for the main floor, mezzanine, balcony, and gallery.

¶ These prices are grouped in 11 different concert categories, which reflect the varied classical tastes of our patrons. These groupings also consider preferences for day of the week, time of day, and season of the year.

¶ Please see me in my office at 3 p.m. on March 10 so that we can review our ticket sales campaign. Last year's season ticket holders have had ample time to renew their subscriptions; we must now concentrate on attracting new season subscribers. I shall look forward to reviewing your plans.

urs | Attachment

Correspondence 62-59
E-Mail Message

Mr. Phillips:

¶ We are interested in implementing a new security program for the personal computers in our main office and would like to study the specifications and features your system provides.

(continued on next page)

In Word, when you type an e-mail address and then a space, an e-mail hyperlink is inserted automatically.

¶ Please send information and prices on your state-of-the-art security software. The ready availability of the Internet to the general public and others has made the prevention of identity theft, phishing, and other types of related scams a top security priority in our firm.

¶ Thank you for your assistance.

Charles | Charles Cox | E-mail: chcox@mailserver.net | Phone: 770-555-2843

Correspondence 62-60 Memo

MEMO TO: Eduardo Bocelli, Cabaret pops Conductor

FROM: Marcia Greene, Executive Director

Date: March 2, 20--

SUBJECT: Irving Berlin Concert

Our Patron Advisory Program Committee has included several recommendations in it's *its* attached letter. They would like the Irving Berlin concert to begin with some pre-World War I hits, followed by ~~music~~ *songs* from the 1920s and 1930s. The first part of the ~~program~~ *evening* will focus on favorite hit songs from the 1920s and 1930s. After the intermission, the program will focus on hit songs from the 1940s and 1950s. A planning meeting has been scheduled for you, Dolly Carpenter (the Rehearsals Coordinator), and me on Mar. 9 at 10 A.M. at Orchestra Hall. I look forward to seeing you then.

urs

Attachments

c:Dolly Carpenter

Correspondence 62-61 Memo

MEMO TO: Dolly Carpenter, Rehearsals Coordinator
FROM: Sam Steele, Executive Director
DATE: March 3, 20--
SUBJECT: Summer Cabaret Pops Concerts

¶ We are pleased that you will be our rehearsals coordinator for this summer's Cabaret Pops concerts. The five biweekly concerts will run from June 13 through August 8.

¶ As the concert schedule is much lighter during the summer months, I am quite confident that you will be able to use the Orchestra Hall stage for all rehearsals. This is the preference of Eduardo Bocelli, who will be the conductor for this summer's Cabaret Pops concerts.

¶ I look forward to seeing you on June 1.

¶ urs

Skillbuilding and Report Review

63

Goals

- Demonstrate improved speed and accuracy while typing.
- Demonstrate acceptable proofreading skills by comparing lines.
- Correctly format a business report and an academic report.

A. WARMUP

alphabet

practice: *u* and *y*

easy

1 Just keep examining every low bid quoted for zinc etchings.
2 yum buy duly yuck fury your guy July busy yuk quay you jury
3 Pam blames all her problems on the rituals of the sorority.

Skillbuilding

B. MAP+: NUMBERS

Follow the GDP software directions for this exercise to improve keystroking accuracy.

PPP

PRETEST » PRACTICE » POSTTEST

PRETEST

Take a 1-minute timed writing. Review your speed and errors.

C. PRETEST: Discrimination Practice

4   Lois said the rear of the long train was right next   11
5 to the column of poplar trees. A robber had entered a red   22
6 car and stolen a case of grapefruit juice and ten cases of   34
7 soda pop. The officer quickly arrested him on the street.   45

  1 | 2 | 3 | 4 | 5 | 6 | 7 | 8 | 9 | 10 | 11 | 12

PRACTICE

Speed Emphasis:
If you made no more than 1 error on the Pretest, type each *individual* line 2 times.

Accuracy Emphasis:
If you made 2 or more errors, type each *group* of lines (as though it were a paragraph) 2 times.

D. PRACTICE: Left Hand

8 rtr trip trot sport train alert courts assert tragic truest
9 asa mass salt usage cased cease astute dashed masked castle
10 sds sad used suds said pods based drips curds stride guards
11 rer rear rest overt rerun older before entire surest better

E. PRACTICE: Right Hand

12 mnm menu numb hymns unmet manly mental namely manner number
13 pop post coop opera pools opens polite proper police oppose
14 olo tool yolk loon spoil lodge color stroll lottery rolling
15 iui unit quit fruit suits built medium guided helium podium

POSTTEST
Repeat the Pretest timed
writing and compare
performance.

F. POSTTEST: Discrimination Practice

Language Arts

Compare this paragraph
with the last paragraph
of the timed writing
on page 239. Edit the
paragraph to correct any
errors.

G. PROOFREADING

16   Another advantage of digital photography is that the
17 the expense of developing your own photos is less because you
18 do not have to buy any rolls of film, nor do you have
19 to have your photos developed by others. Also, your photos
20 can be edited if you do not like what you see. You can crop
21 the photo, adjust it's color or contrast, take out red-eye
22 imperfections and even add or delete elements from the photo
23 or from other photographs you have taken.

REFER TO
Word Manual

L. 31, L. 32, L. 34 &
L. 46

Report
63-34
Business Report

Document Processing

VIDEO-BASED TRAINING PROGRAMS
Rodolfo Madison, Training Consultant

¶ Video-based training programs are being implemented at an ever-increasing
rate across the country. While this type of training should certainly not be the
only method that is used to train your employees, it is very effective and can offer
significant advantages over other training methods.

ADVANTAGES

¶ There are many advantages to video-based training. However, only the most
significant ones are discussed here.

Save Development Time. You can shorten your training cycle because you will have
the ability to deliver "just-in-time" training where and when you need it. Facilitation
materials with activities and discussion points can be used in whole or in part to
create training events that run anywhere from one to four hours.

Add Variety to the Delivery Mix. Workshops and lectures can become routine and
boring. Video provides a change of pace and can add an entertainment factor that
is not possible in a live presentation. Videos can also be used to supplement a face-
to-face workshop to stimulate discussion, demonstrate concepts that could not
otherwise be presented, and provide meaningful examples of the topic at hand. The
more the senses are engaged in the content, the more the participants will learn.

Build a Resource Library. Building a video and/or DVD library allows you to offer
a broader range of training. You will no longer be limited to custom in-house
development or scheduled classroom events. Trainees can check out a DVD or
access video training online.

(continued on next page)

RECOMMENDATION

¶ Video-based training materials save your organization time and money, and they make your business look progressive. Because they help build learning retention, they can also improve the return on your training investment. The next step should be a formal review of your training needs and an evaluation report to be completed by a professional video-based training firm with a proven track record.

Report
63-35
Academic Report

REFER TO
Reference
Manual

R-8C–D: Multipage
Academic Report

BECOMING A FITNESS WORKER
Cal Jordan

According to the U.S. Department of Labor's Bureau of Labor Statistics, "Jobs for fitness workers are expected to increase much faster than the average for all occupations."[1] Fitness workers should have good job prospects due to rapid job growth in health clubs, fitness facilities, and other settings where fitness workers are concentrated.

NATURE OF THE WORK

Fitness workers primarily instruct and motivate individuals or groups in a variety of exercise activities. A rising trend is providing fitness trainers in the workplace as an employee benefit. There are several categories of fitness workers.

Personal Trainers. Personal trainers work one-on-one with individuals to help them assess their level of physical fitness and set and reach fitness goals. Trainers can also demonstrate exercises to help clients improve their exercise techniques. They may keep records of exercise sessions for monitoring progress and offer advice regarding lifestyles outside of the gym to improve fitness. They often work in a variety of places—health clubs, hospitals, fitness studios, resorts, and private homes are typical.

When you type text followed by two hyphens (--), followed by more text and then a space, a formatted em dash (—) will automatically be inserted.

Group Exercise Instructors. Group exercise instructors conduct group exercise sessions, including aerobic exercise, stretching, and muscle conditioning. Classes are often set to music, and Pilates and yoga are often incorporated. Exercise classes should be motivating, safe, and challenging. Louise Byron says that classes that incorporate Pilates and yoga can be more effective than weight training for overall strength and toning.[2]

Fitness Directors. Fitness directors oversee health club or fitness center activities. They might create programs for member orientations, fitness assessments, and workout incentive programs. They also select fitness equipment; coordinate training programs; hire, train, and supervise fitness staff; and carry out other administrative duties.

RELATED OCCUPATIONS

Other workers that focus on physical fitness include athletes, coaches, and physical therapists. For example, a physical therapist is often required to create exercise plans to improve their patients' flexibility, strength, and endurance. Dietitians and nutritionists also have related careers because they offer advice on improving and maintaining good health.

Remove any automatic hyperlinks for electronic references enclosed by angle brackets immediately after they appear, and replace the angle brackets as needed.

[1] U.S. Department of Labor, *Occupational Outlook Handbook*, <http://www.bls.gov/oco/ocos296.htm>, accessed on April 22, 2010.

[2] Louise Byron, *Pilates and Yoga for Strength and Fitness*, 2nd ed., Midwest Publishing, Chicago, 2010, p. 20.

Report
63-36
Left-Bound Business
Report

REFER TO
Reference
Manual

R-9A: Left-Bound
Business Report

Open the file for Report 63-34 and make the following changes:

1. Change the report from a business report to a left-bound business report.
2. Add this new paragraph heading and paragraph as the last paragraph in the ADVANTAGES section of the report:

Supplement Existing Training Resources. Videos can often be used to support more than one of your training initiatives. For example, you can use a video like *Leadership for the New Millennium* to enhance workshops on decision making, leadership, teamwork, or communication.

3. Add a page number to display on the second page only.

Strategies for Career Success

Looking for a Job

Don't waste time! Start your job search early. Scan the Help Wanted sections in major Sunday newspapers or their Web sites for job descriptions and salaries. The Internet provides access to worldwide job listings at sites like Monster.com, Dice.com, Craigslist.com, and on company and government Web sites, such as the federal government's jobs site (http://www.usajobs.gov/).

Consult references such as the U.S. Department of Labor's *Occupational Outlook Handbook* (http://www.bls.gov/oco/) to research types of jobs in various fields and the requirements for those jobs. Visit your college placement office. Sign up for interviews with companies that visit your campus.

Talk with people in your field to get advice. Look for an internship or join a professional organization in your field. Attend local chapter meetings to network with people in your chosen profession.

Taking the initiative in your job search will pay off!

Your Turn: Visit the Internet site for the *National Business Employment Weekly* at http://www.employmentguide.com, which provides more than 45,000 national and international job listings online.

Skillbuilding and Table Review

Goals

- Type at least 40wpm/5′/5e.
- Correctly format a boxed table, an open table, and a ruled table.

A. WARMUP

alphabet   1 George W. Bush quickly fixed prize jam cakes on television.

frequent digraphs   2 ti tie anti tic site tilt tin tithe stir tide tick tip tint

easy   3 I may make a quantity of maps to aid me when I visit Japan.

Skillbuilding

B. PROGRESSIVE PRACTICE: NUMBERS

Follow the GDP software directions for this exercise to improve keystroking speed.

C. TECHNIQUE PRACTICE: SHIFT KEY

Type each line 2 times. After striking the capitalized letter, return the SHIFT KEY finger immediately to home-row position.

4 Aldo Bonilla skied. Clara Duarte typed. Ellen Fuller filed.
5 Guy Hayes ate dinner. Isabella Jayne hid. Kevin Lee sobbed.
6 Megan Newsome sat. Otis Petrov tried. Quincy Rogers hummed.
7 Syd Tia wed Ursula Vivian. Willie Xin and Yvonne Zola lied.

Take two 5-minute timed
writings. Review your
speed and errors.

Goal: At least
40wpm/5'/5e

D. 5-MINUTE TIMED WRITING

8	The computer has changed the way you do things in the	11
9	office today. Jobs that used to take many hours to complete	23
10	now can be done in less time. A quick review of ways in	34
11	which the computer can help you streamline your work may	46
12	be in order.	48
13	Most software programs include helpful wizards that	59
14	can guide you through any project. You can use a stored	70
15	template, or you can create your own style. You do not need	82
16	to write your thoughts in longhand on paper before you type	94
17	them. Composing and revising documents as you type them	105
18	will save you lots of time.	111
19	Your computer is valuable for more than just writing	122
20	letters. Using different software applications, you can	133
21	create dazzling presentations for all to see. You can also	145
22	build databases for sorting and storing all types of data,	156
23	format spreadsheets, create your own calendar and colorful	169
24	charts, and perform calculations. You can even publish your	180
25	own newsletter and make business cards. It is exciting to	192
26	consider the ways you can use a computer.	200

1 | 2 | 3 | 4 | 5 | 6 | 7 | 8 | 9 | 10 | 11 | 12

REFER TO
Word Manual

L. 28 & L. 36–39

Table
64-23
Boxed Table

REFER TO
Reference
Manual

R-13A: Boxed Table

Document Processing

$700 COMPOUNDED ANNUALLY FOR 7 YEARS AT 7 PERCENT		
Beginning of Year	**Interest**	**Value**
First	$00.00	$ 700.00
Second	49.00	749.00
Third	52.43	801.43
Fourth	56.10	857.53
Fifth	60.03	917.56
Sixth	64.23	981.79
Seventh	68.72	1,050.51
Eighth	78.68	1,129.19

Table
64-24
Open Table

REFER TO
Reference Manual

R-13B: Open Table

SALES CONFERENCES All Sessions at Regional Offices		
Date	City	Leader
October 7	Boston	D. G. Gorham
October 17	Baltimore	James B. Brunner
October 24	Miami	Becky Taylor
November 3	Dallas	Rodney R. Nordstein
November 10	Minneapolis	Joanne Miles-Tyrell
November 17	Denver	Becky Taylor
November 26	Los Angeles	Rodney R. Nordstein

Table
64-25
Ruled Table

REFER TO
Reference Manual

R-13C: Ruled Table

COMPARISON OF SALES QUOTAS AND ACTUAL SALES
July to December

Month	Sales Quotas	Actual Sales
July	$ 935,400	$ 950,620
August	970,750	896,230
September	974,510	725,110
October	990,270	990,110
November	975,890	968,290
December	1,960,470	1,978,690
Totals	$6,807,290	$6,509,050

Keyboarding Connection

Finding Business Information on the Internet

Finding information about businesses on the Internet is easy. If you want to research a company, you can go to its Web site, or you can use a search engine to find out what resources and information are available. Sites like Bloomberg.com and Yahoo! have articles about business trends and companies. Professional organizations like the American Management Association and the Chamber of Commerce also have Web sites where you can learn about their member businesses.

Start by using a search engine like Google, and you'll find plenty of business information available on the Internet. Company Web sites often have an About Us link, where you can learn more about specific companies.

Your Turn: Access the *Selected Business Resources on the Web* site at http://www.bls.gov and explore its offerings.

Correspondence

Multipage Letters

66

Goals

- Type at least 41wpm/5′/5e.
- Correctly format a multipage letter.

A. WARMUP

alphabet 1 A puzzled woman bequeathed idiotic jerks very exotic gifts.
concentration 2 nonrepresentational counterinsurgencies individualistically
easy 3 A new toxic problem may ensue if we burn the old cornfield.

Skillbuilding

B. SUSTAINED PRACTICE: ROUGH DRAFT

Take a 1-minute timed writing on the boxed paragraph to establish your base speed. Then take a 1-minute timed writing on the following paragraph. As soon as you equal or exceed your base speed on this paragraph, move to the next, more difficult paragraph.

4   The possibility of aging and not being able to live as 11
5 independently as we want to is a prospect that no one wants 23
6 to recognize. One resource designed to counter some of the 35
7 negative realities of aging is called the Handyman Project. 47

8   This type of ~~project~~ *program* helps support elders and disabled 12
9 residents in their efforts to maintain the*ir* homes. As the 24
10 name implies, "handy" volunt*e*ers per for*m* minor home repairs 36
11 such as tight*e*ning leaky faucets and fixing broken windows. 48

12 Other type*s* of work include painting, plumbing, yard 11
13 work, and carpent*r*y. The volunteers are all as divers*i*fied 23
14 as the wor*k* itself. You may find a retire*e* working next to 35
15 an executive or a student ~~helping~~ *assisting* a li*c*ensed electrician. 47

16   Their back gr*o*unds may vary, but *w*hat they share is the 11
17 *desire* ~~hope~~ to put their capabilities to good use. Volunteers ~~take~~ *find* 23
18 a high level of personal satisfaction after ~~doing~~ *finishing* a job 35
19 ~~but~~ *and* spending time with *an elder who really needs the help.* 47

1 | 2 | 3 | 4 | 5 | 6 | 7 | 8 | 9 | 10 | 11 | 12

C. 5-MINUTE TIMED WRITING

20	Making a successful presentation to an audience is a	11
21	skill that is absolutely essential in your career. The art	23
22	of speaking before a group requires planning and hard work.	35
23	Although different speakers prepare in many different ways,	47
24	a speaker should try to adhere to certain rules.	56
25	As the speaker, you are quite visible to people in the	68
26	audience. Therefore, you should always try to make a good	79
27	first impression. When you walk to the podium to speak, you	91
28	give the audience a chance to notice your neat appearance,	103
29	good posture, and confident manner. You will improve the	114
30	quality of your voice if you stand up straight and hold	126
31	your shoulders back and stomach in.	133
32	As you talk, use your eyes, face, and hands to help	143
33	you connect with your listeners. Maintain eye contact by	155
34	just moving your eyes over the group without focusing on	166
35	any one person. Use hand movements and facial expressions	178
36	to convey meanings to your audience. By utilizing these	189
37	techniques, you will improve your speaking skills, and your	201
38	effort may be noted.	205

```
1 | 2 | 3 | 4 | 5 | 6 | 7 | 8 | 9 | 10 | 11 | 12
```

Formatting

D. MULTIPAGE LETTERS

To format a multipage letter:

1. Type the first page on letterhead stationery, and type continuation pages on plain paper that matches the letterhead.

2. Insert a page number in the top right-hand corner of the page header of all continuing pages, and remove the page number from the first page.

> 2
>
> I have never been involved with anything like this before. Any help that you give me will be appreciated. I look forward to working with you.
>
> Sincerely,
>
> Gerald H. Fordham
> Attorney at Law
>
> smr
> Enclosure

Document Processing

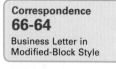

Correspondence
66-64
Business Letter in
Modified-Block Style

REFER TO
Reference
Manual

R-5A–B: Multipage
Business Letter

July 13, 20-- | Miss Florence B. Glashan | Attorney at Law | 2932 Point Street | Providence, RI 02903 | Dear Miss Glashan:

¶ It was a pleasure to meet you at the convention for trial attorneys in New York last week. In addition to the interesting program highlights of the regular sessions, the informal discussions with people like you are an added plus at these meetings. Your contribution to the program was very beneficial and highly informative.

¶ You may recall that I had just been appointed by the court to defend a woman here in Providence who has been charged with embezzling large sums of money from her previous employer. The defendant had been employed at a large department store for more than 25 years. Because of her valuable years of experience in accounting with the store, she was in charge of accounts receivable at the store. Her previous employer, the plaintiff in the case, claims that she embezzled $18,634 three years ago, $39,072 two years ago, and $27,045 last year.

¶ You mentioned that you had represented defendants in similar cases in previous years. Your assistance would be invaluable as I prepare for this defense. If you are willing to lend your professional expertise in this case, here is what is needed:

1. Within the next week, send the appropriate citations for all similar trials in which you participated.
2. Provide any other case citations that you think might be helpful in this case.
3. Meet with me in approximately two weeks for a case consultation. At that time we can discuss compensation for your work on this matter.

¶ A copy of the formal complaint is enclosed for your review. I will call you in about a week to arrange a time and place for our meeting. Please let me know if there is additional information that would be helpful in preparing for this case.

¶ This type of case will present unique challenges, but I know your guidance and years of experience will be invaluable. I look forward to working with you.

Sincerely, | Gerald H. Fordham | Attorney at Law | urs | Enclosure

Correspondence
66-65
Business Letter in
Block Style

April 3, 20--

Mr. ~~Tom~~ *Thomas* Crawford | District Product Manager | Office Supplies of America | 2101 Pennsylvania Avenue, ~~N.W.~~ *nw* | Washington, ~~dc~~ 20006 | Dear Tom:

¶ The Sales Conference in Atlanta last week was out standing. Your winning the "Gold Key" award for the most sales for the year was well deserved indeed.

¶ When you first became part of our salesteam, you showed great enthusiasm for your job immediately. There is no doubt in my mind that Office Supplies of America is well represented in the Washington Metro area.

¶ I particularly want to commend you for obtaining the McKinley account. Acquiring this account ~~have~~ *has* been a major objective for a number of years. None of our other sales representatives ~~has~~ *have* been able to accomplish this feat. What approach did you take, Tom? Did you:

(continued on next page)

1. Spend consider able time with the president, Mr. Arch Davis or one of his associates? If so, who were the individuals involved?

2. Conduct a series of presentations for key personel?

3. Develop a special marketing campaign for McKinley itself?

4. Use a regular campaign model and customize it for McKinley?

5. Combine various strategies in your efforts to obtain this important account?

¶ Please let me know what approaches you used to make this sale. Successes of this nature do _not_ happen without a lot of hard work. You to are be commended for putting forth your best efforts to sign the account.

¶ If we can arrange a time at our annual sales meeting, we would like to have you make a presentation to our Sales Representatives. They would benefit greatly from having you share your success story. Our annual meeting will be held in late September in Richmond, VA.

¶ Again, congratulations on receiving this very prestigious award. All of us here in the home office are greatly ~~very~~ pleased with the performance of our entire sales team. Indications that are this will be a year when our sales records will be broken and we will again be in the media spotlight.

Sincerely yours, | Leonard d. Manchester | President | urs | bc: Maria Olson, Director of Sales

Correspondence 66-66
Business Letter in Modified-Block Style

Open the file for Correspondence 66-64 and make the following changes:

1. Change the inside address to this:

   ```
   2632 East Main Road
   Portsmouth, RI 02871
   ```

2. Replace the last sentence in the first paragraph with these:

   ```
   Networking with colleagues
   like you is always
   ```

   ```
   enlightening and beneficial.
   I value your input greatly.
   ```

3. Add this sentence after the last sentence in the letter:

   ```
   I will call you in a few
   days to discuss this matter
   further.
   ```

Special Correspondence Features

Goals

- Demonstrate improved speed and accuracy while typing.
- Demonstrate acceptable language arts skills in using hyphens, in subject and verb agreement, and in using abbreviations.
- Correctly use Word's sort feature.
- Correctly format correspondence with multiple addresses, on-arrival notations, and subject lines.

A. WARMUP

alphabet	1	How quickly the daft jumping zebras were vexed by the boys.
one hand	2	career uphill gas pin awards homonym read yummy grade lumpy
easy	3	He has on a tux and she has on a tan gown for their social.

Skillbuilding

MAP+

B. MAP+: ALPHABET

Follow the GDP software directions for this exercise to improve keystroking accuracy.

C. PROGRESSIVE PRACTICE: ALPHABET

Follow the GDP software directions for this exercise to improve keystroking speed.

Language Arts

Study the rules at the right.

RULE
- compound adjective

D. HYPHENS

Hyphenate compound adjectives that come before a noun (unless the first word is an adverb ending in -ly).

> We reviewed an up-to-date report on Wednesday.
> But: The report was up to date.
> But: We reviewed the highly rated report.

Note: A compound adjective is two or more words that function as a unit to describe a noun.

E. AGREEMENT

RULE
agreement singular
agreement plural

Use singular verbs and pronouns with singular subjects; use plural verbs and pronouns with plural subjects.

> I <u>was</u> happy with <u>my</u> performance.
> <u>Janet and Phoenix</u> <u>were</u> happy with <u>their</u> performance.
> Among the items discussed <u>were</u> our <u>raises and benefits</u>.

F. ABBREVIATIONS

RULE
abbreviate none

In general business writing, do not abbreviate common words (such as *dept.* or *pkg.*), compass points, units of measure, or the names of months, days of the week, cities, or states (except in addresses).

> Almost one-half of the audience indicated they were at least 5 feet 8 inches tall.

Note: Do not insert a comma between the parts of a single measurement.

Edit each sentence to correct any errors.

4 The Sabins visited Hickory to look at four bedroom homes.

5 Cindy Wallace has a part time job after school.

6 The accountants was extremely busy from March through April.

7 Lydia and Margaret were invited to present their report.

8 The portfolio include several technology stocks.

9 The planning committee will meet on Tue., Sept. 26.

10 Please credit the acct. for the amt. of $55.48.

11 The mgr. said the org. will move its headquarters to NC.

12 Appearing last on the agenda was the reports about the
13 urgently needed parts.

Formatting

G. MULTIPLE ADDRESSES

Often a letter may be sent to two or more people at the same address or to different addresses:

1. If a letter is addressed to two people at the same address, type each name on a separate line above the same inside address.
2. If a letter is addressed to two people at different addresses, type each name and address, one under the other. Press ENTER 2 times between the addresses.
3. If a letter is addressed to three or more people, type the names and addresses side by side, with one at the left margin and another beginning at the center-point. Press ENTER 2 times before typing the third name and address at the left margin.

↓5X
November 19, 20--
↓4X

Dr. Albert Russell, Professor
Department of English
Appalachian State University
Boone, NC 28608
↓2X
Dr. Kay Smith, Professor
Director of Business
Grove City College
Grove City, PA 16127
↓2X
Dear Dr. Russell and Dr. Smith:
↓2X
It is with great pleasure that I announce the scholarship winners for this year's
awards banquet to be held in the next month. The awardees' names are listed
below.
↓2X

H. ON-ARRIVAL NOTATIONS

On-arrival notations (such as *CONFIDENTIAL*) should be typed on the second line
below the date, at the left margin. Type the notation in all-caps. Press ENTER 2 times to
begin the inside address.

↓5X
November 19, 20--
↓2X
CONFIDENTIAL
↓2X
Mr. and Mrs. Earl Walters
3408 Washington Boulevard
New Tripoli, PA 18066
↓2X
Dear Mr. and Mrs. Walters:
↓2X
We are very pleased to tell you that your daughter will be the recipient of a
prestigious scholarship this semester. She will be recognized at a banquet to be
held next month.
↓2X

I. SUBJECT LINES

A *subject line* indicates what a letter is about. Type the subject line below the salutation at
the left margin, preceded and followed by 1 blank line. (The term *Re* or *In re* may be used
in place of *Subject*.)

↓5X
November 19, 20--
↓4X

Mr. and Mrs. Earl Walters
3408 Washington Boulevard
New Tripoli, PA 18066
↓2X
Dear Mr. and Mrs. Walters:
↓2X
Subject: Scholarship Awarded
↓2X
We are very pleased to tell you that your daughter will be the recipient of a very
prestigious scholarship this semester. She will be recognized at a banquet to be
held next month.
↓2X

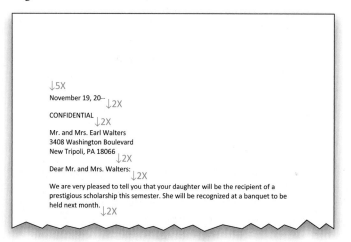

↓5X

J. WORD PROCESSING: SORT

GO TO
Word Manual

Study Lesson 67 in your Word Manual. Complete all of the shaded steps while at your computer. Then format the documents that follow.

Document Processing

Correspondence
67-67
Business Letter in Block Style

- compound adjective

Sort the bulleted list in ascending alphabetical order.

abbreviate none

November 8, 20-- | CONFIDENTIAL | Mrs. Katie Hollister | 11426 Prairie View Road | Kearney, NE 68847 | Dear Mrs. Hollister: | Subject: Site for New Elementary School

¶ As you are aware, your farm, located in the northeast quarter of Section 26 in Tyro township, is a part of Independent School District 17. Each of our three elementary schools occupies 11 acres and is adjoined by an 18-acre park. We are now in the early planning stages for a fourth elementary school. Because your farm is centrally located, the District 17 Board has directed me to initiate discussions with you on the following topics regarding 11 acres of your land:

- Purchasing options
- Time frames for purchasing
- Alternative sites

¶ Please call me to arrange a meeting with you and your attorneys, Jonathan Beck and Myra Colter, no later than November 13. They informed me that they will coordinate their schedules around yours. I look forward to our discussions.

Yours truly, | Irvin J. Hagg | Superintendent | urs | c: District 17 Board

agreement plural

Sort each bulleted list in
ascending alphabetical
order.

October 4, 20-- | Ms. Deborah Campbell Wallace | 7835 Virginia Avenue, NW |
Washington, DC 20037 | Mr. Thomas E. Campbell | 3725 Stevens Road, SE |
Washington, DC 20020 | Dear Ms. Wallace and Mr. Campbell:

¶ We received your letter requesting instructions for transferring stock. The most
common stock transfer situations are provided below. Determine which type of
transfer you require, and select the instructions that apply to your stock transfer.

- Transferring shares to another individual
- Transferring shares to a minor
- Transferring shares from a deceased shareholder (multiple owners)
- Transferring shares from a deceased shareholder (individual ownership)
- Transfers involving a trust
- Transfers involving a power of attorney
- Changing a name

agreement singular

¶ Every transfer requires a letter of instruction specifying how you want your shares
transferred. The following items are required for all types of transfers:

- Name and address of new owner
- Social security number or taxpayer identification number
- Dated and signed form
- Preferred form of ownership (that is, joint tenants or tenants in common)
- Total number of shares being transferred

abbreviate none

¶ Please be sure to submit all required documentation no later than November 1, and
note that all documents submitted become part of the permanent record of transfer
and will not be returned. All transfers must have your signature guaranteed by a
financial institution participating in the Medallion Signature Guarantee Program.

- compound adjective

¶ If you need additional information, you may visit our Web site for step-by-step
instructions, or you may call one of our customer service representatives at our toll-
free number.

Sincerely, | William J. Shawley | Shareholder Services | urs

Nov. 17, 20--

~~Doctor~~ Dr. Francesca Tuscany | 953 Foster Street | Durham, NC 27701 | Dear Dr. Tuscany: |

SUBJECT: January Meeting Book Selection

¶ Your new book, The Iron Hand *ital*, has gotten excellent reviews across the nation. The

agreement plural

citizens of durham are pleased that a respected member of one of their local colleges

is receiving national attention. ¶ Our book discussion group in ~~Morehead~~ Durham, composed

of members of the AAUW (American Association of University Women), is going to

select 1 of your books below for discussion at our January meeting. All the topics

agreement plural

we agreed to discuss were related to your books. We would like you very much to

recommend one of these books:

Sort the bulleted list in
ascending alphabetical
order.

Format book titles
in italic.

SS

- *The Iron Hand*
- *Peace in Troubled Times*
- *A House Divided*

I will call you next week. Your ~~presence~~ attendance at our meeting would be a real highlight.

Sincerely | Theresa Mayfield | 2901 Garfield Court | Durham, NC 27701

More Special Correspondence Features

68

Goals

- Type at least 41wpm/5'/5e.
- Correctly use Word's table shading and e-mail blind copy features.
- Correctly format a table within a document.
- Correctly format correspondence with a company name, delivery notation, blind copy notation and postscript.

A. WARMUP

alphabet

practice: *f* and *d*

easy

1 My folks proved his expert eloquence was just a big hazard.
2 fad fold fodder fed doff defy find fled deaf fund deft fade
3 Sign the forms to pay for the ivory bowl she got in Durham.

Skillbuilding

B. PACED PRACTICE

Follow the GDP software directions for this exercise to improve keystroking speed and accuracy.

C. 5-MINUTE TIMED WRITING

Take two 5-minute timed writings.

Goal: At least 41wpm/5'/5e

4 Taking photos with a digital camera is a process that	11
5 is somewhat unique and different from taking photos with	22
6 film. Most digital cameras store images on a device such as	34
7 a memory card or a memory stick. The number of photos you	46
8 can store on a card or stick depends on how many megabytes	58
9 it can hold. Once you reach the limit of the memory device,	70
10 you can store no new images until you either transfer or	81
11 delete the old ones to make room for new ones.	91
12 The advantages of using a memory device are many. For	102
13 example, the card or stick can be used over and over; or,	113
14 when the device is full, just simply remove it and put in a	125
15 new device. You can also move the images to the computer,	137
16 where they can reside on the hard drive for as long as you	149
17 want. If the memory card or stick you have does not have	160
18 enough memory, you can upgrade the size.	168
19 Finally, you will see instantly any images you have	179
20 taken with the camera. If you decide not to keep an image	190
21 in the camera, you can delete it to make space for other	202
22 exciting images.	205

1 | 2 | 3 | 4 | 5 | 6 | 7 | 8 | 9 | 10 | 11 | 12

D. TABLES WITHIN DOCUMENTS

To format a table that is part of a letter, e-mail message, memo, or report:

1. In a single-spaced document, press ENTER 2 times before and 1 time after the table. Be sure you are outside the table structure before pressing ENTER 1 time.
2. In a double-spaced document, press ENTER 1 time before and after the table.
3. Single-space the body of the table.
4. Adjust the column widths, and center the table within the margins of the document.
5. Never split a table between two pages if it will fit on one page. If a table will not fit at the bottom of the page on which it is first mentioned, place it at the top of the next page.

MEMO TO: Leo Guthrie

FROM: Paul Forester

DATE: January 10, 20--

SUBJECT: Sales Comparison

Listed below are the sales totals for the last two quarters. Please review the information before our staff meeting on Friday. ↓2X

SALES SUMMARY December 31, 20		
Region	Third Quarter	Fourth Quarter
Northeast	$ 956,321	$912,980
Southeast	735,765	775,112
Northwest	825,666	857,034
Southwest	1,081,546	995,478

↓1X

Come to the meeting prepared to discuss plans for the upcoming sales promotions that will take place in our district.

mjd

E. COMPANY NAMES IN CLOSING LINES

Some business firms show the company name in the closing lines of a letter. Type the company name in all-caps on the second line below the complimentary closing. Then press ENTER 4 times and type the writer's name.

Thank you for inviting me to participate in the discussion concerning this issue. It has been very informative and helpful. ↓2X

Sincerely, ↓2X

HENDERSON AND SONS, INC. ↓4X

Mark Henderson, President ↓2X

mjd

F. DELIVERY NOTATIONS

Type a delivery notation (such as *By fax*, *By e-mail*, *By FedEx*, or *By messenger*) on the line below the enclosure notation (if used) or on the line below the reference initials. A delivery notation comes before a copy notation.

Thank you for inviting me to participate in the discussion concerning this issue. It has been very informative and helpful. ↓2X

Sincerely, ↓4X

Mark Henderson
President ↓2X

imz
Enclosure
By e-mail
c: Mary Stevenson

G. BLIND COPY NOTATIONS

Use the blind copy (*bc:*) notation when the addressee is *not* intended to know that someone else is receiving a copy of the letter. Type the *bc* notation on the file copy at the left margin on the second line after the last item in the letter.

When preparing a letter with a blind copy, print one copy of the letter; then add the blind copy notation and print another.

Thank you for inviting me to participate in the discussion concerning this issue. It has been very informative and helpful. ↓2X

Sincerely, ↓4X

Mark Henderson
President ↓2X

imz ↓2X

bc: Mary Stevenson

H. POSTSCRIPTS

If a postscript (*PS:*) is added to a letter, it is typed as the last item in the letter, preceded by 1 blank line. If a blind copy notation and postscript are used, the blind copy notation follows the postscript.

Thank you for inviting me to participate in the discussion concerning this issue. It has been very informative and helpful. ↓2X

Sincerely, ↓4X

Mark Henderson
President ↓2X

imz
Enclosure ↓2X

PS: You will be reimbursed for all expenses. Complete an expense report and submit it to your supervisor. ↓2X

bc: Mary Stevenson

I. E-MAIL WITH BLIND COPIES

Use the blind copy (*bcc:*) feature when the addressee in the To box is *not* intended to know that someone else is receiving a copy of the e-mail.

To format an e-mail message with a blind copy:

- Format the e-mail message as usual.
- No special formatting steps are needed when a blind copy is sent. Therefore, do *not* type a blind copy notation at the bottom of the e-mail message.

- Type e-mail addresses for recipients as desired in the Bcc box.

J. WORD PROCESSING: TABLE—SHADING AND E-MAIL—BLIND COPIES

GO TO
Word Manual

Study Lesson 68 in your Word Manual. Complete all of the shaded steps while at your computer. Then format the documents that follow.

Document Processing

Correspondence
68-70
Business Letter in Block Style

March 1, 20-- | Ms. Ramona Gutierrez | Austin Communications | 5 Gulf Street | Concord, NH 03301 | Dear Ms. Gutierrez:

¶ We are indeed interested in designing a new corporate logo and the corresponding stationery for your fine company. As I indicated in our recent telephone conversation, we have a design staff that has won many national awards for letterhead form design.

¶ Within a couple of weeks, we will submit several basic designs to you and your committee for consideration. Here is a modified price list for the printed stationery:

Use 25 percent shading for Row 1.

Stationery	Cost
Letterhead (500 sheets)	$ 80.00
Business cards (1,000 cards)	39.50
Coated brochures (1,000 sheets)	219.30
Envelopes (1,500)	92.00

¶ In the meantime, please call me if we can be of further service.
Sincerely yours, | Samantha A. Steele | General Manager | urs | By fax | bc: Design Department

Hi, Renee:

¶ Samantha Steele of Imperial Graphic Design sent me a modified price list for our printed stationery. I added our own budget to the last column in the table below.

Use 100 percent shading for Row 1.

Stationery	Cost	Budget
Letterhead (500 sheets)	$ 80.00	$120.00
Business cards (1,000 cards)	39.50	25.00
Coated brochures (1,000 sheets)	219.30	300.00
Envelopes (1,500)	92.00	85.50

¶ Let me know your reaction to her proposed price list after reviewing our budget.

Ramona | Ramona Gutierrez | E-mail: gutierrez@acmail.com | Phone: 603-555-3363

November 5, 20-- | Burlington Fitness Center | 31 Battery Street | Burlington, VT 05401 | Ladies and Gentlemen:

¶ We have 494 apartments at Fountain Ridge. As the recreation coordinator, I have concerns not only about the leisure-time activities of our residents but also about the health and physical fitness of the more than 1,100 people who call Fountain Ridge home.

¶ Our recreation facilities are excellent. In addition to our two outdoor tennis courts, putting green, and swimming pool, we have the following indoor facilities: two racquetball courts, swimming pool, whirlpool bath, sauna, steam room, and two billiard tables. However, we have no workout equipment.

¶ During the next few months we will be equipping a new gymnasium. The dimensions of the gym and schematics are enclosed. We would like to provide our residents with classes that will incorporate the equipment below:

Use 100 percent shading for Row 1 and 25 percent shading for Row 2.

CLASS SCHEDULE	
Fountain Ridge Sports Complex	
Equipment	**Proposed Classes**
Exercise bicycles	Spinning
Treadmills	Aerobics
Rowing machines	Toning and conditioning

(continued on next page)

¶ The needs and interests of our residents are varied. Some residents will take full advantage of the gymnasium equipment. However, many of our residents have expressed interest in an indoor track for walking; others would like to add a track for running. We hope to accommodate as many of the suggestions as we feel are feasible.

¶ The population of the residents in the Fountain Ridge complex consists of a mixture of young and middle-age adult couples as well as single residents. Some of the couples have children who would be old enough to enjoy the facilities. Therefore, safety and durability of the equipment are very important considerations. In addition, we would like to continue to develop our complex in a way that would invite family participation in our recreational activities.

¶Do you have a sales representative serving this area who could meet with me to discuss this proposal? In the meantime, please send any related information and prices.

Sincerely yours, | FOUNTAIN RIDGE | Rosa Bailey-Judd | Recreation Coordinator | urs | Enclosure | By fax | PS: Please contact me no later than November 10. | bc: Ramona Garcia

Keyboarding Connection

Creating an E-Mail Signature File

Creating a signature file saves you time and adds a personal touch to your e-mail messages. A signature file is a tag of information that is automatically included at the end of your e-mail messages. It may include your signature, a small graphic, your address, your phone number, or a quotation. Use the following guidelines to create a signature file.

Open your e-mail software. Open the menu item that allows you to create a signature file. Type the information you want to include in your signature, and then save and close the file.

Some companies don't allow graphics or quotations in e-mail signature files. E-mailing graphics uses extra bandwidth, which can slow down the network. For this reason, some e-mail software doesn't display graphics at all, instead displaying e-mail in plain text. Quotations may not align with the corporate culture or mission. Check to find out whether your company has corporate guidelines on e-mail signatures before you create your own signature file. When sending e-mail to potential employers, it's useful to add a professional signature to your e-mail that contains your contact information.

Your Turn: Create a signature file, then address an e-mail to yourself. Type "Test" in the Subject box. In the body, type "This is a test of the signature file." Send the e-mail; then open it to see how your signature file looks.

Multipage Memos With Tables

Goals

- Demonstrate improved speed and accuracy while typing.
- Demonstrate acceptable language arts skills in spelling.
- Correctly use Word's find and replace feature.
- Correctly format a multipage memo with a table.

A. WARMUP

alphabet	1	The lazy judge was very quick to pay tax money for the bar.
frequent digraphs	2	or orb for door fort more boor nor odor port orator ore ort
easy	3	The neighbor will do the fieldwork when she is in the glen.

Skillbuilding

B. MAP+: SYMBOL

Follow the GDP software directions for this exercise to improve keystroking accuracy.

PPP PRETEST » PRACTICE » POSTTEST

PRETEST
Take a 1-minute timed writing.

C. PRETEST: Horizontal Reaches

4	The legal facts gave our lawyers a sense that we could	11
5	be ready to wrap up this case quickly. Until a written copy	23
6	of our testimony is given to us, we shall all be extremely	35
7	anxious. We added every ounce of our energy to your case.	46

1 | 2 | 3 | 4 | 5 | 6 | 7 | 8 | 9 | 10 | 11 | 12

PRACTICE
Speed Emphasis:
  If you made no more than 1 error on the Pretest, type each *individual* line 2 times.
Accuracy Emphasis:
  If you made 2 or more errors, type each *group* of lines (as though it were a paragraph) 2 times.

D. PRACTICE: In Reaches

8	wr wrap wren wreak wrist wrote writer unwrap writhe wreaths
9	ou pout ours ounce cough fouls output detour ousted coupons
10	ad adds dead adult ready blade advice fading admits adheres
11	py pyre copy pygmy pylon happy pyrene choppy pyrite pyramid

E. PRACTICE: Out Reaches

12	yo yoga your youth yodel yowls yogurt joyous yonder younger
13	fa fact farm faith sofas fakes faulty unfair famous defames
14	up upon soup upset group upper upturn supply uplift upsurge
15	ga gate gave cigar gains legal gazing legacy gawked garbage

F. POSTTEST: Horizontal Reaches

Language Arts

G. SPELLING

16 personnel information its procedures their committee system
17 receive employees which education services opportunity area
18 financial appropriate interest received production contract
19 important through necessary customer employee further there
20 property account approximately general control division our

21 The revised systom was adopted by the finantial division.

22 Four employes want to serve on the new property commitee.

23 Approximatly ten proceedures were included in the contract.

24 Further informasion will be recieved from the customers.

25 Their was much interest shown by the production personal.

26 The services in that aria are necesary for needed control.

Formatting

H. WORD PROCESSING: FIND AND REPLACE

GO TO
Word Manual

Study Lesson 69 in your Word Manual. Complete all of the shaded steps while at your computer. Then format the documents that follow.

Document Processing

Correspondence
69-73
Memo

Highlighted words are spelling words from the language arts activities; do *not* highlight them when you type.

MEMO TO: L. B. Chinn, Station Manager | **FROM:** Mitzi Grenell, News Director | **DATE:** May 5, 20-- | **SUBJECT:** FCC European Trip

¶ This memo and others to follow will keep you informed about my upcoming trip to Europe. I have been invited by the Federal Communications Commission to lead a committee that will study television news in European countries. This opportunity came about because Jill Andrews received advance notice about the study and made the necessary arrangements so that I would be invited to participate. I am delighted to take part in this important project, which should be of great interest to all of our employees.

(continued on next page)

¶ A major focus of this study will be to compare the types of technologies used in different European countries to report and broadcast the news. Our study group will visit six European countries to gather further information. We will be visiting England, France, Denmark, Germany, Spain, and Portugal from August 24 through September 23. Four other members will offer their services to this committee:

Sandra Holton	News Director, WSVN	Miami, Florida
Manuel Cruz	News Director, National Public Radio	Boise, Idaho
Jason Chan	Station Manager, WLBZ	Bangor, Maine
Richard Logan	Operations Manager, Cable News System	Provo, Utah

Our initial plans are to spend approximately five full days in each country, meet with the news personnel of one or two of the major networks, tour their facilities, view recent broadcasts, and observe their general operations and various divisions. It should be quite an education.

¶ If you need to contact me during my absence, Barbara Brooks, our liaison at the Federal Communications Commission, is the appropriate contact. She, or any employee on her staff, will be able to provide a location and phone number.

¶ An amendment has been made to my contract that will allow production to continue as usual here at Channel 5 while I am gone. Dave Gelson will assume financial control of the department and will also supervise its day-to-day activities. Further procedures are being finalized so that Dave can make a smooth transition during my absence.

¶ As you can imagine, this is an exciting time for me. Thank you for supporting the project and for taking into account the long-term implications of this important study. urs | PS: Thank you also for suggesting that I visit John Jacobs, one of our most valued customers. I understand that he owns property in England and France and will be at his estate in France at a time that coincides with my schedule. I will be sure to give him your best wishes.

**Correspondence
69-74
Memo**

Open the file for Correspondence 69-73 and make the following changes:

1. Address the memo to "All Employees."
2. Change each occurrence of the words "News Director" to "News Analyst." A total of three replacements should be made.
3. Change each occurrence of the word "France" to "Switzerland." A total of three replacements should be made.
4. Delete the fourth paragraph.
5. Add this as the second-to-the-last paragraph:

```
When I return from this
trip, my committee will
compile a comprehensive
report and analysis that
will be distributed to all
personnel. I will then
organize some internal
focus groups so that we can
discuss the implications of
the study on our day-to-day
operations.
```

6. Delete the postscript at the end of the memo.

MEMO TO: Terri Hackworth Property Manager

FROM: Rosa Bailey-Judd, recreation coordinator

DATE: Apr. 14, 20--

Subject: Fitness Center

¶ The new fitness center will be ready for our residents to use in approximately one month, and interest continues to grow. Your leadership in constructing a fitness center on this property is sincerely appreciated. ¶ As soon as appropriate research is completed, I will be requesting further financial support to purchase the following equipment in the quantity specified:

Single-space the table.

No.	Equipment
15 ~~20~~	Exercise Bicycles
10	Treadmills
8	rowing machines

¶ Three types of other equipment were seriously considered, but ~~the ones~~ *those* listed above are the most important in terms of what is necesary to schedule our proposed fitness classes. I am *ital* not quite ready to sign a contract with a specific supplier. We expect that there will be *very* heavy usage of the *#* specified equipment and are requesting inforamtion from vendors regarding durability, warranties, and the support of service personnel. I will receive that information within the week and will read through it carefully before signing a final contract.

SS ¶ Thank you again for your full support and cooperation with this project. The general contractor you hired has received rave reviews. The new ~~gym~~ *fitness center* is a golden opportunity for all our residents to ~~vastly~~ improve their quality of life.

urs

Memo Reports

Goals

- Type at least 41wpm/5′/5e.
- Correctly format a memo report with report headings and a bibliography.
- Successfully complete a Progress and Proofreading Check with zero errors on the first scored attempt.

A. WARMUP

alphabet

number/symbol

easy

1 Those five lazy movers quit packing the hard jewelry boxes.
2 (fay237@yahoo.com) 33% Coe & Tan 6/8 Hi! $2.41 *Oct. #95-01
3 One half of the endowments may be paid by the town members.

Skillbuilding

B. 12-SECOND SPEED SPRINTS

Take three 12-second timed writings on each line. The scale below the last line shows your wpm speed for a 12-second timed writing.

4 That new city law may help us to fish for cod on the docks.
5 He may sign over the title to his autos when he is in town.
6 She may go with me to the city to visit my son and his pal.
7 The doe and buck by the old bush may dig up the giant oaks.
' ' ' 5 ' ' ' 10 ' ' ' 15 ' ' ' 20 ' ' ' 25 ' ' ' 30 ' ' ' 35 ' ' ' 40 ' ' ' 45 ' ' ' 50 ' ' ' 55 ' ' ' 60

C. TECHNIQUE PRACTICE: BACKSPACE KEY

Type each line 2 times, using your Sem finger to strike the BACKSPACE key when you see the ← symbol. For example, type *bud*, backspace, and type *m*, thus changing *bud* to *bum*.

8 bud←m gig←n dew←n rag←m tad←n own←l get←m tie←n toe←n
9 car←p hoe←g yea←n pie←n vat←n hug←m rug←m pod←i per←p
10 job←y yaw←m bus←y pad←l lad←p the←y nag←p fur←n nub←n
11 fad←n max←y jag←m fig←n ice←y oaf←k add←o mow←p log←o

Take two 5-minute timed writings.

Goal: At least 41wpm/5'/5e

D. 5-MINUTE TIMED WRITING

```
12        In most offices, many products that are used each day    11
13   are made of materials that can now be recycled. Amazingly,    23
14   items made of glass, steel, aluminum, plastics, and paper     34
15   can be recycled to make many products that we need. Also,     46
16   the recycling process can help the environment.               56
17        Some unique examples of the process of recycling the     66
18   items we often throw away are listed here. Those old coffee   78
19   filters can be used to make soles for new shoes. Pieces of    90
20   paper that are thrown away each day can be used to make       101
21   tissue paper or paper towels. Most plastics that are used     113
22   in soda bottles can be recycled for insulation for jackets    125
23   and auto interiors. Used lightbulbs and some glass products   137
24   can also be used to replace the surface on our streets.       148
25        Look around the room in which you are working. If you    159
26   are not already taking part in a recycling program, you may   171
27   want to recycle some items that you no longer need. Items     183
28   such as used paper, file folders, and aluminum cans can be    194
29   collected very quickly. What other items can you add?         205
     1 | 2 | 3 | 4 | 5 | 6 | 7 | 8 | 9 | 10 | 11 | 12
```

Formatting

E. REPORT HEADINGS IN MEMOS

REFER TO
Reference Manual

R-9C: Memo Report

There are times when a memo report is used rather than a cover memo to accompany a report. The memo and the report are combined into one, and headings are formatted as they are in a report. If a table is included in the body of the report, it should be formatted as it would be in a report. Use reference initials at the end of a memo report.

Document Processing

Report
70-38
Memo Report

MEMO TO: All Employees | **FROM:** Frank Reynolds, Director | **DATE:** February 24, 20-- | **SUBJECT:** New Security System

¶ Beginning April 1, we will be using a new security access system. Various security system options were researched thoroughly before a final decision was made to implement a fingerprint access system. Complete installation should occur by the end of March, but the system will not be activated until April 1. The system includes digital surveillance cameras and a fingerprint access system at all entrances. This will provide a more secure working environment, especially in the evenings and on weekends. Please carefully read the specifications below and follow the detailed instructions for using the new system:

(continued on next page)

FINGERPRINT ACCESS SYSTEM

Description	Specifications
Fingerprint memory capacity	78 people
Password capacity	78 people
False identification rate	Less than 0.0001%
Password length	8 bytes
Unlock methods	Fingerprint or keypad code

FINGERPRINT AND KEYPAD CODES

¶ Once the new system is installed, you simply touch the fingerprint keypad lock with your index finger for access during nonworking hours. You will also receive a keypad code for alternate access. Although mechanical keys can be used, they will <u>not</u> be created or distributed. Human Resources will begin programming fingerprint codes during the week of March 20. Further instructions will be issued at that time.

ENTRANCE AND EXIT PROCEDURES

¶ Entrances will unlock automatically each day at 8 a.m. and lock automatically at 5 p.m. To enter, touch the fingerprint keypad lock with your index finger. When the green light comes on, open the door. Do <u>not</u> hold the door open longer than 30 seconds when you enter or exit, or the alarm will sound. When you exit the building, do <u>not</u> use the special latch handle to open the door, or the alarm will sound. Instead, use the push bar. Sign in and sign out at the front desk each time you enter and exit.

¶ If you have questions about our new security access system and procedures, send an e-mail message to me at <u>freynolds@infotech.com</u>.

urs

Report
70-39
Bibliography

REFER TO
Reference Manual

R-9B: Bibliography

BIBLIOGRAPHY

"Biometric Fingerprint Keypad Locks," *OfficeSecuritySystems,* January 11, 2010, <http://www.officesecuritysystems.com/fingerprint>, accessed on January 15, 2010.

"Business Alarm Monitoring," *SecurityZone,* December 11, 2009, <http://www.securityzone.com/securitymonitoring>, accessed on January 16, 2010.

De La Cruz, Stacey, "Digital Surveillance Systems," *Security Systems Today,* November 19, 2009, p. 18.

Paisley, Robert, "What's New in Business Security Systems," *The Daily Sentinel,* January 12, 2010, p. D6.

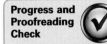

Report
70-40
Memo Report

Progress and Proofreading Check ✓

Documents designated as Proofreading Checks serve as a check of your proofreading skill. Your goal is to have zero typographical errors when the GDP software first scores the document.

MEMO TO: All Employees
FROM: Won Chul Lee, President
DATE: March 2, 20--
SUBJECT: New Administrative Center

¶ You will all be very pleased to know that after extensive consultation with several architectural firms, I have finalized plans for a new administrative center to be constructed at 3900 Rockefeller Plaza. This memo will

(continued on next page)

provide you with general information about the exciting plans for the center's exterior and interior development.

ARCHITECTURE AND LANDSCAPING

¶ Exterior plans will maintain the historical integrity and beauty of the surrounding area and reflect the architecture of other buildings in the office park. Landscaping plans include a park area, a picnic area, and a small pond. Paseos (winding walkways) will connect the various businesses within the complex and include both bike paths and foot paths.

DEPARTMENTAL LOCATIONS

¶ Staff will be located within the new facility as follows:

1. Accounting will be located on the first floor in the west wing.
2. Sales and marketing will be located on the first floor in the east wing. All staff will be grouped according to product line.
3. Technical support will be located in the basement level of the east wing. All staff will be grouped according to product support.
4. All other staff will be located on the second floor. Exact locations will be determined at a later date.

SPECIAL FACILITIES

¶ Conference rooms will be located in the center of the building on the first floor to provide easy access for everyone. All rooms will be equipped with state-of-the-art technology. Our new center will also include a full-service cafeteria, a copy center, a library, an athletic center, and an on-site day-care center.

¶ Construction of the new center will begin when the necessary permits have been obtained. I hope you are looking forward to our new location as much as I am. More information will be forthcoming as plans are finalized.

urs

Reports

Itineraries

Goals

- Demonstrate improved speed and accuracy while typing.
- Demonstrate acceptable language arts skills in using commas.
- Correctly format an itinerary.

A. WARMUP

alphabet
concentration
easy

1 My faxed jokes won me a pager from the cable TV quiz shows.
2 electromagnetically antirevolutionaries overdiversification
3 The big dog down by the lake may bury the eighty fishbowls.

Skillbuilding

B. MAP+: ALPHABET

Follow the GDP software directions for this exercise to improve keystroking accuracy.

C. PROGRESSIVE PRACTICE: ALPHABET

Follow the GDP software directions for this exercise to improve keystroking speed.

Language Arts

Study the rules at
the right.

RULE
, nonessential expression

D. COMMAS

Use a comma before and after a nonessential expression.

Andre, who was there, can verify the statement.
But: Anyone who was there can verify the statement.
Van's first book, *Crisis of Management,* was not discussed.
Van's book *Crisis of Management* was not discussed.

Note: A nonessential expression is a group of words that may be omitted without changing the basic meaning of the sentence. Always examine the noun or pronoun that comes before the expression to determine whether the noun needs the expression to complete its meaning. If it does, the expression is *essential* and does *not* take a comma.

Use a comma between two adjacent adjectives that modify the same noun.

We need an intelligent, enthusiastic individual for this job.
But: Please order a new bulletin board for our main conference room.

Note: Do not use a comma after the second adjective. Also, do not use a comma if the first adjective modifies the combined idea of the second adjective and the noun (for example, *bulletin board* and *conference room* in the second example).

Edit each sentence to correct any errors.

4 The school president Mr. Roberts will address the students.

5 The fall planning meeting which is held in Charlotte has been
6 canceled.

7 Students planning to take the certification test must
8 register for the orientation class.

9 The sleek luxury car is scheduled for delivery next week.

10 Margaret brought her fast reliable laptop to the meeting.

11 A stamped addressed envelope should be included with the
12 survey.

Formatting

E. ITINERARIES

REFER TO
Reference Manual

R-11C: Itinerary

An itinerary is a proposed outline of a trip that provides a traveler with information, such as flight times and numbers, meeting times, travel dates, and room reservations. An itinerary may also include notes of special interest to the traveler.

To format an itinerary:

1. Press ENTER 5 times to begin the first line of the itinerary 2 inches from the top of the page.
2. Insert an open table with 2 columns and enough rows to accommodate the completed itinerary.
3. Insert 1 blank line between each part of the heading block in Row 1.
4. Type the date in Row 2, Column A, in all-caps and bold; press ENTER 1 time.
5. Type the time in Column A and the corresponding information in Column B; press ENTER 1 time as shown after each group of lines in Column B.
6. Repeat these steps until the itinerary is finished, and adjust the column widths as needed.

↓5X

14 pt **RESOURCE CONSULTANTS SALES MEETING** ↓2X

12 pt↓ **Itinerary for Linda Padilla** ↓2X

March 12-14, 20-- ↓2X

THURSDAY, MARCH 12 ↓1X	
9:39 a.m.-10:07 a.m.	Flight from Atlanta to New Orleans; Delta 1585 (800-555-1222); e-ticket; Seat 8D; nonstop. ↓2X Sharon Lee (Cell: 504-555-8029; Office: 504-555-7631) will meet your flight on Thursday, provide transportation during your visit, and return you to the airport on Saturday morning. Airport Embassy Suites (504-555-4032) King-sized bed, nonsmoking room; late arrival guaranteed; Reservation No. 0312010-AZ. ↓1X
FRIDAY, MARCH 13	
9 a.m.	Resource Consultants Sales Meeting Royal New Orleans Hotel 730 Rue Bienville, Bourbon Street Suite New Orleans, LA 70130 (503-555-7631)
7 p.m.	Dinner at the Royal New Orleans Hotel—The French Quarter Bistro.
SATURDAY, MARCH 14	
6:30 a.m.	Meet Sharon Lee, who will accompany you on the return flight, in the lobby of the Airport Embassy Suites for transportation to the airport.
8:30 a.m.-10:50 a.m.	Flight from New Orleans to Atlanta; Delta 5995; e-ticket; Seat 10D; nonstop.

, nonessential expression

(Note: Table shown with "View Gridlines" active.)

**Report
71-42**
Itinerary

, nonessential
expression

, adjacent adjectives

RSA TECHNOLOGY CONFERENCE | Itinerary for Mrs. Norma McKinley |

September 25-29, 20-- | WEDNESDAY, SEPTEMBER 25 | 1:50 p.m.-4:10 p.m. | Flight from Columbus to Boston; US Airways 2053; Seat 13F; nonstop. | Boston Inn (617-555-3982) | King-sized bed, nonsmoking room; late arrival guaranteed. | Judith Greenburg, who will be at the same conference, will meet you in the lobby at 6 p.m. for dinner. | **THURSDAY, SEPTEMBER 26 |** 8:30 a.m.-5 p.m. | RSA Technology Conference, Suite 201 | A compact, full-featured presentations projector will be ready in the suite no later than 8 a.m. | **FRIDAY, SEPTEMBER 27 |** 9 a.m.-10:17 a.m. | Flight from Boston to New York City; US Airways 454; Seat 10D; nonstop. | **SUNDAY, SEPTEMBER 29 |** 2:07 p.m.-4:18 p.m. | Flight from New York City to Columbus; US Airways 324; Seat 9A; nonstop.

**Report
71-43**
Itinerary

, adjacent adjectives

, nonessential
expression

HEALTH EFFECTS INSTITUTE CONFERENCE | Itinerary for Dr. Ron Jacobs |

July 8-10, 20-- | MONDAY, JULY 8 | 2:45 p.m.-4:05 p.m. | Flight from Houston to Los Angeles; United 834; Seat 10C; nonstop. | Marriott (310-555-1014) | King-sized bed; nonsmoking room; late arrival guaranteed; Reservation No. 45STX78. | **TUESDAY, JULY 9 |** 6 a.m.-7:15 a.m. | Flight from Los Angeles to Sacramento; American 206; Seat 4A; nonstop. | Sacramento Garden Inn (916-555-7373) | King-sized bed; nonsmoking room; late arrival guaranteed; Reservation No. QRR6H. | A spacious, well-equipped welcome booth, including computers with Internet access, will be available in the Executive Center, Room 12B. | 10 a.m.-4:30 p.m. | Health Effects Institute Conference, Executive Center, Room 12A. | **WEDNESDAY, JULY 10 |** 7 a.m.-11:15 a.m. | Flight from Sacramento to Houston; United 307; Seat 7B; nonstop.

Strategies for Career Success

Successful Interviewing Techniques

The interview is a useful tool for gathering more information about a company. Here are some steps to effective interviewing.

Conduct preliminary research so you can ask intelligent questions and make efficient use of the interview time. Prepare a list of questions to use in the interview. Make sure questions are open-ended, unbiased, and geared toward gathering insights you can't gain through reading about the company. Be prepared to take notes, listen actively, and ask follow-up questions, as needed.

Remember that an interview, whether for a job or for information gathering, is also your opportunity to find out if a company or career would be a good fit for you. It is in everyone's best interest to find out during a job interview if you will be happy at the company, so ask questions about things that are important to you. These might be things like potential for advancement, various career paths within a specialty, and corporate culture (e.g., does the company promote a work-life balance, or is it a place where overtime is routine and can lead to better opportunities?).

Greet the interviewer by name, and thank him or her for taking time to talk to you. If it's not a job interview, explain why you are interested in interviewing him or her. Stay within the scheduled time. In closing the interview, thank the person again, and ask if you can get in touch if other questions come to mind.

Your Turn: Prepare a list of questions you might use in interviewing someone concerning what his or her company does.

Agendas and Minutes of Meetings

Goals

- Type at least 42wpm/5'/5e.
- Correctly format an agenda and the minutes of a meeting.

A. WARMUP

alphabet   1 Quick brown foxes jumped over the lazy dog who was resting.

one hand   2 adverb hookup was ply target minimum beat knoll acted kinky

easy   3 The quantity of profits for the coalfield is a big problem.

Skillbuilding

B. SUSTAINED PRACTICE: SYLLABIC INTENSITY

Take a 1-minute timed writing on the boxed paragraph to establish your base speed. Then take a 1-minute timed writing on the following paragraph. As soon as you equal or exceed your base speed on this paragraph, move to the next, more difficult paragraph.

4   Each of us has several bills to be paid on a monthly   11
5 basis. For most of us, a checkbook is the tool that we use   23
6 to take care of this chore. However, in this electronic   34
7 age, other ways of doing this have received rave reviews.   45

8   You will likely be surprised to learn that the most   11
9 basic way and the cheapest way to pay bills electronically   22
10 involves the use of a Touch-Tone phone. The time required   34
11 is approximately a third of that used when writing checks.   46

12   Several banking institutions offer or plan to offer   11
13 screen phones as a method for paying bills. It is possible   22
14 to buy securities, make transfers, and determine account   34
15 balances. You will save time by using a Touch-Tone phone.   45

16   A third type of electronic bill processing involves   11
17 using a microcomputer and a modem. Software programs have   22
18 on-screen checkbooks linked to bill-paying applications.   34
19 Other microcomputers use online services through a modem.   45

     1 | 2 | 3 | 4 | 5 | 6 | 7 | 8 | 9 | 10 | 11 | 12

Take two 5-minute timed writings.

Goal: At least 42wpm/5'/5e

C. 5-MINUTE TIMED WRITING

```
20      Whether you are searching for your first job or are      11
21  looking to change jobs, your networking skills may play a     22
22  crucial role in how successful you are in that endeavor.      34
23  Networking can be defined in some respects as a group of      45
24  people who are linked closely together for the purpose of     57
25  achieving some sort of end result. In this case, the end      68
26  result will be to establish new contacts who might be able    80
27  to assist you in your job search.                             87
28      Your network is made up of dozens of people you have      97
29  met. You can never be sure who has the potential of helping  109
30  you the most in your job search. Therefore, it is important  121
31  that you consider all acquaintances. You should certainly    133
32  network with business associates, and especially those you   145
33  have met at various meetings or conferences. And don't       158
34  forget former teachers in whose classes you were enrolled.   168
35      Former classmates provide an excellent base on which     178
36  to build your network, and friends and family should also    190
37  be included. Also, use the Internet to nurture any online    202
38  contacts you may have made over the years.                   210
       1 | 2 | 3 | 4 | 5 | 6 | 7 | 8 | 9 | 10 | 11 | 12
```

Formatting

REFER TO Reference Manual

R-11A: Meeting Agenda

D. AGENDAS

An agenda is a list of topics to be discussed at a meeting. It may also include a formal program of a meeting and consist of times, rooms, speakers, and other related information.

To format an agenda:

1. Press ENTER 5 times to begin the first line of the agenda 2 inches from the top of the page.
2. Center and type the name of the company or committee in all-caps, bold, and 14-point font.
3. Press ENTER 2 times; then center and type Meeting Agenda in upper- and lowercase, bold, and 12-point font.
4. Press ENTER 2 times; then center and type the date in upper- and lowercase, bold, and 12-point font.
5. Press ENTER 2 times and turn off bold.
6. Type all agenda items as a numbered list using Word's default format.

↓5X

14 pt **BECKER CORPORATION STAFF MEETING**
↓2X

12 pt↓ **Meeting Agenda**
↓2X

February 17, 20--
↓2X

default
format

1. Call to order
2. Approval of minutes of January 15 meeting
3. Progress report on the remodeling of the staff lounge, copy center, and reception area
   (Roger Wilcox)
4. Discussion of plans for group presentations at the National Advanced Technology
   Institute meeting
5. Annual company picnic (Rachel Morris)
6. Announcements
7. Adjournment

E. MINUTES OF MEETINGS

REFER TO
Reference Manual

R-11B: Minutes of a Meeting

Items discussed during a meeting are officially recorded as the minutes of a meeting.
To format the minutes of a meeting:

1. Press ENTER 5 times to begin the first line of the minutes 2 inches from the top of the page.
2. Insert an open table with 2 columns and enough rows to accommodate the completed meeting minutes.
3. Insert 1 blank line between each part of the heading block in Row 1.
4. Type the first section heading in Row 2, Column A, in all-caps and bold.
5. Type the corresponding information in Column B; press ENTER 1 time after the final line in Column B.
6. Move to the next row and repeat steps 4 and 5 until all remaining sections have been completed.
7. Type the closing and signature lines in Column B of the final row; press ENTER 4 times to allow room for the signature.
8. Adjust the width of Column A to accommodate the longest heading as shown in the illustration that follows.

↓5X

14 pt **PLANNING COMMITTEE** ↓2X

12 pt↓ **Minutes of the Meeting** ↓2X

February 10, 20-- ↓1X

ATTENDANCE	The Planning Committee meeting was called to order at 1 p.m. on February 10, 20--, by Michelle North, chairperson. Members present were Cal Anderson, L. T. Braddock, Lisa Samson, Sharon Owens, and J. R. Stern. ↓1X
APPROVAL OF MINUTES	The minutes of the January 10 meeting were read and approved as presented.
OLD BUSINESS	The committee reviewed bids for the purchase of a new computer for the Cheyenne office. The committee will accept the lower of two bids that have been submitted.
NEW BUSINESS	The committee reviewed a proposal for a new complex in Helena. After much discussion, the committee agreed to contact the Helena county clerk's office to get information on zoning ordinances.
ADJOURNMENT	The meeting was adjourned at 2:45 p.m. The next meeting is scheduled for March 22 in Room 26 at 1 p.m. ↓2X Respectfully submitted, ↓4X *Barbara Cheng* Barbara Cheng, Secretary

(Note: Table shown with "View Gridlines" active.)

Document Processing

Report 72-44
Agenda

Use Word's default numbering format.

FOX ASSOCIATES STAFF MEETING
Meeting Agenda
April 15, 20--

1. Call to order
2. Approval of minutes of March 15 meeting
3. Progress reports for the construction of new media center
4. Discussion of the upcoming time management seminar (F. Pryor and J. Harrington)
5. Discussion of Internet security and antivirus software (T. Rashid)
6. Annual charity event (J. Simpatico)
7. Announcements
8. Adjournment

GREENWAY SECURITY CORPORATION
Meeting Agenda
October 13, 20--

1. Call to order
2. Approval of minutes of September 10 meeting
3. Progress reports on biometric access control technology (Marie Newsome)
4. Upgrading of 8.0 presentation media
5. Handheld scanners and readers product development (Andrew Slovinsky)
6. Visitor registration and tracking (Juan Mendoza)
7. Announcements
8. Adjournment

ADVISORY COMMITTEE
Minutes of the Meeting
June 10, 20--

ATTENDANCE	The Advisory Committee meeting was called to order at 1 p.m. on June 10, 20--, by Suzanne Higgins-North, chairperson. Members present were Georgia Holton, James Duncan, Mary Benavidez, Pete Bergstrom, Quan Ying Zhao, and Sharon Rose.
APPROVAL OF MINUTES	The minutes of the May 10 meeting were read and approved as presented.
OLD BUSINESS	The committee reviewed recommendations for new hardware and software and new ergonomically sound workstations, lighting, and seating.
NEW BUSINESS	The committee reviewed a proposal for a new classroom complex in Helena. After much discussion, the committee agreed to contact the Helena county clerk's office to get information on zoning ordinances.
ADJOURNMENT	The meeting was adjourned at 2:45 p.m. The next meeting is scheduled for July 10 in Room 16. Respectfully submitted, Nancy Jacobs, Secretary

(Note: Table shown with "View Gridlines" active.)

HUMAN RESOURCES DEPT.

Minutes of The Meeting

May 20, 20--
(14 inserted above 20)

ATTENDING *(ANCE written above, with strikethrough on ING)*

On May 14, 20--, A *(special inserted)* meeting of the Human Resources Department was held in the office of Mr. Choi. Members *(All inserted)* were present except Donald Clark, who was represented by *(# space mark)* Monica Cruz. The meeting was called to order at 10 A.M.

APPROVAL OF MINUTES

The minutes of the Apr. 14 meeting were read and approved as presented.

OLD BUSINESS

Andrea Fields was in charge of a staff-development survey. Ninety-seven questionnaires were returned, and a copy of the staff-development survey was *(distributed and inserted)* discussed. The committee will

ss

consider the findings and be prepared to make recomendations *(m inserted)* for up dated job descriptions at the next ~~monthly~~ meeting.

NEW BUSINESS

Mr. Choi discussed plans to disseminate information about vacancies that occur within the company to prospective job applicants. Monica Cruz will draft a flyer to be sent to the Lakeview Sentinel *(ital)*. Programs for the NPA convention to be held in Los Angeles were distributed to all members. Each committee member was asked to distribute copies to employees all *(circled)* in his or her department.

ADJOURNMENT

The meeting was *(# space)* ~~ended~~ adjourned at 11:45 a.m. The next meeting has been scheduled for ~~July 10~~ June 20 in the Conference Center.

Respectfully submitted,

Brandon Scher Secretary *(, inserted)*

Procedures Manual

Goals

- Demonstrate improved speed and accuracy while typing.
- Demonstrate acceptable proofreading skills by editing a paragraph.
- Correctly use Word's footer feature.
- Correctly format a procedures manual.

A. WARMUP

alphabet
practice *u* and *y*
easy

1 The jobs of waxing linoleum frequently peeved chintzy kids.
2 yum buy duly yuck fury your guy July busy yuk quay you your
3 Laurie may dismantle her tan bicycle and put it in the van.

Skillbuilding

MAP+

B. MAP+: NUMBERS

Follow the GDP software directions for this exercise to improve keystroking accuracy.

PPP

PRETEST » PRACTICE » POSTTEST

PRETEST
Take a 1-minute timed writing.

C. PRETEST: Vertical Reaches

4   Janice and her escort were late for a dance at the   10
5 resort. The drummers in the band had just started to play   22
6 as they came in. It seems Janice injured the back of her   33
7 knee on the bank of the river during a cruise that morning. 45
    1 | 2 | 3 | 4 | 5 | 6 | 7 | 8 | 9 | 10 | 11 | 12

PRACTICE
Speed Emphasis:
If you made no more than 1 error on the Pretest, type each *individual* line 2 times.
Accuracy Emphasis:
If you made 2 or more errors, type each *group* of lines (as though it were a paragraph) 2 times.

D. PRACTICE: Up Reaches

8 at late flatly rebate atomic rather repeat attest atom what
9 dr draft drank dryer drew drain drama dread dream drag drug
10 ju judge juice jumpy junks juror judo julep jumbo jump just
11 es essay nests tests less dress acres makes uses best rests

E. PRACTICE: Down Reaches

12 ca cable caddy cargo scare decay yucca pecan cage calm case
13 nk ankle blank crank blink junk think trunk brink bank sink
14 ba tuba ballot cabana bakery abates global basket balk band
15 sc scar scale scalp scene scent scold scoop scope scan disc

F. POSTTEST: Vertical Reaches

Edit the paragraph to correct any errors.

G. PROOFREADING

16   Many home computer user like the challenge of haveing
17 the latest in both hardware and software technology. Their
18 are those however, who's needs likely can be satisfied at
19 a very low costs. A used Pentium personnel computer with
20 color monitor and keyboard might be your's for under $ 300.
21 Check out th Yellow Page, or visit a used-computer store.

Formatting

H. PROCEDURES MANUAL

Organizations often prepare procedures manuals to assist employees in identifying the steps or methods they must follow to accomplish particular tasks. The illustration depicts a continuation page in a procedures manual for American Bistro. The title of the manual is "Employee Manual" and the report section name is "Training Program."

To format a procedures manual:

1. Type the manual using standard formatting for the body of a business report.
2. Insert a header (suppressed on the first page) with the company name followed by a comma and the manual title at the left margin.

3. Move to the right margin, and type the name of the report section in italics.
4. Insert a footer with the word "Page" followed by a page number field centered in the footer.

Strategies for Career Success

Corrective Feedback

Sometime in your career, you will give someone corrective feedback. You can use positive communication to do this and not appear to criticize the person.

Here are some things you should not do. Do not correct the person in front of others. Avoid giving feedback when you are angry. Stay away from derogatory or dismissive comments (for example, "That's a useless idea!"). Do not dismiss a person's enthusiasm with comments like "We've never done that before" or "It won't work."

Here are some things you should do. Listen to the other person's side of the situation. Ask for ideas on how to fix the situation. Express yourself in a positive way, such as saying, "You're getting much closer" or "That's an interesting idea." Be specific about what the person can do to correct the situation. Follow up within a short time and identify all progress.

Your Turn: Think about the last time you received corrective feedback. Did the person giving you feedback use techniques to create a positive outcome?

American Bistro, Employee Manual   *Training Program* Header
                                                                       italic

A high-quality dining experience doesn't happen without preparation. A careful,
systematic plan for training and then mentoring must occur. Our training program
includes a structured plan for training for the following positions: ↓2X

- Server
- Dishwasher
- Line Cook
- Prep Cook
- Bus Person
- Host or Hostess
- Bartender ↓2X

Each of these positions is discussed in detail and many constructive suggestions
are outlined. ↓2X

SERVER ↓2X

The functions and the responsibilities of the server are many and varied. General
guidelines and specific responsibilities and opening and closing procedures are
critical. Guest service is the goal for all restaurant employees but is particularly
important for those who deal with the customer directly. ↓2X

Quality Control and Ordering. A server must be aware of quality control in terms
of the food being served. Is it fresh, properly prepared, and promptly served?
Ordering procedures must be in place so that the guest feels confident that the
order will arrive promptly, accurately, and as expected.

Personal Appearance. Guests will make a direct correlation between a server's
personal appearance and the overall quality of the dining experience. If the server
is not dressed appropriately, the guest will begin the dining experience with a
negative impression. If the server creates a good first impression in appearance
and attitude, the guest will anticipate a wonderful and very pleasant dining
experience.

Suggestive Selling. Suggestive selling as a guest is ordering and reviewing the
menu is a fine art that must be practiced and rehearsed. The specials and features

Page 8   Footer

I. WORD PROCESSING: FOOTERS

Study Lesson 73 in your Word Manual. Complete all of the shaded steps while at your
computer. Then format the documents that follow.

Document Processing

Report
73-48
Procedures Manual

Abbott Industries, Employee Training Manual   *Introduction*

¶ Managers are responsible for developing training programs for new employees
who have been hired in any of the seven regional branches of Abbott Industries. The
basic content of this employee training program is outlined next.

EMPLOYEE TRAINING MANUAL OUTLINE

¶ Abbott Industries will distribute this manual to all new managers to help familiarize
them with the day-to-day procedures of the company. Also, answers are provided to
the following questions with specific details included in each section:

- Where does the training manual fit within the training program?
- For whom is the manual designed, and what does it contain?
- How should the manual be used?
- Can the manual be used in a classroom setting?
- Can the manual be used as self-paced instructional material?
- Can study guides accompany the manual?

(continued on next page)

EMPLOYEE TRAINING PROGRAM PHILOSOPHY AND GOALS

¶ Well-trained employees are the key to the continued success of Abbott Industries. Studies have shown that the most successful, productive employees are those who have received extensive training. One of the positive results of a training program is that employees often feel they have a strong stake in the company's future. That internalized sense of ownership is highly motivational. The next section in this training manual explains the program guidelines.

Page 2

Report
73-49
Procedures Manual

Studio One Photography, Presentation Software Guide   *Presentation Overview*

PRESENTATION ACTION PLAN

¶ An effective presentation does not happen by accident. It must be designed and formatted in a way that is appropriate to the audience and the topic. It must focus carefully on the subject at hand and include the right amount of text and graphics on each slide without appearing busy. Artwork, tables, and charts should be used purposefully to convey information clearly.

¶ Sound and video must be used with discretion as they can become a distraction rather than an enhancement. The same holds true for animation. It can quickly become annoying unless it is used sparingly. A good presentation should include a closing that provides the audience with an opportunity for questions, answers, and discussion.

PRESENTATION SOFTWARE

¶ There are several different computer-assisted presentation methods. However, Studio One Photography is using PowerPresentation software exclusively at this time. Any presentation can be delivered directly from a computer by connecting to a large external monitor or to a projection system.

¶ The software also allows presentations to be saved in a format for publishing on the Internet. Self-running presentations can be created specifically for the Internet; however, some of the special effects and animation may be lost in the process. Presentations can also be saved to a CD that will start automatically when the CD is inserted into a computer. Because the CD contains both the presentation and special viewer software, distributing the presentation is seamless.

Page 7

Report
73-50
Procedures Manual

1. Open Report 73-49.
2. Edit the header, and type `Clip Art Overview` as the section name.
3. Edit the footer so the page number starts at page 8.
4. Delete the entire content of the report body, and replace it with this:

ADDING Clip Art

Clip art can enhance the appearance of a slide, and it can be easily added to selected slides or to every other slide in your presentation. Several clip art images are included in this presentation package and any 1 of them can be used in slides that you prepare. If you choose, therefore prefer, you can also insert clip art images from other packages. To insert a clip art image from your Presentation software package, follow these steps:

1. In the desired slide, Click the icon for adding a clip art image.

2. Select the image from the software clip art library and size and move it to its new location.

3. Size and move the image to its correct location on the presentation slide.

4. Copy the image to the slide master if it is to appear on all slides.

You can also modify change the appearance of a clip art image by changing the colors used or by changing the contrast or brightness. A mirror image is created by flipping the image so that its horizontal or vertical position is are reversed. To eliminate unwanted sections of an image, crop the unwanted sections. This process is similar to what happens you when take a printed picture and use scissors to cut off portions of the picture except that it happens electronically.

Keyboarding Connection

Observing Netiquette

Netiquette is proper conduct for e-mail users. It shows courtesy and professionalism and conveys a good impression of you and your company. Since e-mail is close to speech, it is the most informal of business documents.

Check your e-mail daily. Try to answer it the same day it arrives. Don't let it accumulate in your mailbox; you risk offending the sender. Use regular capitalization. All-caps indicate SHOUTING; all-lowercase text conveys immaturity. Most readers tolerate an infrequent typo, but if your message is filled with errors, you appear unprofessional. Use your spell checker, and don't overwhelm people with unnecessary e-mail. Use discretion. Don't automatically reply all; make sure the information is relevant to each e-mail recipient.

Be considerate. Be professional. Don't forward jokes or nonwork-related e-mail at work. Anything you write can wind up in your personnel file. E-mail that criticizes another person can be forwarded to him or her without your knowledge.

Your Turn: Review your next e-mail message for the use of netiquette.

Reports Formatted in Columns

Goals

- Type at least 42wpm/5'/5e.
- Correctly use Word's column and hyphenation features.
- Correctly format a magazine article.

A. WARMUP

alphabet
frequent digraphs
easy

1 Amusing quips galvanized a few of the mock jury in the box.
2 th that bath them both math then moth the myth theft thirty
3 The doe and buck by the old bush may dig up the giant oaks.

Skillbuilding

B. PROGRESSIVE PRACTICE: NUMBERS

Follow the GDP software directions for this exercise to improve keystroking speed.

C. TECHNIQUE PRACTICE: SPACE BAR

Type each line 2 times, using your right thumb to strike the SPACE BAR in the center.

4 Mr. Li may ask an arm and a leg for the new car on the lot.
5 The hot sun in the sky led Ann to ask him for a cup of tea.
6 Bo may use an old key to the gym for the new job if he can.
7 One ton of wet tar on the dam may be a bit too hot for him.

D. 5-MINUTE TIMED WRITING

8 Have you ever given any thought to starting your own 11
9 business? Obviously, there is some risk in starting out in 23
10 a venture such as this. However, if you realize there are 34
11 some issues to starting up a business, it may not seem to 46
12 be such a daunting undertaking. Let's quickly look at just 58
13 some of the issues that are involved in this task. 68
14 First of all, you need to think about whether you want 79
15 to do so badly enough to work long hours without knowing if 91
16 you will make any money at the end of the month. It would 103
17 be advantageous if you had worked previously for another 114
18 company as a manager or have managerial experience. 124
19 You have to have some sense for just how much money 135
20 you will need to start your business. It will take some 146
21 working capital to get you started. If you have put money 158
22 aside to invest in the company, there is a good possibility 170
23 you will succeed. If you don't have enough put aside, can 181
24 you get credit from a lending institution to assist you 193
25 through the first few months? And, of course, you'll need 204
26 to get credit from suppliers. 210

1 | 2 | 3 | 4 | 5 | 6 | 7 | 8 | 9 | 10 | 11 | 12

Formatting

E. MAGAZINE ARTICLES

Magazine articles can be formatted as a newspaper-style column in which text flows from the bottom of one column to the top of the next column. Magazine articles are generally formatted as 2-column reports.

To format a magazine article with two columns:

1. Turn hyphenation on.
2. Press ENTER 5 times to begin the first line of the magazine article 2 inches from the top of the page.
3. Center and type the title in all-caps, bold, and 14-point.
4. Press ENTER 2 times; then center and type the byline in upper- and lower-case, bold, and 12-point.
5. Press ENTER 2 times and change to left alignment.
6. Type the article single-spaced; insert 1 blank line before and after all side headings.
7. Select the body of the report, and change to justified alignment.
8. For a multipage article, insert a header (suppressed on the first page) with the author's last name, a space, and the page number aligned at the right.
9. Carefully select text beginning just before the first character in the first paragraph through the last typed character of the document excluding the paragraph formatting following the last character.
10. Format the body into 2 columns.
11. If any heading appears as a one-liner at the bottom of the first page, keep it with the text on the next page.
12. Balance the columns if necessary.
13. Fix any large gaps that might appear between the words of the last line of the body.

14 pt **TIME AND PERCEPTION** ↓2X

12 pt ↓ **Shannon Jones** ↓2X

Time is a method human beings use to measure and sequence events, to compare the durations of events, and to measure the intervals between events. Time is a hot topic in terms of religion, philosophy, and science. However, defining time in an objective, accepted way has been nearly impossible among scholarly types. How, in fact, do you compare one moment to the next?

As human beings, our perception of time has grown out of a natural series of rhythms that are linked to daily, monthly, and yearly cycles. No matter how much we live by our wristwatches, our bodies and our lives will always be somewhat influenced by an internal clock. What is of even greater interest, though, are the many uses and perceptions of time based on individuals and their cultures.

RHYTHM AND TEMPO

Rhythm and tempo are ways we relate to time and are discerning features of a culture. In some cultures, people move very slowly; in others, moving quickly is the norm. Mixing the two types may create feelings of discomfort. People may have trouble relating to each other because they are not synchronized. To be synchronized is to subtly move in union with another person; it is vital to a strong partnership.

In general, Americans move at a fast tempo, although there are regional departures. In meetings, Americans tend to be impatient and want to "get down to business" right away. They have been taught that it is best to come to the point quickly and avoid vagueness. Because American business operates in a short time frame, prompt results are often of more interest than the building of long-term relationships.

PERCEPTION AND MEMORY

Picture yourself in a room watching someone enter, walk across the room, and sit down. By the time the person sits down, your brain must remember the actions that happened previous to the act of sitting down. All these memories and perceptions are filed as bits of data in the brain. The perception of the passing of time from the first event of entering the room to the last event of sitting down occurs only if the observer is aware and comparing the events.

What would happen if the observer could not remember one or more of the events from the time the person entered the room to the time that person was seated? The brain might interpret the scene and assign a time frame, but unless the observer remembers, the perception of time passing would not exist.

LIVING IN THE MOMENT

If a human being perceives himself to be of a certain age, this is because he has accumulated data, remembers that data, and has a basis for a comparison. If a person cannot remember his past, such as a person with dementia, then he would not be aware of the existence of such a past. He would only be experiencing the single "moment" he was living in.

F. WORD PROCESSING: COLUMNS AND HYPHENATION

Study Lesson 74 in your Word Manual. Complete all of the shaded steps while at your computer. Then format the documents that follow.

Document Processing

INTERVIEW TECHNIQUES
Sandra Dolan

¶ The interview process enables a company to gather information about you that was not provided on your resume or application form. This information may include such items as your career goals, appearance, personality, poise, and ability to express yourself verbally.

¶ Regardless of where you went to school or how much experience you have, if you aren't able to interview successfully, you won't get the job. Take note of the information in this article to help you interview successfully and get the job you want.

APPEARANCE

¶ Plan your wardrobe carefully because first impressions are lasting ones when you walk into the interviewer's office. If you are not quite certain about what you should wear, dress conservatively.

¶ Whatever you choose, be sure that your clothing is clean, neat, and comfortable. You should also pay attention to details such as personal hygiene, clean hair, shined shoes, well-groomed nails, and appropriate jewelry and other accessories.

MEETING THE INTERVIEWER

¶ Be sure to arrive at the interview site a few minutes early. Stand when you meet the interviewer for the first time. If the interviewer offers to shake hands, shake hands in a confident, firm manner. A great deal of nonverbal communication occurs even in a simple handshake.

THE INTERVIEW PROCESS

¶ Maintain direct eye contact with the interviewer when you respond to his or her questions. Listen intently to everything that is said. Be aware of any movements you make with your eyes, your hands, and other parts of your body during the interview. Too much movement may be a signal to the interviewer that you are nervous, that you lack confidence, or that you are not certain of your answers.

¶ During the interview, the interviewer will judge not only what you say but also how you say it. As you answer questions, you will be judged on grammar, articulation, vocabulary, and tone of voice. The nonverbal skills that the interviewer may judge are your attitude, enthusiasm, listening ability, and promptness in responding to questions.

ENDING THE INTERVIEW

¶ Let the interviewer determine when it is time to close the interview. When this time arrives, ask the interviewer when he or she expects to make a decision on hiring for this position and when you may expect to hear about the job. Thank the interviewer for taking the time to meet with you, and make a graceful, prompt exit.

¶ After the interview, send a follow-up letter to remind the interviewer of your name and your continued interest in the company. This follow-up letter will set you apart from the competition and provide another example of your communication skills. Let the interviewer know how to contact you by providing a telephone number where you can be reached. A cell phone number is preferable to a home phone number. Make it easy for the interviewer to contact you.

PACIFIC INSURANCE DISCOUNTS
Sharon Brooks

¶ Policyholders of Pacific Insurance (and their dependents) are eligible for a wide range of discount services. These services provide you with a variety of items you can purchase, from automobiles to computers to jewelry. Here are some examples of the merchandise and services that are available to all Pacific Insurance members.

AUTO PRICING

¶ You can order the most sophisticated auto information guide on the market. The guide will give you information on retail prices, vehicle specifications, safety equipment, and factory-option packages.

¶ When you are ready to place your order for an automobile, a team of company experts will work with you and with the prospective dealer to ensure that you are getting the best possible price through a network of nationwide dealers. You are guaranteed to get the best price for the automobile you have chosen.

¶ Once you have purchased your automobile, Pacific Insurance will provide all your insurance needs. Discounts on policy rates are provided for completion of a driver-training program, for installed antitheft devices, and for installed passive restraint systems, such as air bags.

¶ Finally, Pacific Insurance can make your purchase decision an easy one by always providing a low-rate finance plan for you. You can be certain that you are getting the most competitive interest rate for the purchase of your automobile when you finance with Pacific Insurance.

CAR RENTAL DISCOUNTS

¶ When you need to rent an automobile while traveling, take advantage of special rates available to you from five of the largest car rental agencies. Send us an e-mail message at pacificinsurance@mail.com to receive all details regarding car rental rates and participating agencies.

(continued on next page)

ROAD AND TRAVEL SERVICES

¶ You can enjoy the security of specialized coverage for both towing and roadside emergency through the Pacific Insurance Road and Travel Plan. If you're locked out of your car or need a jump start, a tire changed, or a tow, Pacific Insurance is there.

¶ As a Pacific Insurance traveler, you can take advantage of our exclusive discounts and bonuses on cruises and tours. Our travel plan provides daily and weekend trips to over 100 destinations.

MERCHANDISE BUYING

¶ Each quarter a buying services catalog will be mailed to you. This catalog includes a variety of items that can be purchased through Pacific Insurance, and you'll never find better prices! Through the catalog you can purchase jewelry, furniture, sports equipment, electronics, appliances, computers, and much more. To place an order, simply call Pacific Insurance free at 1-800-555-3838 or visit our Web site.

Report 74-53
Magazine Article

Open the file for Report 74-51 and make the following changes:

1. Change the author's name to "Debra Winger."
2. Add the following section just before the section entitled "ENDING THE INTERVIEW."

INTERVIEW QUESTIONS

¶ Be prepared for common interview questions, and be prepared to ask some of your own. You might ask about the company's mission statement, about the typical career path for this position, or about a typical workday at that organization. Ask some questions that show you are interested in learning more about the company and want to make a commitment to its success as a future employee.

75

Report Review

Goals

- Demonstrate improved speed and accuracy while typing.
- Demonstrate acceptable language arts skills in composing paragraphs.
- Correctly format an agenda, the minutes of a meeting, and a magazine article.
- Successfully complete a Progress and Proofreading Check with zero errors on the first scored attempt.

A. WARMUP

alphabet
number/symbol
easy

1 I quickly explained that many big jobs involve few hazards.
2 rlow@juno.com 294% (Dix & Wu) 8/9 Yes! $1.34 *Fri. #1257-60
3 Jane did not blame the busy auditor for her usual problems.

Skillbuilding

B. 12-SECOND SPEED SPRINTS

Take three 12-second timed writings on each line.

4 I may make us one set of maps to aid us when we visit them.
5 I hid a big car in my new lot, but I may not get to it by two.
6 It is a shame she works such odd anthems into her busy art.
7 It is the duty of the busy worker to take apart the panels.
' ' ' '5' ' ' '10' ' ' '15' ' ' '20' ' ' '25' ' ' '30' ' ' '35' ' ' '40' ' ' '45' ' ' '50' ' ' '55' ' ' '60

C. PACED PRACTICE

Follow the GDP software directions for this exercise to improve keystroking speed and accuracy.

Language Arts

D. COMPOSING PARAGRAPHS

Do you think it is safe to make and pay for purchases online? Compose a paragraph of at least three to four sentences answering this question.

Report 75-54
Agenda

UNITED BANK OF THE WEST
Meeting Agenda
May 15, 20--

1. Call to order
2. Approval of minutes of April 15 meeting
3. Installment loans (Gerald Hagen)
4. Mortgage loans (William McKay)
5. Series EE bonds (Francis Montoya)
6. Club memberships (Louise Abbey)
7. Certificates of deposit (Robert Hunt)
8. Closing remarks
9. Adjournment

Report 75-55
Minutes of a Meeting

ART SOCIETY OF MENDOCINO
Minutes of the Meeting
Oct. 19, 20--

ATTENDANCE Linda Scher called the meeting to order at 8 p.m. in the Mendocino Fine Arts Center.

APPROVAL OF MINUTES The minutes of the October 10th meeting were read and approved with 1 correction—the spring arts fair will be held in April rather than in May of next year.

OLD BUSINESS Susan Firtz furnished each member with a list of artists and the names of the watercolor paintings by each artist.

NEW BUSINESS Martha Steward informed members that a new supply of canvas and oil paint arrived. Members can check out any items they need to begin their winter projects. She reminded everyone that The Winter Arts Fair will be held December 14 at the Centennial Convention Center.

ADJOURNMENT The Meeting was adjourned at 9:45 p.m. The December meeting will be canceled and the next meeting will be held January 12.

Respectfully submitted,

Carole Little

PUBLIC SPEAKING TIPS
Donna Barnes

¶ We have all been giving performances since our very early years. The most terrifying part of each performance was probably the fear that we would "freeze" when it came our turn to perform. Whenever we find ourselves in this predicament, we should accept that fear and learn to let it work for us, not against us. We need to recognize that nervousness or fear may set in during our performance. Then, when it does happen (if it does), we will be ready to cope with it and overcome it.

¶ If you forget some lines in a recitation, try to remember other lines and recite them. Doing so may help those forgotten lines to "pop back" into your memory so that you put them in at a later time.

¶ You always want to leave your audience with the idea that you have given them something worthwhile that they can use or apply to their own lives. For maximum impact on your audience and to make sure that they remember what you say, use audiovisual aids to reinforce your message. Remember, however, that audiovisual aids are nothing more than aids. The real message should come in the words you choose when giving your presentation.

¶ Study your speech well; even rehearse it, if necessary. However, do not practice it to the extent that it appears that you are merely reading what is written down on the paper in front of you. Much of your personality should be exhibited while you are giving your speech. If you are an enthusiastic, friendly person who converses well with people face-to-face, then those same qualities should be evident during your speech. A good piece of advice is to just go out there and be yourself—you will be much more comfortable by doing so, and your audience will relate to you better than if you try to exhibit a different personality when at the podium.

¶ No matter how rapidly you speak, slow down when you are in front of a group. The fact that you are nervous can cause your speech rate to increase. The best way to slow down your speaking is to breathe deeply. Doing so also causes your nervous system to relax, allowing you to proceed with your speech calmly.

¶ Finally, the best advice for giving a successful speech is to be prepared. You will be more confident if you are thoroughly prepared. Do your research, rehearse your speech, and make notes about any points you want to emphasize.

Strategies for Career Success

Audience Analysis

Knowing your audience is fundamental to the success of any message. Ask the following questions to help identify your audience.

What is your relationship with your audience? Are they familiar—people with whom you work—or people unknown to you? The latter will prompt you to conduct some research to better communicate your purpose. What is the attitude of your audience? Are they hostile or receptive to your message? How will your message benefit them? What is your anticipated response? Asking these questions first can help prevent message mishaps later.

When writing to a diverse audience, direct your message to the primary audience. These key decision makers will make a decision or act on the basis of your message. Determine the level of detail, organization, formality, and use of technical terms and theory.

Your Turn: Compose a thank-you e-mail to a friend. How would it differ from an interview thank-you letter?

UNIT 16

Tables

Tables With Footnotes or Source Notes

Goals

- Type at least 43wpm/5'/5e.
- Correctly use Word's table features to change text direction and insert or delete rows or columns.
- Correctly format a table with source notes or footnotes.

A. WARMUP

alphabet 1 My wife wove six dozen plaid jackets before the girls quit.

concentration 2 disenfranchisements unconstitutionality contemporaneousness

easy 3 The girl may make a formal gown of fur to go with her hair.

Skillbuilding

B. SUSTAINED PRACTICE: NUMBERS AND SYMBOLS

Take a 1-minute timed writing on the boxed paragraph to establish your base speed. Then take a 1-minute timed writing on the following paragraph. As soon as you equal or exceed your base speed on this paragraph, move to the next, more difficult paragraph.

4	There is a need at this time to communicate our new	11
5	pricing guidelines to our franchise outlets. In addition,	22
6	they must be made aware of inventory implications. They	33
7	will then be in a position to have a successful operation.	45

8   Franchise operators could be requested to use either   11
9 a 20% or a 30% markup. A $50 item would be marked to sell   22
10 for either $60 or $65. Depending on future prospects for   34
11 sales, half of the articles would be priced at each level.   45

12   Ms. Aagard's suggestion is to assign items in Groups   11
13 #1470, #2830, and #4560 to the 20% category. The Series 77   23
14 items* would be in the 30% markup category except for the   34
15 items with a base rate under $100. What is your reaction?   48

16   Mr. Chavez's recommendation is to assign a 30% markup   11
17 to Groups #3890, #5290, #6480, and #7180. About 1/4 of the   23
18 remainder (except for soft goods) would also be in the 30%   35
19 category. Groups #8340 and #9560 would have a 20% markup.   46

  1 | 2 | 3 | 4 | 5 | 6 | 7 | 8 | 9 | 10 | 11 | 12

Goal: At least 43wpm/5'/5e

C. 5-MINUTE TIMED WRITING

```
20        Starting up your own business may mean that you are        11
21  thinking about acquiring an existing business. If so, is        22
22  that business doing well in the community? If you are going      34
23  to buy out an established business, you need to know the         45
24  reason the current owner wishes to sell the company. If          57
25  there are other businesses in the area, you should first         68
26  find out what reputation that business has built up in the       80
27  community. Do other businesses think highly of the company?      92
28        You must also consider what type of advertising you       102
29  plan to use to get your business off to a good start. You        114
30  might use ads in newspapers, on television, in magazines,        128
31  or on the Internet. When you start your ad campaigns, you        137
32  should consider hiring an ad agency to put out the right         149
33  message for your company and its products. You should also       160
34  consider the types of ads being used by your competitors to      172
35  determine what has worked well for them.                         181
36        Yes, there are major issues that need to be addressed      192
37  when starting up your own business; and all of the issues        203
38  should be dealt with before you decide to take such a step.      215
      1 | 2 | 3 | 4 | 5 | 6 | 7 | 8 | 9 | 10 | 11 | 12
```

Formatting

REFER TO
Reference Manual

R-8B: Multipage Business Report
R-13A: Boxed Table

D. TABLES WITH SOURCE NOTES OR FOOTNOTES

To format tables with source notes or footnotes:

1. When you insert a table, include an additional row at the bottom of the table for the source note or footnote.
2. Merge the cells in the bottom row.
3. For a source note, type Note: or Source: as applicable in the bottom row; then type the corresponding information for the source note.
4. For a footnote, type an asterisk (or another symbol) at the relevant point within the table; then in the bottom row, type an asterisk and the corresponding information for the footnote.

E. WORD PROCESSING: TABLE—TEXT DIRECTION AND TABLE—INSERT, DELETE, AND MOVE ROWS OR COLUMNS

GO TO
Word Manual

Study Lesson 76 in your Word Manual. Complete all of the shaded steps while at your computer. Then format the documents that follow.

Document Processing

Table
76-26
Boxed Table

1. In Row 1, set the text direction to display vertically from bottom to top, and change the alignment to bottom center.
2. Adjust the row height so that none of the column heading lines wrap to a second line.

3. In the merged cells in the bottom row, type the table note as shown.

Portfolio Counselor	Years of Experience	Fund Title Code	MSC World Index	Maxim Global Funds Index	Class A Management Fees	Class B Management Fees	Class C Management Fees
Steven Burgess	16	529-A	40.33%	38.78%	.37%	.37%	.37%
Jean Carol	5	529-B	38.78%	5.65%	.23%	1.00%	.25%
Mark Denning	12	361-A	21.42%	1.23%	.15%	.15%	.14%
Rex Humber	3	361-B	38.29%	3.99%	.75%	1.52%	.76%
Note: This information is subject to change.							

Table
76-27
Boxed Table

Open the file for Table 76-26 and make the following changes:

1. Delete the table note row.
2. Delete Column H.
3. Insert a row above Row 3. Type this:

   Marie Alexander | 20 | 436-C
   | 26.17% | 24.39% | .52% |
   1.25%

4. Insert a column to the left of Column F. Type this:

   United Fund Index | 31.29%
   | 19.07% | 9.73% | 2.75% |
   5.41%

5. Adjust the alignment of the new column heading to bottom center.
6. Move Column D to the right one column so it will become Column E.
7. Move Row 3 up one row so it becomes Row 2.
8. Insert a row at the bottom of the table, merge the cells, and type this left-aligned note: Note: This information will be updated next quarter.
9. Apply a 25 percent shading to Row 1.

Table
76-28
Boxed Table

1. In Row 1, set the text direction to display vertically from bottom to top, and change the alignment to bottom center.
2. Adjust the row height so that none of the column heading lines wrap to a second line.
3. In the merged cells in the bottom row, type the table footnote as shown.

Office Supply Account*	LED Laser Printer	Internal Fax Modem	Cash Management System	Plain-Paper Laser Fax
OE-9	$405	$181	$199	$249
DD-7	395	150	205	234
US-2	410	125	183	252
OB-1	420	167	179	245
*Codes are subject to change.				

Keyboarding Connection

Virus and Spam Prevention

Use caution when opening e-mail attachments or downloading files from the Internet. Download files only from reliable Web sites. Do not open files attached to an e-mail from an unknown source. Also question files attached to e-mail from a known source. Some viruses replicate themselves and are sent through e-mail without users' knowledge.

Delete any e-mail with an odd subject, a chain e-mail, or electronic junk mail, commonly known as spam. If you're given the opportunity to unsubscribe from a spammer's list, think twice. Your reply will stop the messages from a reputable mailing list, but replying to e-mail spam lets the spammers know your e-mail address is legitimate and can actually increase the amount of spam you receive.

To protect against lost data, back up your files on a regular basis. Then you will be prepared if a virus infects your computer. New viruses are discovered daily, so update your antivirus software regularly.

Your Turn: How do you handle junk mail via snail mail? Do you notice similarities when dealing with spam?

Tables With Braced Column Headings

77

Goals

- Demonstrate improved speed and accuracy while typing.
- Demonstrate acceptable language arts skills in capitalization.
- Correctly format a table with braced column headings.

A. WARMUP

alphabet   1   Grumpy wizards made toxic brew for Jack and the evil queen.

one hand   2   assets linkup bat kin tested phonily wave imply refer puppy

easy   3   Kent may fish with me for cod at the docks on their island.

Skillbuilding

B. MAP+: ALPHABET

Follow the GDP software directions for this exercise to improve keystroking accuracy.

C. PROGRESSIVE PRACTICE: ALPHABET

Follow the GDP software directions for this exercise to improve keystroking speed.

Language Arts

Study the rules at the right.

RULE
≡ noun #

D. CAPITALIZATION

Capitalize nouns followed by a number or letter (except for the nouns *line, note, page, paragraph,* and *size*).

Please read Chapter 5, which begins on page 94.

RULE
≡ compass point

Capitalize compass points (such as *north, south,* or *northeast*) only when they designate definite regions.

From Montana we drove south to reach the Southwest.

4 The marketing manager had a reservation on flight 505 to
5 Atlanta.

6 Please order two model 6M printers.

7 The desktop publishing seminar will be held in Room 101.

8 Study pages 120-230 for the unit test.

9 Please contact all representatives in the northern states.

10 Didn't line 9 of the directions say to drive south?

11 The population of the south continues to increase.

Formatting

E. TABLES WITH BRACED COLUMN HEADINGS

A braced column heading is a heading that applies to more than one column (for example, *Explore Chicago Pass* and *Chicago City Pass* in the table shown below). To create a braced column heading:

1. Position the insertion point where you want the braced heading to appear.
2. Merge the cells that will hold the braced heading.
3. Center the braced column heading over the appropriate columns.

Document Processing

Table
77-29
Boxed Table

CHICAGO ATTRACTION DISCOUNT CARDS Spring Rates*					
Explore Chicago Pass			Chicago City Pass		
Month	Adult	Child	Month	Adult	Child
March	$60	$45	March	$55	$40
April	70	55	April	65	50
May	90	75	May	85	70
*Read page 2 of "Big City on a Budget" for details.					

≡ noun #

Table
77-30
Boxed Table

CHICAGO TRAVEL BOOKS Sales Trends			
Midwest Publishing		Total Sales	
Region	Sales Representative	Last Year	This Year
Illinois	Jeff Meyer	$1,956,250	$2,135,433
Wisconsin*	Marjorie Matheson	859,435	1,231,332
Indiana	Valerie Harper	737,498	831,352
*Includes only eastern Wisconsin.			

≡ compass point

Table
77-31
Boxed Table

Single-space the table.

AMERICA DISCOVERY TOURS			
Illinois Tour Highlights		San Francisco tour Highlights	
Attraction	**Location**	**Attraction**	**Location**
Land Øf Lincoln	Springfield	Golden Gate Park	Central Richmond
Adler Planetarium	South Shore of Chicago	Exploratorium	Presidio
Lincoln Park	North Side of Chicago	Yerba Buena Gardens	South Beach
The Navy Pier	Downtown Chicago	Coit Tower	The Embarcadero
Aquarium Shedd	South Shore of Chicago	Fishermans Wharf	North Beach
Wrigley Building	North Side of Chicago	Palace of Fine Arts	Persidio

Tables in Landscape Orientation

Goals

- Type at least 43wpm/5'/5e.
- Correctly use Word's page orientation feature.
- Correctly format a table in landscape orientation.

A. WARMUP

alphabet

practice *r* and *t*

easy

1 Those heavy boxers performed quick waltzes and lively jigs.
2 rat try rotate trust tort tutor treat Trent trite trot hurt
3 His body of work may disorient the visitors in the chapels.

Skillbuilding

B. PACED PRACTICE

Follow the GDP software directions for this exercise to improve keystroking speed and accuracy.

C. 5-MINUTE TIMED WRITING

Take two 5-minute timed writings.

Goal: At least 43wpm/5'/5e

```
 4      This is the third in a series of timed writings on      10
 5  starting up a new business. In this presentation, you will  22
 6  consider some expense and merchandise issues as well as     33
 7  some thoughts on the building you will move into or build.  45
 8      There are several expenses that you will have to look   56
 9  at for your new business. For example, do you realize how   68
10  much construction costs will be, or, if you are going to    79
11  rent a building, how much that expense will amount to? You  91
12  must also project expenses for insurance on the building    102
13  and its contents, utilities costs for running the business, 114
14  interest expense on any loans you secure to purchase or     128
15  renovate the building, and any new advertising expenses.    137
16      You must also consider the amount of merchandise you    148
17  will have on hand when you first open your store. If you    159
18  have several lines of merchandise, you need to determine    171
19  how many products and how much of each product you will     182
20  keep on the shelves and how much you will keep in inventory 194
21  in your warehouse. To acquire this merchandise, you must    205
22  locate suppliers who will sell you what you need.           215
        1 | 2 | 3 | 4 | 5 | 6 | 7 | 8 | 9 | 10 | 11 | 12
```

D. TABLES IN LANDSCAPE ORIENTATION

The default page orientation for 8.5- by 11-inch paper is vertical (also known as *portrait*). Sometimes, however, the content of a document would fit better or appear more attractive in horizontal orientation (called *landscape*). Format all tables in this lesson in landscape orientation.

Portrait orientation.

TEEN DRIVING SCHOOL					
6-Month Class Schedule					
Date	Instructor	Street Address	City	State	ZIP
January 29	Stephen Kepplinger	3959 Sierra Highway	Acton	California	93510
February 14	Gina Rowella	6329 Victory Boulevard	Burbank	California	91501
March 9	Marcus Barelas	901 San Fernando Road	Newhall	California	91321
April 12	Peng Lim	6624 Foothill Boulevard	Tujunga	California	91042
May 10	Sylvia Chavez	19241 Roscoe Boulevard	Northridge	California	91324
June 12	Lisa Bonine	8329 Ventura Canyon	Sherman Oaks	California	91401

Landscape orientation.

TEEN DRIVING SCHOOL					
6-Month Class Schedule					
Date	Instructor	Street Address	City	State	ZIP
January 29	Stephen Kepplinger	3959 Sierra Highway	Acton	California	93510
February 14	Gina Rowella	6329 Victory Boulevard	Burbank	California	91501
March 9	Marcus Barelas	901 San Fernando Road	Newhall	California	91321
April 12	Peng Lim	6624 Foothill Boulevard	Tujunga	California	91042
May 10	Sylvia Chavez	19241 Roscoe Boulevard	Northridge	California	91324
June 12	Lisa Bonine	8329 Ventura Canyon	Sherman Oaks	California	91401

E. WORD PROCESSING: PAGE ORIENTATION

GO TO
Word Manual

Study Lesson 78 in your Word Manual. Complete all of the shaded steps while at your computer. Then format the documents that follow.

Strategies for Career Success

Developing Confidence as a Presenter

Public speaking anxiety is quite common. As many as 77 percent of experienced speakers admit to having some anxiety on each speaking occasion. Normally, stage fright decreases with experience.

Even if there are no physical expressions of anxiety, speakers often assume others can see through their smiles to their fears. However, listeners are actually poor judges of the amount of anxiety that speakers experience.

A little anxiety can actually stimulate a better presentation. The best way to control your anxiety is to be well prepared for the presentation. Carefully analyze your audience, research your topic, organize the speech, practice your delivery, and believe in the ideas. Being well prepared puts you in an excellent position to control your anxiety.

Your Turn: "I'm glad I'm here. I'm glad you're here. I know that I know." What are the benefits of repeating this to yourself before each presentation?

Table
78-32
Boxed Table

THE TRAVEL SHOP
Travel Agent Contact Information*

Name	Street Address	City	State	ZIP	Telephone	E-Mail
Ronald Dahl	8787 Orion Place	Columbus	OH	43240	614-555-4951	rdahl@tts.com
Ming Dai	1415 Elbridge Payne Road	Chesterfield	MO	63017	636-555-9940	mdai@tts.com
Amber Palmer	3100 Breckinridge Boulevard	Duluth	GA	30096	770-555-7007	apalmer@tts.com
Anita Mills	21600 Oxnard Street	Woodland Hills	CA	91367	818-555-2675	amills@tts.com

*Contact information was last updated on July 1.

Table
78-33
Boxed Table

Open the file for Table 78-32 and make the following changes:

1. Change Ronald Dahl's address to this:

   376 West Lane Avenue

2. Add this information for another travel agent in a new row just above the table note:

   Mike Cassidy | 2739 Idaho Avenue | Kenner | LA | 70062 | 504-555-0089 | mcassidy@tts.com

3. Change the table note to read as follows:
   *For a complete listing of all travel agents, visit http://www.thetravelshop.com and click "Contact Us."

Table
78-34
Boxed Table

Ohio CUSTOMER SURVEY RESULTS

Office Products Unlimited

July 1 20--

Customer	Address	City	Zip	Telephone No	Most Recent Purchase
Becker, Steve	121 North Summit Street	Toledo	44426	419-555-2384	Label maker
Cross, Mario	20604 Lucile Rd. South	Columbus	43230	614-555-2074	Book case and Shelving
Dusenberry, Rich	322 West Lyons Road	Cleveland	44902	261-555-2002	Portable hard drive
Ferrer, Marie	5914 Bay Oaks Place	Chillicothe	45601	614-555-1399	Portable DVD player
Goodrich, Mike	10386 Power Drive	Steubenville	43952	614-555-7821	Digital camera
Juarez, Ismael	231 East Front Street	Youngstown	44502	216-555-3885	Postal scale
Lancaster, Robert	6823 Creekwood Dr.	Columbus	43085	614-555-2934	Wireless router
Pastor, Sandra	26044 Manzano Court	Youngstown	44505	216-555-1777	Cordless keyboard
Wee, Ju Jong	936 East Wind Drive	Cleveland	44121	216-555-8239	Industrial shredder

Tables With Predesigned Formats

80

Goals

- Type at least 43wpm/5'/5e.
- Correctly use Word's table styles feature.
- Correctly format a predesigned table.

A. WARMUP

alphabet	1	Judge Hank Powell quickly gave six embezzlers a stiff fine.
number/symbol	2	(ali41@cs.com) (10%) Guy & Lee 7/8 In! $5.40 *f.o.b. #26-39
easy	3	Claudia may sign the title to her auto when she is in town.

Skillbuilding

B. 12-SECOND SPEED SPRINTS

Take three 12-second timed writings on each line.

4 Jake moved to amend the law to let the worker take the job.
5 Jan and her son may make a bowl of fish and a cup of cocoa.
6 Jane can buy fuel for the old blue auto at the nearby lots.
7 Kay and she may both visit us in May when they are in town.
' ' ' '5' ' ' '10' ' ' '15' ' ' '20' ' ' '25' ' ' '30' ' ' '35' ' ' '40' ' ' '45' ' ' '50' ' ' '55' ' ' '60

C. TECHNIQUE PRACTICE: TAB KEY

Press TAB 1 time between words. Type each line 2 times.

Press TAB where you see the → symbol.

8	are→	Mag→	Uzi→	Lew→	Mel→	adz→	ace→	ale→	Jew→	air→	Poe
9	axe→	Job→	Leo→	Mia→	Jon→	Peg→	arc→	ago→	ate→	Pia→	Una
10	aha→	Ott→	Ivy→	zag→	ape→	Obi→	Ike→	Hsu→	and→	asp→	zip
11	May→	Liz→	Lou→	Kit→	Ned→	Kim→	Ham→	age→	aft→	zoo→	Mel

Take two 5-minute timed writings.

Goal: At least 43wpm/5'/5e

D. 5-MINUTE TIMED WRITING

```
12      Finding a job is a challenge in today's job market,    11
13  but there are some steps you can take to remain competitive  23
14  in the job market. First of all, be sure you know something  35
15  about the company. Does it have offices in a location to     48
16  which you would move, and is the position in that company    58
17  one in which you would like to spend the next five to ten    69
18  years of your working life?                                  75
19      To be successful during the interview, you need to      85
20  know yourself. What are your strengths, and what are your    97
21  weaknesses, if any? Be sure to emphasize your unique skills 109
22  both in your resume and during the interview. Let others    120
23  know what makes you the best candidate for the job. Some    132
24  excellent traits to emphasize would be enthusiasm, a high   143
25  motivation level, and an excellent work ethic.              153
26      When you go for your interview, take into account how   164
27  you dress. Choose your wardrobe as you would for your first 178
28  day on the job. If you are uncertain as to the particular   187
29  dress code, always err on the side of conservatism. Also,   199
30  be mindful of your personal grooming. Make certain your     210
31  hair is trimmed and neat.                                   215
     1 | 2 | 3 | 4 | 5 | 6 | 7 | 8 | 9 | 10 | 11 | 12
```

Formatting

E. PREDESIGNED TABLES

Predesigned table styles are used to quickly refine the look and layout of a table and to format major table elements, such as title blocks and total lines, in unique ways. Bolding and varying font sizes have been used up to this point to distinguish the title, subtitle, and column headings in a table. A table style will distinguish these table elements in a more refined way through colorful, customized designs. As with any style, repeating a table style also ensures design consistency.

Table styles help comprehension by giving readers visual style cues for different content. For example, if the bottom table row includes a total line, a table style option could be used to format that row in a distinct way. Likewise, a unique treatment could be applied to the first column if the content calls for it.

F. WORD PROCESSING: TABLE—STYLES

GO TO Word Manual

Study Lesson 80 in your Word Manual. Complete all of the shaded steps while at your computer. Then format the documents that follow.

Document Processing

1. Apply a table style of your choice.
2. In Rows 1 and 2, verify that all text is bolded.
3. In Row 2, align the column headings at the bottom center.

HIGH-YIELD CD RATES 1-Year Deposits			
Institution	**Rate**	**APY**	**Minimum Deposit**
ADSCapital.com	2.45%	2.70%	$10,000
Amber Direct	2.50%	2.50%	10,000
Arizona First National Bank	2.18%	2.20%	5,000
Chorus Bank	2.71%	2.74%	10,000
GCBank.com	2.57%	2.60%	1,000
GMBC Bank	2.71%	2.75%	500
HTSM Direct	2.27%	2.30%	10
New Mercantile	2.35%	2.38%	10,000
Nexus Bank	2.53%	2.56%	1,000
Regal Capital Bank	2.45%	2.45%	2,000
State Bank	2.51%	2.54%	500
State Bank of Indiana	2.30%	2.32%	5,000
UTCDirect.com	2.52%	2.55%	8,000
Average	2.47%	2.51%	$ 4,847

1. Apply a table style of your choice.
2. In Rows 1 and 2, verify that all text is bolded.
3. In Row 2, align the column headings at the bottom center.

BUILDING DIRECTORY National Convention Center			
No.	**Room Name**	**Seating**	**Square Feet**
102	Alabama	35	400
104	Colorado	150	1,600
106	Delaware	25	350
108	Georgia	50	600
202	Montana	35	400
204	Nevada	50	600
206	New Jersey	300	3,200
208	Pennsylvania	350	3,600

Table
80-40
Predesigned Table

1. Apply a table style of your choice.
2. In Rows 1 and 2, verify that all text is bolded.
3. In Row 2, align the column headings at the bottom center.

ABC MEMBER VACATIONS Promotional Sailing Prices*						
	7-Day Cruises			**12-Day Cruises**		
Location	**Interior**	**Ocean-View**	**Balcony**	**Interior**	**Ocean-View**	**Balcony**
Alaska	$ 599	$ 699	$1,299	$1,199	$1,299	$1,899
Canada	965	1,290	1,445	1,565	1,890	2,045
Caribbean	739	839	1,239	1,139	1,239	1,839
Hawaii	699	799	1,999	1,299	1,399	2,699
Mexico	599	749	849	999	1,149	1,249
Panama Canal	1,299	1,749	2,099	1,699	2,049	2,449

*All prices are subject to change.

Progress and Proofreading Check

Documents designated as Proofreading Checks serve as a check of your proofreading skill. Your goal is to have zero typographical errors when the GDP software first scores the document.

Strategies for Career Success

Cell Phone Manners Matter

Mind your cell phone manners! Although the cell phone allows you to keep in touch with your boss, coworkers, and clients, it also requires you to consider your communication etiquette. One of the worst violations of etiquette and safety is driving and talking at the same time. Several states now have laws restricting or forbidding cell phone use while driving. It is much safer to pull off the road to make or answer a call.

Consider others when you use a cell phone in a public place (for example, a restaurant). Don't use your cell phone at the movies or in a public restroom. If you use the phone in public, talk quietly and watch what you say. Cell phones in meetings can distract others or interrupt the meeting completely; some companies prohibit them in business meetings.

Your Turn: Observe cell phone users in a public place. Are they mindful of others when they use their phones?

Outcomes Assessment on Part 4

Test 4

1   Many business firms create their own special documents   11
2 today by using software packages that are designed to do   23
3 the job. These packages help people with limited design   34
4 skills create pages with very little effort. The challenge,   48
5 though, is for the person to design the pages effectively   57
6 so that the readers will read them. After all, the reason   69
7 for putting in all that time and money is to get people to   81
8 read the articles.   85
9   Designing pages that are easy to read is not quite as   98
10 easy as it seems. For example, a reader may be confused if   107
11 a page has too many headlines. Instead, a reader may want   119
12 to read fewer headlines that are printed in large type.   130
13   Desktop publishers require just a few good tools to   141
14 interest the reader. A good plan to use is to be sure to   152
15 put the most important articles at the top of the first   164
16 page and the less important articles on the inside pages.   175
17 The use of bullets or side headings is also a helpful guide 187
18 to help a reader zip through pages. A final suggestion is   199
19 to use pictures and graphics that can make the text much   210
20 more interesting to read.   215

1 | 2 | 3 | 4 | 5 | 6 | 7 | 8 | 9 | 10 | 11 | 12

MEMO TO: All ~~Members~~ _Employees_

FROM: Judy Greenburg

DATE: ~~June~~ _July_ 23, 20--

SUBJECT: Understanding Your Dental Plan

The Fulton # Community College district sent out a quarterly news letter early in ~~July~~ _June_ explaining the dental plan benefits offered to all of our employees. The highlights of each plan were reviewed and many of you requested further information.

Vanguard Dental PPO

If you are a ~~Dental Vanguard~~ Plan member, ask the dentist specifically if he or she is a Vanguard Dental provider and if he or she is in the ppo or Premiere network. Your benefits _will_ vary greatly depending upon the dentists affiliation. The table below includes examples of the costs you might pay with each _of the three_ types of Vanguard Dental providers.

Bottom-align column headings. Single-space the table.

		Out-of-Network	Out-of-Network _Noncontracted_ ~~Non-Contracted~~
Category	PPO Dentist	Premiere Dentist	Dentis_t_
Dentists charge	$1,000	$1,000	$1,000
Vanguard's approved fee	640	800	800
Plan payment	512	640	640
Member payment	128	160	360

VANGUARD DENTAL PPO

Charges For a Crown*

*Dentist's charges and approved fees are hypothetical.

HEALTHGUARD DENTAL HMO

If yuo are a Healthguard Dental _Plan_ member remember that you may change your dentist any at time and as often as you wish as long as your dentist is a participating provider. Other covered family members do _not_ have to choose the same dentist. Visit www.vanguard.net and www.healthguard.net for further details and a Directory of Dentists.

urs

January 10, 20-- | Mr. James F. Duncan | 229 Foster Street | Durham, NC 27701 | Dear Mr. Duncan:

¶ I am sorry that I had to end our phone call so abruptly yesterday. I would like to respond to both of your questions more specifically and give you a few more details regarding the tax consequences of hiring your daughter as an employee in your business.

1. You will need to issue her a W-2 form if you are paying her as an employee this year.
2. You cannot deduct her wages as a business expense on Schedule C because she is over the age of 19 and because you have paid her more than $600 this year.

¶ Please check with your tax attorney, and read IRS Publication 15 for further details. Sincerely yours, | Arlene R. Weiser | Attorney at Law | urs | PS: You may want to discuss this matter with your daughter before calling your tax attorney for an appointment. | bc: Peggy Jennings

Apply a 100 percent shading to Row 1 and a 25 percent shading to Row 3 and Row 11.

VALENCIA MEADOWS POOL Lesson Schedule*			
Session A		**Session B**	
Time	**Code**	**Time**	**Code**
7:10-8:10 a.m.	3508.310	7:05-8:05 a.m.	4001.910
8:20-9:20 a.m.	3509.311	8:25-9:25 a.m.	4002.911
9:30-10:30 a.m.	3510.312	9:40-10:30 a.m.	4003.912
10:45-11:15 a.m.	3511.313	10:35-11:35 a.m.	4004.913
12:05-1:05 p.m.	3512.314	12:15-1:15 p.m.	4005.914
5:40-6:40 p.m.	3513.315	5:10-6:10 p.m.	4006.915
7:15-8:15 p.m.	3514.316	7:15-8:15 p.m.	4007.931
*Session A begins June 15; Session B begins August 1.			

Formal Report Project

Formal Report Project—A

86

Goals

- Type at least 45wpm/5′/5e.
- Correctly use Word's styles feature.
- Correctly format a multipage business report.

A. WARMUP

alphabet 1 A zoo quickly bought a jinxed mauve dog with pink fur ears.
concentration 2 superstitiousnesses comprehensibilities incomprehensibility
easy 3 Dudley may then dismantle the tan bicycle out on the lanai.

Skillbuilding

B. SUSTAINED PRACTICE: PUNCTUATION

Take a 1-minute timed writing on the boxed paragraph to establish your base speed. Then take a 1-minute timed writing on the following paragraph. As soon as you equal or exceed your base speed on this paragraph, move to the next, more difficult paragraph.

4 One of the strengths you must have if you are going to 11
5 be a success in business is good writing skills. You must 23
6 practice your writing skills every day if you want them to 35
7 improve. Perfection of writing skills takes much practice. 46

8 You must always strive to write clearly, concisely, 11
9 and accurately. Remember always that your writing can be 22
10 examined by more people than just the one to whom you have 34
11 written. It's often looked at by other readers as well. 45

12 You want to be sure that your letters always convey a 11
13 positive, helpful attitude. Don't forget, you represent 22
14 more than yourself when you write--you also represent your 34
15 company! This is an important, useful rule to remember. 45

16 Try to stay away from negative words like "can't" or 11
17 "won't." Readers also do not like phrases such as "because 23
18 of company policies" or "due to unforeseen circumstances." 34
19 Using these words and phrases never helps resolve problems. 46

 1 | 2 | 3 | 4 | 5 | 6 | 7 | 8 | 9 | 10 | 11 | 12

Goal: At least 45wpm/5'/5e

C. 5-MINUTE TIMED WRITING

20	During upbeat economic times, businesses have trouble	11
21	finding and keeping their skilled workers. As a result,	22
22	some places may offer great benefits to the workers. These	34
23	could include such things as sick leave, life insurance,	45
24	profit sharing, paid time off each year, and flextime.	56
25	The concept of flextime was brought to the workforce	67
26	quite a few years ago. Companies implemented this concept	78
27	for a lot of reasons. Among the top reasons for flexible	90
28	work schedules at that time were to reduce the number of	101
29	cars on the road, to help workers to meet their families'	113
30	needs and demands, and also to attract more women back to	124
31	the workforce.	127
32	Businesses can manage such a schedule in a few ways.	138
33	Employees may have a chance to choose when to arrive and	150
34	leave for the day. This policy allows people who like to	161
35	work early in the day to start early and end early and vice	173
36	versa. Other companies may allow their employees to work	184
37	extended hours for four days and then enjoy three days off.	196
38	This type of benefit has assisted both workers and	206
39	companies. Companies recognize that their workers are more	218
40	productive and absences are lower.	225

1 | 2 | 3 | 4 | 5 | 6 | 7 | 8 | 9 | 10 | 11 | 12

Formatting

D. WORD PROCESSING—STYLES

GO TO Word Manual

Study Lesson 86 in your Word Manual. Complete all of the shaded steps while at your computer. Then format the document that follows.

Document Processing

You will begin typing Report 86-60, a formal business report project, in this lesson and will continue adding pages and features to the report in Lessons 87, 88, and 89.

- In Report 86-60, you will apply a Title style and Subtitle style to the title block and a Heading 2 style to the side headings. You will also insert a header and lists.
- In Report 87-61, you will apply styles, insert a list and two tables, format a displayed paragraph, and insert footnotes.

- In Report 88-62, you will apply styles, format a displayed paragraph, and insert clip art and footnotes.
- In Report 89-63, you will apply styles, insert a table, format a displayed paragraph, insert clip art and a footnote, and create bookmarks and hyperlinks.

Follow these steps to create the first two pages of the business report. Do not apply any styles until directed to do so:

1. Press ENTER 5 times, type the title in all-caps, and press ENTER 1 time.
2. Type the byline information in upper- and lowercase letters, and press ENTER 1 time after each line; then type the date, and press ENTER 2 times.
3. Type the first paragraph; then press ENTER 1 time.
4. Type the side heading in all-caps, and press ENTER 1 time. (Additional spacing will be added above the side heading later when the Heading 2 style is applied.)
5. Continue in like manner until all paragraph and side headings have been typed.
6. Insert a header that will display on all pages except the first page; type Human Resources Department at the left margin, and type Page followed by a space and an automatic page number at the right margin.
7. Select all header text and format it using Cambria 10 pt. Italic.
8. Add a bottom border; then close the header.

After you finish typing the part of the report shown in Lesson 86, do this:

1. Apply the Title style to the report title. (The title style automatically bolds the text.)
2. Apply the Subtitle style to the byline information and date line; then bold these lines.
3. Apply the Heading 2 style to the side headings. (The Heading 2 style automatically applies italic and bold and inserts blank space above the heading.)

↓5X
Title style **INTERCULTURAL SEMINARS** ↓1X

Subtitle style **Heath R. Watkins, Director** ↓1X

Human resources department ↓1X

March 10, 20-- ↓2X

Calibri 12 pt

¶ The Marketing department has been conducting surveys of our world wide offices, foreign customers, and *prospective* foreign customers over the last several months. Information received through the use of ~~our~~ mailed questionnaires has made us aware of an urgent need to improve our communication skills at the international level. Therefore, we are going to conduct a series of seminars to focus on intercultural awareness issues. *This* ~~The~~ report addresses the process involved in developing the seminars, the ~~instructional~~ approach to be used, the seminar content that will be provided, and the schedule for conducting the seminars. ↓1X

Heading 2 style **PROBLEM**

¶ Some incidents have been reported to us in which we have failed to negotiate contract with foreign customers and foreign prospective customers because of ~~serious~~ breakdowns in communication. Some of these setbacks have been the result of conscious negative acts on the part of our employees. However, the main culprit seems to be lack of awareness of cultural differences and lack of appreciation for the nuances that reflect these cultural differences. Indeed, there are unlimited possibilities almost for misunderstandings, insults, miscues, and avenues for people of good intent to *mis*communicate. These issues must be addressed immediately to preclude any *future* breakdowns in communications.

Heading 2 style **INTERCULTURAL SEMINARS**

¶ Three day seminars designed to improve intercultural communication skills will be held at regional sites in the United States and in selected foreign cities where we have offices: ↓2X

- Beijing
- Hamburg
- Madrid
- Melbourn*e*
- Oslo
- Rio *de* Janeiro
- Tokyo
- Warsaw ↓2X

¶ It will be our intent that all employees who have direct contact with people from other countries will participate in *these* seminars over a four-month period. Depending on

(continued on next page)

the success of these seminars, the programs will be made available in the company to others who express an interest in acquiring or enhancing their cultural awareness. Any future seminars will ~~always~~ be scheduled on an as-needed basis during the upcoming calendar year.

¶ It would be unreasonable to assume that a small team of people from our company would have the ~~breadth of~~ knowledge needed to conduct these seminars in eight foreign cities. However, Celeste Fuhrmann, Robert Driscoll, and Han Lee have agreed to work together as the coordinating team for this effort. Ms. Fuhrman, Mr. Driscoll, and Mr. Lee will be soliciting volunteers to work with them in their areas of expertise. They hope to gain representative views and opinions for the purpose of molding an impressive array of ~~seminar~~ topics. Please contact one of these individuals if you believe you have the necessary background and/or experience and would like to volunteer.

¶ Each of these individuals has worked over the past 2 months with the managers of our international offices as well as with natives in specific countries to formulate a preliminary plan for these in-service programs. Their ~~There~~ plan will use the expertise of our employees ~~in each~~ country who have had negotiating experience in each and who have knowledge of local customs as demonstrated by natives. We are confident that through this team approach, everyone will gain an understanding of problems not only from the position of our company but also from the perspective of those with whom they conduct business.

BENEFITS OF ATTENDING THE SEMINARS *(Heading 2 style)*

¶ Besides the obvious benefits that seminars such as these provide, ~~invited~~ speakers will lead discussions on a variety of topics to provide answers to questions such as the following:

- How can I develop a good working relationship with other colleagues?
- How can I avoid offending people?
- Do I need to adapt to another people's culture when I travel abroad?
- Is cultural stereotyping harmful or helpful?
- How do people from different cultures approach the decision-making process?
- How can we improve international cooperation?

¶ It is our hope that the seminars will help all participants gain a much greater awareness and understanding of the cultural environment in which they work. We believe the seminars will assist all participants in avoiding cultural mistakes that might be costly to the company. Finally, for those employees who frequently work in one of our foreign branches, the seminars will enable these people to adapt much more quickly to the cultures of the country in which they work.

Save this unfinished report. You will resume work on it in Lesson 87.

352   Unit 18 • Lesson 86

Formal Report Project—B

Goals

- Demonstrate improved speed and accuracy while typing.
- Demonstrate acceptable language arts skills in using abbreviations.
- Correctly format a multipage business report.

A. WARMUP

alphabet	1	Freight to me sixty dozen quart jars and twelve black pans.
one hand	2	career uphill gas pin awards homonym read yummy grade lumpy
easy	3	The Auburn sorority may dock in England for a formal visit.

Skillbuilding

B. MAP+: ALPHABET

Follow the GDP software directions for this exercise to improve keystroking accuracy.

C. PROGRESSIVE PRACTICE: ALPHABET

Follow the GDP software directions for this exercise to improve keystroking speed.

Language Arts

Study the rules at the right.

RULE
abbreviate measures

RULE
abbreviate lowercase

RULE
abbreviate ≡

D. ABBREVIATIONS

In technical writing, on forms, and in tables, abbreviate units of measure when they occur frequently. Do not use periods.

> 14 oz   5 ft 10 in   50 mph   2 yrs 10 mo

In most lowercase abbreviations made up of single initials, use a period after each initial but no internal spaces.

> a.m.   p.m.   i.e.   e.g.   e.o.m.
> Exceptions: mph   mpg   wpm

In most all-capital abbreviations made up of single initials, do not use periods or internal spaces.

> OSHA   PBS   NBEA   WWW   VCR   MBA
> Exceptions: U.S.A.   A.A.   B.S.   Ph.D.   P.O.   B.C.   A.D.

4 A mixture of 25 lb of cement and 100 lb of gravel was used.

5 The desk height must be reduced from 2 ft. 6 in. to 2 ft 4
6 in.

7 The 11 a. m. meeting was changed to 1 p. m. because of a
8 conflict.

9 The eom statement was published over the Internet on the
10 W.W.W.

11 She enlisted in the U.S.M.C. after she received her MBA
12 degree.

13 His Ph. D. dissertation deals with the early history of NATO.

Document Processing

When you type the remaining report pages in Lessons 87, 88, and 89, do this:

1. Type all lists, tables, displayed paragraphs, and footnotes in standard format.

2. Apply styles as the last step in each lesson.

Report
87-61
Business Report
(Continued)

INSTRUCTIONAL APPROACH

¶ Fruehauf and Chang suggest a framework of instruction that *has been* was recognized by several international groups, and has been used by seminar groups around the globe. This approach includes the following ③ components:

1. The Cognitive component

2. The Affective component

3. The Experiential component

¶ The cognitive component includes information about co*m*municating with people of other cultures. The *a*ffective component is the area in which attention is given to attitudes, emotions, and resulting behaviors as they are affected by human interaction in a multicultural environment. The experiential component is the "hands-on" element that suggests several *different* possibilities. Others who have used this instructional approach have found that the use of simulations is a natural. *for this type of experience* Writing letters, memos, e-mails, and reports to persons in other cultures also provides beneficial learning experiences. In addition, the use of tutors can be very helpful to workers unfamiliar with a particular culture.[1]

---

[1] Faye Fruehauf and Chao Chang, "Communication Across Cultures," *International Business World*, April *Monthly* 2010, pp. 33-47.

(continued on next page)

SEMINAR CONTENT

¶ The cognitive, affective, and experiential components would be applied as appropriate for each of the topics included. The coordinating ~~team~~ members have used the resources available to them at ~~our three~~ several local universities, including MIT and UMASS.

abbreviate ≡

¶ The coordinating team has found that most colleges and universities now provide instruction in international communication. Many offer separate degrees in international Communication, and the number of majors and minors in this discipline ~~have~~ has been growing rapidly for the past several years. While the content of international communication is integrated into several Business Administration and Psychology courses, there has been a trend in recent years to provide a course or courses specifically designed for business interaction in an intercultural setting. The very nature of this type of study makes it ~~very~~ difficult to segment the broad topical areas, as all elements are so closely intertwined.

¶ The seminars must reflect the broad involvement of our international operations. There is a need for many workers in our domestic offices to develop an appreciation of the intercultural challenge. This is true not only for those in the marketing and sales areas. Those in ~~our~~ the finance department and ~~our~~ the legal department are increasingly involved |only/not| with foreign companies but also with huge multinational corporations that, at times, are as large as or larger than the biggest companies in the U.S. Table 1, page 4, provides a summary of the largest multinational corporations with whom we have worked on numerous projects since the early 1980s. around the globe

REFER TO
Reference
Manual

R-8B: Tables in Reports

Table 1. Largest International Companies		
(Doing Business With CanCom, Inc.)		
Company Name	**Location**	**Global Rank**
HSBC Holdings	United Kingdom	1
Royal Shell Dutch	Netherlands	6
Toyota Motor	Japan	8 7
BNP Paribas	France	13
Allianz	Germany	14
Gaz Prom	russia	19
Banco Santander	Spain	21 24
ENI	Italy	28
China Petro	China	30
Nokia	Finland	69

(continued on next page)

¶ Several seminar topics have been suggested to the coordinating team members, and the literature reviewed by the team suggests that there might be possibly more than a dozen from which to choose. Because of time constraints, however, we have decided to include 8 topics that are recommended by Chernov, Uda, and Kapoor. The topics and presentation times are displayed in Table 2 below.[2]

abbreviate measures

Table 3. SEMINAR TOPICS	
Instructional Topic	**Time**
Body positions and movements	2 hrs
Concept of Culture	3 hrs
Conflict Resolution	2 hrs
Intimacy in Relationships	3 hrs
Language	2 hrs
Male and Female roles	2 hrs
Space & Time	2 hrs
Religion, Values, and Ethics	4 hrs

¶ **Body Positions and Movements.** Body language—that is, facial expressions, gestures, and body movements—convey messages about attitude and may be interpreted differently by people in different cultures. For example, firm handshakes are the normal in the U.S.; loose handshakes are the custom in some other countries. The way we stand, sit, and hold our arms may convey different messages in different cultural settings.

¶ **concept of culture.** This session will be an over view of the various cultures in which we conduct business, including ecommerce. Boucher identifies the needs for varied marketing strategies within the different economic, political, and cultural environments:

Indent the long quotation ½ inch from each margin.

> International web use and access are growing exponentially, and many businesses are wanting to capitalize on this trend and grab their fair share of this global market. English-speaking audiences are not expected to continue to dominate this market. Certainly, more than a literal translation will be required to reach this culturally diverse audience.[3]

¶ Case studies will be reviewed that are considered classics in the field of international communication. In addition, summaries of some of our own successes and failures will be reported.

---

[2] Vasily Chernov, Yoshifumi Uda, and Deepak Kapoor, *The Dynamics of Intercultural Seminars*, Gateway Publishing, St. Louis, 2009, p. 42.

[3] Sandra Boucher, "Cultural Comparisons in E-Commerce," January 17, 2010, <http://www.ecommerce.com/news.htm>, accessed on February 23, 2010.

Save this unfinished report. You will resume work on it in Lesson 88.

Formal Report Project—C

88

Goals

- Type at least 45wpm/5′/5e.
- Correctly use Word's clip art feature.
- Correctly format a multipage business report.

A. WARMUP

alphabet

practice: *a* and *s*

easy

1 Jeff had his size to help him quickly win over Gene Baxter.
2 ask has say sales bases areas scans seams sodas visas tasks
3 Duane may try to fix the auditory problems in the city gym.

Skillbuilding

B. PACED PRACTICE

Follow the GDP software directions for this exercise to improve keystroking speed and accuracy.

C. 5-MINUTE TIMED WRITING

Take two 5-minute timed writings.

Goal: At least 45wpm/5′/5e

```
 4        Technology surrounds us. It is everywhere you look.      11
 5   People use cellular phones to speak to one another just       22
 6   about anywhere. They carry their pagers so that they can be   34
 7   reached at any time. Everyone, from the busy executive to     45
 8   the college student, is now quite used to being available     57
 9   at all hours of the day or night.                             64
10        In recent years, busy travelers have become used to      74
11   using their laptops everywhere. They use computer ports in    86
12   airports, hotel rooms and lobbies, and even taxis. This       97
13   technology allows the busy traveler to have access to the    109
14   Internet while on the go. Using the laptop, the user can     120
15   access the latest weather report, sports scores, and news,   132
16   almost as soon as they happen.                               138
17        Using the latest technology, you can keep up with your  150
18   work and maintain contact with your office. You can even     161
19   access your bank accounts and pay bills while waiting in     172
20   traffic. Also, if you are in a new place, you can find a     184
21   restaurant or call for directions as needed. The technology  196
22   options that have become available to almost everyone are    207
23   quite amazing. We are living in a small world that seems to  219
24   be getting smaller each day.                                 225
     1  |  2  |  3  |  4  |  5  |  6  |  7  |  8  |  9  |  10 |  11 |  12
```

GO TO
Word Manual

D. WORD PROCESSING: CLIP ART—INSERT

Study Lesson 88 in your Word Manual. Complete all of the shaded steps while at your computer. Then format the document that follows.

Document Processing

Report
88-62
Business Report
(Continued)

Insert clip art related to communication, similar to the above example.
Set the clip art width to 1 inch, set the wrap style to square, and align the clip art at the right margin, even with the first line of the Language paragraph.

¶ **Conflict Resolution.** Whether people are involved in negotiating a contract, working together to remedy product quality issues, or resolving contract interpretations, the need for tact and skill is particularly important in the foreign setting. Many of the seminar topics have implications in the area of conflict resolution. While every effort should be made to prevent conflict, there is a need for guidance in resolving disagreements in foreign cultures.

¶ **Intimacy in Relationships.** The degree of physical contact that is acceptable varies considerably. Hugs and kisses are the standard, even in the business office, in some countries. By contrast, the act of touching a person is considered an extreme invasion of privacy in other places. The use of first names may or may not be acceptable. To ask a personal question is extremely offensive in some cultures. While socializing with business clients is to be expected in some countries, it would be highly inappropriate in others. These are only a few of the relationship concerns that will be explored.

¶ **Language.** It is obvious that language differences play a major part in business miscommunication. Whenever there is an interpreter or a written translation involved, the chances for error are increased. There are over 3,000 languages used worldwide. Just as with English, there are not only grammar rules but also varied meanings as words are both spoken and written. Even with the English language, there are differences in usage between the English used in the United States and that used in England.

¶ Although English is the language usually used in international communication, the topics identified in Table 2 illustrate the complexity of communicating accurately; and the problem continues to grow. For example, literal translations of American advertising and labeling have sometimes resulted in negative feelings toward products. As world trade increases, so does the need for American businesses to understand the complexities of cultural differences. Matthews offers this example:

> A businessperson must change his or her expectations and assumptions away from what is customary and acceptable in the United States in terms of personal and social conduct to what is customary and acceptable within the culture of the country where he or she is conducting business. Any other assumption can have serious consequences and undesirable results. In the other person's mind, you are the foreigner, and therefore you will be the one who might look out of place or act in a way that is considered socially unacceptable.[4]

[4] Craig Matthews, *Comparing Cultural Differences*, Grant Publishing Company, Los Angeles, 2010, p. 37.

(continued on next page)

Insert clip art related to shaking hands, similar to the above example.

Set the clip art width to 1 inch, set the wrap style to square, and align the clip art at the right margin, even with the first line in the Male and Female Roles paragraph.

¶ A good sense of humor is an asset not only in our personal lives but also in the business environment. However, it probably should be avoided in multicultural settings because the possibilities for misinterpretation are compounded. Do not use humor that makes fun of a particular individual, group, or culture. Remember that what may appear to be humorous to you may have a negative connotation in another culture.

¶ **Male and Female Roles.** There are major contrasts in the ways male and female roles are perceived in different cultures. The right to vote is still withheld from women in countries all over the world. Opportunities for female employment in the business environment vary considerably. Pay differentials for men and women continue to exist. Opportunities for advancement for men and women often are not the same.

¶ **Space and Time.** The distance one stands from someone when engaged in conversation is very important. If a person stands farther away than usual, this may signal a feeling of indifference or even a negative feeling. Standing too close is a sign of inappropriate familiarity. However, it should be recognized that different cultures require a variety of space for business exchanges to take place. In the United States, that space is typically from three to five feet, but in the Middle East and in Latin American countries, this distance is considered too far.

abbreviate lowercase

abbreviate lowercase

¶ There is also the element of time—a meeting that is scheduled for 9 a.m. likely will start on time in the United States, but in other cultures the meeting may not start until 9:30 a.m. or even 10 a.m. Punctuality and time concepts vary with the customs and practices of each country. Patience really can be a virtue.

Save this unfinished report. You will work on it again in Lesson 89.

Keyboarding Connection

Protecting Your Files With Antivirus Programs

A virus is a computer program intentionally written to contaminate your computer system. Viruses can enter your system from files downloaded from the Internet or can be acquired from infected files sent to you via e-mail, instant message or chat, or other storage media.

You can protect your computer by purchasing an antivirus program. These programs periodically scan your computer system for viruses. They also scan files that you bring into the system. Some antivirus manufacturers allow you to download a trial copy of their software from their Web site. You can try the software for a few days before you decide if you want to buy it.

Your Turn: If you want to visit antivirus sites to find out what they have to offer, search for *antivirus software* in your search engine.

Formal Report Project — D

Goals

- Demonstrate improved speed and accuracy while typing.
- Demonstrate acceptable language arts skills in spelling.
- Correctly use Word's features to insert a file, add bookmarks, and add hyperlinks.
- Correctly format a boxed table and a multipage business report.

A. WARMUP

alphabet   1 Quick goblins jumped over a lazy dwarf with the onyx rings.

frequent digraphs   2 in ink nine chin pin kind main sin mind tin skinny win inns

easy   3 The right bicycle may fix the problems of the ban on autos.

Skillbuilding

B. MAP+: SYMBOL

Follow the GDP software directions for this exercise to improve keystroking accuracy.

PPP

PRETEST » PRACTICE » POSTTEST

PRETEST

Take a 1-minute timed writing.

C. PRETEST: Close

```
4     Old Uncle Bert lived northeast of the swamp, opposite   11
5  a dirty old shop. Last week we asked him to agree to allow  23
6  Aunt Gretel to purchase a jeweled sword for her birthday.   34
7  He fooled all of us by getting her a new topaz necklace.    46
      1 | 2 | 3 | 4 | 5 | 6 | 7 | 8 | 9 | 10 | 11 | 12
```

PRACTICE

Speed Emphasis:
   If you made no more than 1 error on the Pretest, type each *individual* line 2 times.

Accuracy Emphasis:
   If you made 2 or more errors, type each *group* of lines (as though it were a paragraph) 2 times.

D. PRACTICE: Adjacent Keys

```
8  as asked asset based basis class least visas ease fast mass
9  op opera roped topaz adopt scope troop shops open hope drop
10 we weary wedge weigh towed jewel fewer dwell wear weed week
11 rt birth dirty earth heart north alert worth dart port tort
```

E. PRACTICE: Consecutive Fingers

```
12 sw swamp swift swoop sweet swear swank swirl swap sway swim
13 un uncle under undue unfit bunch begun funny unit aunt junk
14 gr grade grace angry agree group gross gripe grow gram grab
15 ol older olive solid extol spool fools stole bolt cold cool
```

F. POSTTEST: Close Reaches

Language Arts

G. SPELLING

16 means valve entry patient officer similar expenses industry
17 quality judgment academic provisions previously cooperation
18 foreign closing indicated secretary especially construction
19 monitoring assessment continuing registration manufacturing
20 products policies capacity presently accordance implemented

21 Every company offiser will have simaler expenses next week.

22 In my judgement, we must insist on co-operation from all.

23 My secertary said that she traveled to a foriegn country.

24 We must continue monitering the progress for assesment.

25 The new policeis must be implimented for all products.

26 We must implement continuing registeration during the
27 closeing weeks.

Formatting

H. WORD PROCESSING: FILE—INSERT AND BOOKMARKS AND HYPERLINKS

GO TO
Word Manual

Study Lesson 89 in your Word Manual. Complete all of the shaded steps while at your computer. Then format the documents that follow.

Document Processing

Table
89-46

Boxed Table

This table will later be inserted into Report 89-63.

Table 3. FOREIGN-CITY SEMINARS

City	First Seminar	Second Seminar
Melbourne	May 2–4	July 5–7
Rio de Janeiro	May 9–11	July 11–13
Beijing	May 16–18	July 18–20
Hamburg	May 23–25	July 25–27
Tokyo	June 6–8	August 1–3
Warsaw	June 13–15	August 8–10
Oslo	June 20–22	August 15–17
Madrid	June 27–29	August 22–24

Report
89-63

Business Report (Continued)

¶ **Religion, Values, and Ethics.** While we can recognize the difficult challenge presented by language differences, this category (religion, values, and ethics) is in some ways the area that can bring about the most serious breakdowns in relations with those from other cultures.

¶ The very nature of religious beliefs suggests that this is a delicate area, especially for those involved in business transactions in foreign countries. Also, religious beliefs affect the consumption of certain products throughout the world. Examples are tobacco, liquor, pork, and coffee.

¶ Values are a reflection of religious beliefs for most people. We have previously heard of references to right and wrong as applied to the ideals and customs of a society. Values relate to a range of similar topics, and they may pertain to areas such as cleanliness, education, health care, and criminal justice. Such values are often very personal and as such can have a variety of interpretations. The more interpretations there are, the more likely it is that miscommunication will occur.

¶ Ethics can be considered as standards of conduct that reflect moral beliefs as applied to both one's personal life and one's business life.

¶ Delaney suggests that now more than ever, a code of ethics is essential within the business environment. When this code of ethics is missing or if it is not enforced, chaos and financial ruin for everyone associated are often the result.

(continued on next page)

Insert clip art related to world travel, similar to the above example.

Set the clip art width to 1 inch, set the wrap style to square, and align the clip art at the right margin, even with the first line of the first paragraph in the TENTATIVE SEMINAR SCHEDULE section.

A quality code of ethics is presently being recognized as an intrinsic and critical component in any business environment. Newspapers are filled with reports of scandalous, unconscionable, unethical behavior that has led to the downfall of otherwise successful businesses.[5]

TENTATIVE SEMINAR SCHEDULE

¶ As indicated earlier, all employees who have direct contact with people in other cultures will participate in these continuing seminars. That means that we need to have two identical three-day seminars scheduled at each site. These seminars will be conducted in the cities shown in Table 3.

(Insert Table 89-46 here)

¶ The Marketing Department is to be commended for calling our attention to the seriousness of our international communication problem. Celeste Fuhrmann, Robert Driscoll, and Han Lee also deserve our sincere thanks for their planning efforts for implementing the intercultural communication seminars. Through their efforts, we have experienced a high level of cooperation from all departments.

¶ As can be seen, special attention is being given to the seminar topics for these in-service programs. Efforts are also being made to identify instructors and resource persons who will develop instructional strategies that will be effective, interesting, and well received by the participants. These seminars will help significantly in increasing our market share in the international market.

---

[5] Denise C. Delaney, *Business Ethics and Workplace Compliance,* Empire Publishing Company, San Francisco, 2009, p. 35.

After completing Report 89-63, add three bookmarks and three hyperlinks by following these directions:

1. Add the first bookmark to Table 1 in the table title on page 4 of the report. Add a text hyperlink to the words "Table 1" found on page 3, last paragraph, to link to this bookmark.
2. Add the second bookmark to Table 2 in the table title on page 4 of the report. Add a text hyperlink to the word "top-ics" found on page 8, last paragraph, to link to this bookmark.
3. Add the third bookmark to Table 3 in the table title on page 7 of the report. Add a text hyperlink to "seminars," found on page 2, second paragraph, to link to this bookmark.

Formal Report Project—E

Goals

- Type at least 45wpm/5'/5e.
- Correctly use Word's feature to insert a cover page.
- Correctly format a cover page, a table of contents, and a bibliography.
- Successfully complete a Progress and Proofreading Check with zero errors on the first scored attempt.

A. WARMUP

alphabet   1   The wizard's main job was to vex the chimps quickly in fog.

number/symbol   2   jjoy@aol.com 66% (Ott & Poe) 5/8 Out! $2.16 *et al. #73-490

easy   3   Did the fiendish old men fight a duel down by the lakeside?

Skillbuilding

B. 12-SECOND SPEED SPRINTS

Take three 12-second timed writings on each line.

4   We may take a number of maps to aid us when we visit there.
5   Alan may then take apart both of the toys out on the lanai.
6   The eight old books are to be thrown into the fields today.
7   Andy will use eight hand signals if he is able to see them.
' ' ' '5' ' '10' ' '15' ' '20' ' '25' ' '30' ' '35' ' '40' ' '45' ' '50' ' '55' ' '60

C. TECHNIQUE PRACTICE: SHIFT KEY

Type each line 2 times. After striking the capitalized letter, return the SHIFT KEY finger immediately to home-row position.

8   Ann Bonn asked for lunch. Colin Dix and Elaine Fochs moved.
9   Glen Hans filed as Iris James typed. Kay Lee talked loudly.
10   Maya Nevins and Orin Parks tried. Quinn Roberts lost a bet.
11   Skye Tynch sat. Uriah Vin and Winn Xung ate. Yates Zyd hid.

Goal: At least 45wpm/5′/5e

D. 5-MINUTE TIMED WRITING

12	Anyone with a supervisory position will occasionally	11
13	have to deal with a problem employee. If you learn to deal	23
14	with this type of worker in a good way, it will benefit	34
15	everyone within the organization.	41
16	As a manager, you should address the problem as soon	51
17	as you are made aware of it. However, if you are extremely	63
18	upset, it may be best to wait until you calm down and have	75
19	time to plan what you will say. Avoid using an approach	86
20	based on reaction, which can often be ineffective and too	98
21	emotional. Speaking up too quickly might bring you some	109
22	unwanted results.	113
23	When you talk to an employee, be sure you get to the	123
24	real issue. Present the facts and tell the employee exactly	135
25	what he or she is doing wrong on the job. Do not express	147
26	your own personal opinion. You need to present a positive	158
27	and mutually fair solution to the employee in question to	170
28	solve a problem.	173
29	At the end of the meeting, ask the person to explain	184
30	his or her problems to you and the changes that are needed.	196
31	By following this procedure, you know everyone understands	208
32	what is happening. Set up a time to meet in a few days to	220
33	follow up with this person.	225

1 | 2 | 3 | 4 | 5 | 6 | 7 | 8 | 9 | 10 | 11 | 12

Formatting

E. WORD PROCESSING: COVER PAGE—INSERT

GO TO
Word Manual

Study Lesson 90 in your Word Manual. Complete all of the shaded steps while at your computer. Then format the documents that follow.

Document Processing

Report 90-64
Cover Page

Create a cover page for Report 89-63 using the Insert Cover Page feature in Word. Use the following information to complete the cover page:

- Select a suitable cover page from the Word gallery that includes (1) company name, (2) report title, (3) author, and (4) name. Delete any extra elements on the page.
- Type CanCom Inc. as the company name.
- Type INTERCULTURAL SEMINARS as the document title.
- Delete the document subtitle.
- Type Heath R. Watkins as the author name.
- Use the current year.
- Delete the company address.

Create a table of contents for Report 89-63 as a separate document. Use the illustration that follows as an example. The table of contents shown is incomplete. You must refer to Report 89-63 to compose and complete all of the entries for the table of contents. Make these changes:

1. Type the title in Calibri 14 pt. Bold. A title style will be applied later to conform with the title in your report.
2. Refer to Report 89-63 to compose and type the table of contents. The entries should include all side headings and paragraph headings from the report, as well as the appropriate page numbers for each heading.

3. Type the side headings in all-caps at the left margin.
4. Type the paragraph headings in upper- and lowercase, indented 0.5 inch from the left margin.
5. When you are finished typing the table of contents, apply the Title style to "CONTENTS."

Use a Title style for CONTENTS.

REFER TO
Reference Manual

R-7D: Table of Contents

CONTENTS

Report
90-66
Bibliography

Type the bibliography for Report 89-63, shown on page 367, as a separate document using standard format. Follow these steps:

1. Type the title in Calibri 14-pt. Bold. A title style will be applied later to conform with the title in your report.
2. Type the bibliography in standard format.

3. When you are finished typing the bibliography, apply the Title style to "BIBLIOGRAPHY."

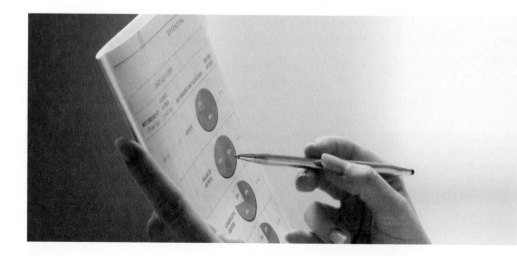

Use a Title style for
BIBLIOGRAPHY.

REFER TO
Reference
Manual

R-9B: Bibliography

Progress and
Proofreading
Check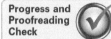

Documents designated
as Proofreading Checks
serve as a check of
your proofreading skill.
Your goal is to have
zero typographical
errors when the GDP
software first scores
the document.

BIBLIOGRAPHY

Boucher, Sandra, "Cultural Comparisons in E-Commerce," January 17, 2010, <http://www.ecommerce.com/news.htm>, accessed on February 23, 2010.

Chernov, Vasily, Yoshifumi Uda, and Deepak Kapoor, *The Dynamics of Intercultural Seminars,* Gateway Publishing, St. Louis, 2009.

Delaney, Denise C., *Business Ethics and Workplace Compliance*, Empire Publishing Company, New York, 2009, p. 35.

Fruehauf, Faye, and Chao Chang, "Communication Across Cultures," *International Business World,* April 2010, pp. 33-47.

Matthews, Craig, *Comparing Cultural Differences*, Grant Publishing Company, Los Angeles, 2010, p. 37.

Finalize the report project:

- Proofread all the pages for format and typing errors.
- Assemble the pages in this order: cover page, table of contents, body, bibliography, and a blank page for a back cover sheet.
- Staple the report pages in the upper-left corner.

Strategies for Career Success

Business Communication

There are five components to the communication process, whether written or oral.

The sender is the person who initiates the communication process. The message is the information that needs to be communicated (for example, "There will be a meeting at . . ."). The channel is the method for transmitting the message (for example, e-mail, letter, memo, or orally). The audience is the person(s) who receives the message. Feedback is the response given to the sender by the audience that enables the sender to determine if the message was received as intended.

The most effective communication within companies must flow not only downward but also upward.

Your Turn: Suppose you send an e-mail to 20 people in your department announcing a meeting to discuss your company's new policy on flextime. Who is the sender? What is the message? What is the channel you use to transmit the message? Who is the audience? What is the ultimate feedback?

Using and Designing Business Documents

Keyboarding in Legal Services Careers

A career in legal services can take many forms. Lawyers, of course, are responsible for legal work, but a number of other positions in the legal services field are available. Often, lawyers assign tasks to paralegals. Paralegals—also referred to as legal assistants—have taken on a larger percentage of responsibilities in recent years. Another profession in the law field, that of court reporter, requires excellent communication skills. Court reporters must take exact notes of proceedings. Keyboarding skills are important for many job functions in legal services careers, and they can prove to give a job candidate an advantage.

Paralegals can work in many different business settings, but they are found most commonly in law firms and government offices. Court reporters are responsible for providing an accurate and detailed legal record of any proceeding. For individuals working in the legal services field, strong communication skills, written and spoken, are very important, but being able to convey ideas in a typed report in a timely manner is even more important.

Goals

Keyboarding

- Demonstrate improved speed and accuracy when operating the keyboard by touch.
- Type at least 50 words per minute on a 5-minute timed writing with no more than 5 errors.

Language Arts

- Demonstrate acceptable proofreading skills, including using proofreaders' marks correctly.
- Demonstrate acceptable language arts skills in punctuation, grammar, and mechanics.
- Demonstrate acceptable language arts skills in composing and spelling.

Word Processing

- Use appropriate word processing commands necessary to complete document processing activities successfully.

Document Processing

- Correctly format office forms, office publications, online resumes, and form letters.

Objective Test

- Answer questions with acceptable accuracy on an objective test.

Using and Designing Office Forms

Designing Letterheads

Goals

- Demonstrate improved speed and accuracy while typing.
- Demonstrate acceptable proofreading skills by comparing lines.
- Correctly use Word's features for small caps and text boxes.
- Correctly format a letterhead form.

A. WARMUP

alphabet
practice: *v* and *b*
easy

1 Jackson believed that we quizzed the old sphinx from Egypt.
2 verb bevel bevy above Bev livable vibe bovine brave visible
3 Rodney may risk half of his profits for the old oak mantel.

Skillbuilding

MAP+

B. MAP+: NUMBERS

Follow the GDP software directions for this exercise to improve keystroking accuracy.

PPP

PRETEST » PRACTICE » POSTTEST

PRETEST
Take a 1-minute
timed writing.

C. PRETEST: Vertical Reaches

```
4       The senior lawyer was able to tackle the case in June.   11
5  He knew he would be making himself available to the court     23
6  for a fourth time in a month. He said he needed to revamp     34
7  his vacation plans to guard against whatever might go awry.   45
    1 | 2 | 3 | 4 | 5 | 6 | 7 | 8 | 9 | 10 | 11 | 12
```

PRACTICE

Speed Emphasis:
If you made no more
than 1 error on the
Pretest, type each
individual line 2
times.
Accuracy Emphasis:
If you made 2 or
more errors, type
each *group* of lines
(as though it were a
paragraph) 2 times.

D. PRACTICE: Up Reaches

```
8  aw awry away paws drawer awakes spawns brawny awards aweigh
9  se self seen sewn bosses paused senior seller seizes itself
10 ki kiln kilt kite skirts joking kinder bikini making unkind
11 rd hard lard cord hurdle overdo lizard inward boards upward
```

E. PRACTICE: Down Reaches

```
12 ac acid ache aces jacked facial actors tacked jackal places
13 kn knot knee knob knives kneels knight knotty knocks knaves
14 ab able blab ably tables fabric babies rabbit cabana cables
15 va vase vain Vail evades revamp valley avails ravage canvas
```

F. POSTTEST: Vertical Reaches

Language Arts

G. PROOFREADING

Compare these lines with lines 38–42 on page 419. Edit the lines to correct any errors.

16   If you have conflicts with your boss or with others at
17 your office, try to work them out by discusing the issue
18 with the people involved to be curtain they understand all
19 all aspects of the conflict. Work together to minimize any
20 any future conflict.

Formatting

H. DESIGNING A FORM

Use the following guidelines to design an attractive, effective form:

1. Keep all elements of your design simple and balanced.
2. Limit the number of fonts, attributes (bold, italics, and so on), and sizes. Using no more than two fonts is a good rule of thumb.
3. Use white space liberally to separate and open up text and graphics.
4. Use different alignments (left, center, right, and full) to add interest and emphasis and to improve readability.
5. Experiment and change—Word makes both easy to do.

I. WORD PROCESSING: FONT—SMALL CAPS AND TEXT BOXES

GO TO Word Manual

Study Lesson 103 in your Word Manual. Complete all of the shaded steps while at your computer. Then format the documents that follow.

Form 103-6

Letterhead Form

REFER TO
Word Manual

L. 88: Clip Art—Insert

1. Change the top, left, and right margins to 0.3 inch.
2. Insert a text box at the top of the page that is 1.4 inches high and 7.8 inches wide.
3. Center the text box horizontally and position it relative to the top margin.
4. Click inside the text box, and change the text alignment to right.
5. Change to Calibri 24 pt. Bold, Small Caps, and type this:

   ROCKWALL REAL ESTATE

6. Press ENTER 1 time, change the font to Calibri 11 pt., and type this:

   ```
   893 Shoreview Drive
   Rockwall, TX 75032
   972-555-8900
   ```

7. Change the font to Calibri 11 pt. Italic, and type this:

   www.rockwallhomes.com

8. Click outside the text box, and then insert clip art related to real estate.
9. Set the clip art wrap style so the clip art is on top of the text box; and then size and move it so that it fits inside the text box as shown in the illustration below.
10. Change the text box and clip art shapes to appear as rounded rectangles.
11. Select a text box border and shading that complement the colors in the clip art.
12. Select all text, and change the font color to one that complements the colors in the clip art.
13. Compare your finished letterhead to the illustration that follows. Make any necessary changes, including removing any automatic hyperlink.

1. Change the top, left, and right margins to 0.3 inch.
2. Insert a text box at the top of the page that is 1.1 inches high and 7.8 inches wide.
3. Click inside the text box, and change the text alignment to center.
4. Change to Cambria 24 pt. Bold Italic, Small Caps, and type this:

   JACK'S MATTING AND FRAMING

5. Press ENTER 1 time, and change the font to Calibri 12 pt. Bold, and type this:

   123 Pearl Street

6. Press the SPACE BAR 2 times, and then insert a square bullet symbol from the Wingdings font group.
7. Press the SPACE BAR 2 times and type this:

   Boulder, CO 80306

8. Press the SPACE BAR 2 times, insert a square bullet symbol, press the SPACE BAR 2 times, and type this:

   303-555-9022

9. Press ENTER 1 time, then change the font to Calibri 12 pt. Bold Italic, and type this:

   www.weframe.com

10. Click outside the text box, and then insert clip art related to picture framing.
11. Set the clip art wrap style so the clip art is on top of the text box; and then size and move it so that it fits inside the left side of the text box as shown in the illustration below.
12. Copy the clip art; then paste it to the right side of the text box, in a position similar to the clip art on the left side of the text box as shown in the illustration below.
13. Change the text box and clip art shapes to appear as rounded rectangles.
14. Select a text box border and shading that complement the colors in the clip art.
15. Select all text, and change the font color to one that complements the colors in the clip art.
16. Compare your finished letterhead to the illustration that follows. Make any necessary changes, including removing any automatic hyperlink.

Cambria 24 pt Bold Italic, Small Caps

Calibri 12 pt Bold
Calibri 12 pt Bold Italic

Form
103-8
Letterhead Form

1. Create a letterhead design of your own—for you personally, for your institution, or for a business.
2. Insert at least one picture that enhances the theme of the letterhead.
3. Remember to include complete information in the address block.
4. Try using fonts that you have not yet applied—experiment with point sizes and attributes.

Strategies for Career Success

Managing Business Phone Time

The average American spends an hour a day on the phone. Phone calls can be extremely distracting. Time is spent taking care of the call and following up after the call. You can take steps to reduce wasted time on the phone.

Before you make an outgoing call, organize the topics you want to discuss. Have all the materials you need: pens, paper, order forms, and so on. Consider sending an e-mail when appropriate, rather than making a phone call. E-mail is less intrusive and can be answered when the recipient has time instead of when it's sent. If you do decide to use e-mail, be prepared to follow up later if you don't get a response.

When you take an incoming call, answer it promptly. Identify yourself. It is common to answer the phone with your first and last name (for example, "Mary Smith speaking" or "Mary Smith"). Limit social conversation; it wastes time. Give concise answers to questions. At the end of the call, summarize the points made. End the conversation politely.

Your Turn: Keep a log of your time on the phone for one day. What is your average conversation time? What can you do to reduce your average phone conversation time?

Designing Miscellaneous Office Forms

Goals

- Demonstrate improved speed and accuracy while typing.
- Demonstrate acceptable language arts skills in composing an e-mail message.
- Correctly format a directory form, a sign-in form, and a memo template.
- Successfully complete a Progress and Proofreading Check with zero errors on the first scored attempt.

A. WARMUP

alphabet	1	Xylophone wizards quickly begat a lively form of jive beat.
number/symbol	2	pnoe@att.net 270% Ivy & Day 3/8 Go! $17.59 *sic (#6423-145)
easy	3	The turkeys and hogs may spend the day in the mango fields.

Skillbuilding

B. 12-SECOND SPEED SPRINTS

Take three 12-second timed writings on each line.

4 The man with the rifle may signal us to take the sign down.
5 Hale saw a bible of the gospel in the chapel near the lake.
6 Half of the maps may be for the land and half for the lake.
7 The firm did not sign a form that may name me to the panel.
` ' ' ' '5' ' ' '10' ' ' '15' ' ' '20' ' ' '25' ' ' '30' ' ' '35' ' ' '40' ' ' '45' ' ' '50' ' ' '55' ' ' '60`

C. PACED PRACTICE

Follow the GDP software directions for this exercise to improve keystroking speed and accuracy.

Language Arts

D. COMPOSING AN E-MAIL MESSAGE

Compose the body of an e-mail message to explain basic design guidelines. Refer to page 423—Section H, Designing a Form. Using your own wording, include the following ideas:

Paragraph 1. Explain that a simple, balanced design is essential and that typefaces (fonts), attributes, and sizes should be limited.

Paragraph 2. Explain that white space should be used to make text easier to read and graphics easier to see.

Paragraph 3. Explain that word processing software is a powerful tool that makes experimenting easy.

Document Processing

1. Change the page orientation to landscape.
2. Change the top margin to 2 inches, the bottom margin to 0.75 inch, and the side margins to 0.5 inch.
3. Insert clip art associated with a home about the same size in the same position as the one in the illustration. **Note:** Change text wrap to In Front of Text before moving the clip art.
4. Click outside the clip art; then insert a text box, about the same size in the same position as the one in the illustration, to hold the headings.
5. Press ENTER 1 time, then change to Calibri 48 pt. Bold, Small Caps.
6. Center and type this:

   ARBOR STATION SUBDIVISION

7. Change the font color to complement the clip art inserted in step 3.
8. Press ENTER 1 time; then change to Calibri 24 pt. Bold, Small Caps.
9. Center and type DIRECTORY OF RESIDENTS as the subtitle.
10. Remove the border around the text box.
11. Click outside the text box; then insert a boxed table with 4 columns and 17 rows.
12. Move the table below the clip art and text box, as shown in the illustration.
13. Select the entire table, and change the font to Calibri 18 pt. Bold.
14. Type these column headings in Row 1: Name | Address | Telephone | E-Mail
15. Change the alignment in Row 1 to center.
16. Add shading to Row 1, using a color that complements the picture.
17. Change the font color to white.

ARBOR STATION SUBDIVISION — Calibri 48 pt Bold, Small Caps
DIRECTORY OF RESIDENTS — Calibri 24 pt Bold, Small Caps
Name | Address | Telephone | E-Mail — Calibri 18 pt Bold

1. Change the top margin to 2 inches, the bottom margin to 0.75 inch, and the side margins to 0.5 inch.
2. Insert a boxed table with 4 columns and 28 rows.
3. Select the entire table, and change the font to Calibri 16 pt. Bold.
4. Type these column headings in Row 1: Name | Time In | Time Out | Date, and then change the alignment in Row 1 to center.
5. Add shading of 25 percent to Row 1.
6. Move to the top of the document, and insert clip art, associated with a check mark, in the same position and about the same size as the one in the illustration that follows. **Note:** Before moving the clip art, set text wrapping so that the image appears on top of the text without rearranging the text.
7. Click outside the clip art, then insert a text box, about the same size and in the same position as the one in the illustration, to hold the heading and the doctors' names.
8. Remove the border around the text box.
9. Change to Calibri 36 pt. Bold, Small Caps; then center and type this:

PHYSICIAN SIGN-IN SHEET

10. Press ENTER 1 time, and change the alignment to left.
11. Press TAB 2 times; turn off Small Caps; then insert a round bullet using Wingdings 20 pt. Bold.
12. Press TAB 1 time, then type Dr. Eleanor Clemmons and press ENTER 1 time.
13. Repeat steps 11 and 12 for the remaining names in the list: Dr. Paul Davis and Dr. Jeanine Sordhoff.

PHYSICIAN SIGN-IN SHEET — Calibri 36 pt Bold, Small Caps

● Dr. Eleanor Clemmons — Calibri 20 pt Bold
● Dr. Paul Davis
● Dr. Jeanine Sordhoff

Wingdings 20 pt Bold

Name	Time In	Time Out	Date

Calibri 16 pt Bold

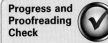

Progress and Proofreading Check

Documents designated as Proofreading Checks serve as a check of your proofreading skill. Your goal is to have zero typographical errors when the GDP software first scores the document.

Type this memo using the preselected blank memo template that has opened automatically.

To: All Employees

CC: Shelley Castle, Benefits Department

From: Brett R. Cecoli, Human Resources Dept.

Date: November 10, 20--

Re: Company Wellness Program

¶ With the flue season just around the corner, we are again planning to administer free flu shots to all company employees. Last year we administered a similar program, and employee absence due to illness was considerably reduced. ¶ A signup schedule will be distributed to all Departments on December 5th. The schedule will list all dates, times, and locations for flu shots to be administered given. Please put December 5 on your calendar, and be sure to sign up for your flu shot. | urs

---

Keyboarding Connection

Choosing a Different Home Page

You don't have to start at the same home page every time you start your browser. You can change the browser's home page to start at one of your favorite Web pages or even a blank page. Refer to your browser's help feature for details.

Some companies require all browser windows to open with the company's home or internal use page. Check your company's Internet usage policy before making any changes to your computer or browser settings.

Your Turn: Using your browser, access a favorite Web page. Make it your browser's home page.

Designing Office Publications

Designing Cover Pages

Goals

- Type at least 49wpm/5'/5e.
- Correctly use the WordArt feature.
- Correctly format a cover page.

A. WARMUP

alphabet
concentration
easy

1 Few black taxis drove up major roads on a quiet hazy night.
2 nonrepresentational professionalization straightforwardness
3 Glen may dismantle the authentic robot when he is downtown.

Skillbuilding

B. SUSTAINED PRACTICE: NUMBERS AND SYMBOLS

Take a 1-minute timed writing on the boxed paragraph to establish your base speed. Then take a 1-minute timed writing on the following paragraph. As soon as you equal or exceed your base speed on this paragraph, move to the next, more difficult paragraph.

4 Shopping in the comfort and convenience of your own	11
5 living room has never been more popular than it is right	22
6 now. Shopping clubs abound on cable channels. You could	33
7 buy anything from exotic pets to computers by mail order.	45

8 Sometimes you can find discounts as high as 20% off 11
9 the retail price; for example, a printer that sells for 22
10 $565 might be discounted 20% and be sold for $452. You 33
11 should always investigate quality before buying anything. 44

12 Sometimes hidden charges are involved; for example, 11
13 a printer costing $475.50 that promises a discount of 12% 22
14 ($57.06) has a net price of $418.44. However, if charges 34
15 for shipping range from 12% to 15%, you did not save money. 45

16 You must also check for errors. Several errors have 11
17 been noted so far: Invoice #223, #789, #273, and #904 had 22
18 errors totaling $21.35, $43.44, $79.23, and $91.23 for a 34
19 grand total of $235.25. As always, let the buyer beware. 45

1 | 2 | 3 | 4 | 5 | 6 | 7 | 8 | 9 | 10 | 11 | 12

Take two 5-minute timed writings.

Goal: At least 49wpm/5'/5e

C. 5-MINUTE TIMED WRITING

20   Why do people choose a particular career? Your first   11
21 instinct might likely be to say that people work to make   22
22 money. That may be true, but extensive research has shown   34
23 that many other factors are considered just as important   45
24 and that these factors should be carefully considered when   57
25 you are about to accept a new position.   65
26   There are many rewards that a job can provide, such   76
27 as a chance to be creative, the chance to spend time with   87
28 people whose company you enjoy, or the feeling that you are   99
29 doing something useful for yourself or for your employer.   111
30 The quality of the work environment is also an important   122
31 consideration in choosing a career, as is the chance to   134
32 work closely with people on a daily basis.   142
33   Obviously, your career should allow you to advance in   153
34 your field and to be competitive for promotions. You should   165
35 be able to see a clear line for advancement in your job and   177
36 be given a chance to demonstrate your abilities so that   188
37 your coworkers and supervisors recognize your strengths.   200
38   Parallel to these factors is the need for your job to   211
39 give you adequate challenges on a daily, continuing basis.   223
40 If your work is not challenging, boredom will set in, and   234
41 you might soon be looking for a change in your career.   245

   1 | 2 | 3 | 4 | 5 | 6 | 7 | 8 | 9 | 10 | 11 | 12

Formatting

D. WORD PROCESSING: WORDART

GO TO Word Manual

Study Lesson 106 in your Word Manual. Complete all of the shaded steps while at your computer. Then format the documents that follow.

1. Insert clip art related to health or the medical profession.
2. Drag and size the clip art so that it looks similar to the one shown in the illustration that follows.
3. Apply an attractive visual style of your choice for the clip art.
4. Insert WordArt, about the same size and in the same position as the one shown in the illustration. Type these words for the WordArt:

   `Health Care Basics`

5. Use Calibri 36 pt. Bold for the Word-Art text; choose a style and color for the WordArt to coordinate with the clip art.
6. Create a text box, about the same size and in the same position as the one below the clip art.
7. Type "Making the Right Choice" inside the text box using Cambria 36 pt. Bold Italic. Choose a

font color for the text to coordinate with the clip art.

8. Remove the border around the text box.
9. Create a text box, about the same size and in the same position as the one at the bottom of the page shown in the illustration that follows.
10. Type A SEMINAR SPONSORED BY BOYD MEDICAL CENTER inside the text box using Calibri 24 pt. Bold, Small Caps.
11. Press ENTER 2 times, change to Calibri 20 pt. Bold, and then type this:

    `Tanner Auditorium`

12. Press ENTER 1 time; then type this:

    `1:00 to 2:30 p.m.`

13. Press ENTER 2 times; then type this:

    `July 10, 20--`

14. Remove the border around the text box.

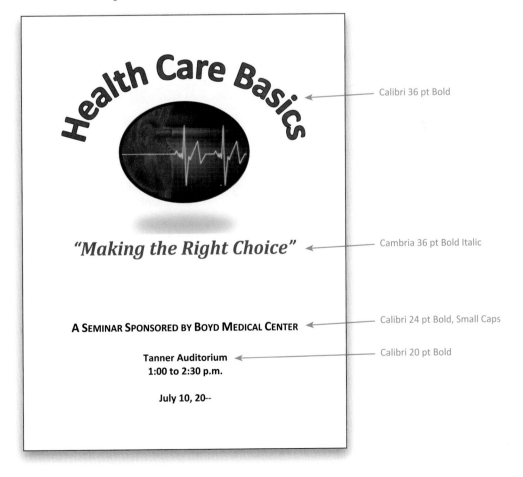

"Health Care Basics" — Calibri 36 pt Bold
"Making the Right Choice" — Cambria 36 pt Bold Italic
A SEMINAR SPONSORED BY BOYD MEDICAL CENTER — Calibri 24 pt Bold, Small Caps
Tanner Auditorium — Calibri 20 pt Bold
1:00 to 2:30 p.m.
July 10, 20--

1. Insert clip art related to the Internet or education.
2. Drag and size the clip art so that it looks similar to the one in the illustration that follows.
3. Apply an attractive visual style of your choice to the clip art.
4. Insert WordArt, about the same size and in the same position as the one at the top of the illustration, and then type Web Page Design on the first line and Online Training on the second line.
5. Use Impact 36 pt. Bold font for the WordArt text; choose a style and color for the WordArt to coordinate with the clip art.
6. Create a text box, about the same size and in the same position as the one shown in the illustration that follows.
7. Use Calibri 24 pt. Bold to type the following inside the text box:

   - Part 1: Page Elements
   - Part 2: Linking Tools

   - Part 3: Search Engines
   - Part 4: Keyword Selection

8. Remove the border around the text box.
9. Create a text box, about the same size and in the same position as the one shown at the bottom of the page in the illustration that follows.
10. Use Calibri 18 pt. Bold to center and type the following inside the text box:

    Cost of 16 hours of instruction is $300. Online training is scheduled for May 4 to May 7, 20--. Each daily program is scheduled from 1 to 5 p.m.

11. Press ENTER 2 times, and then center and type this:

    Enroll at www.webdesign.com/enroll.

12. Add a text box fill color that coordinates with the picture.

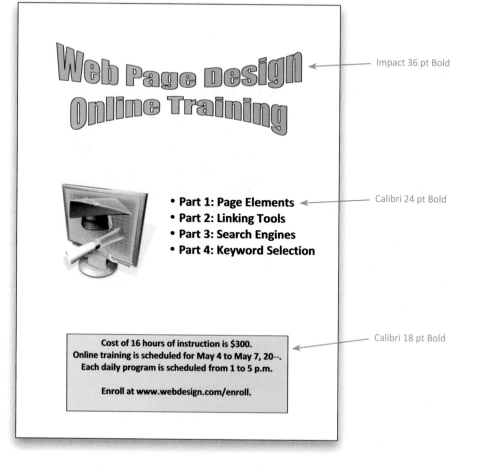

Impact 36 pt Bold

Calibri 24 pt Bold

Calibri 18 pt Bold

1. Create a cover page design of your own to be used as the insert for a view binder that holds information for one of your courses.
2. Insert at least one picture related to the subject of the course.
3. Insert at least one text box with a fill.
4. Insert some WordArt.
5. Change any of the font colors to coordinate with the picture or WordArt as desired.

Designing Announcements and Flyers

107

Goals

- Demonstrate improved speed and accuracy while typing.
- Demonstrate acceptable language arts skills in pronoun usage.
- Correctly use Word's features to move a table and add a background page color.
- Correctly format an announcement and a flyer.

A. WARMUP

alphabet   1 Six big devils from Japan then quickly forgot how to waltz.

one hand   2 revert unhook act him access pumpkin gave lymph fever union

easy   3 Rob's work as the auditor in Lakeland may help us in a way.

Skillbuilding

B. MAP+: ALPHABET

Follow the GDP software directions for this exercise to improve keystroking accuracy.

C. PROGRESSIVE PRACTICE: ALPHABET

Follow the GDP software directions for this exercise to improve keystroking speed.

Language Arts

Study the rules at the right.

RULE
nominative pronoun

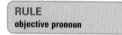

RULE
objective pronoun

See applications of correct pronoun usage in Report 110-88 on pages 456–457.

D. PRONOUNS

Use nominative pronouns (such as *I, he, she, we, they*, and *who*) as subjects of a sentence or clause.

The programmer and <u>he</u> are reviewing the code.
Barb is a person <u>who</u> can do the job.

Use objective pronouns (such as *me, him, her, us, them*, and *whom*) as objects of a verb, preposition, or infinitive.

The code was reviewed by the programmer and <u>him</u>.
Barb is the type of person <u>whom</u> we can trust.

4 We hope they will take all of them to the concert tomorrow.

5 John gave the gift to she on Monday; her was very pleased.

6 If them do not hurry, Mary will not finish her work on time.

7 The book was proofread by her; the changes were made by he.

8 It is up to them to give us all the pages they read today.

9 Me cannot assure they that it will not rain for the picnic.

Formatting

GO TO
Word Manual

E. WORD PROCESSING: TABLE—MOVE AND PAGE COLOR

Study Lesson 107 in your Word Manual. Complete all of the shaded steps while at your computer. Then format the documents that follow.

Document Processing

**Report
107-81
Announcement**

1. Insert WordArt, about the same size and in the same position as the one at the top of the illustration that follows.

2. Use a shape similar to the one shown in the illustration, with the words Dade County; choose the desired font and font size for the text.

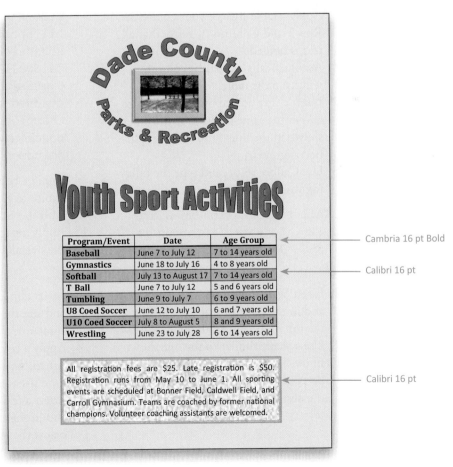

Cambria 16 pt Bold
Calibri 16 pt
Calibri 16 pt

Program/Event	Date	Age Group
Baseball	June 7 to July 12	7 to 14 years old
Gymnastics	June 18 to July 16	4 to 8 years old
Softball	July 13 to August 17	7 to 14 years old
T Ball	June 7 to July 12	5 and 6 years old
Tumbling	June 9 to July 7	6 to 9 years old
U8 Coed Soccer	June 12 to July 10	6 and 7 years old
U10 Coed Soccer	July 8 to August 5	8 and 9 years old
Wrestling	June 23 to July 28	6 to 14 years old

All registration fees are $25. Late registration is $50. Registration runs from May 10 to June 1. All sporting events are scheduled at Bonner Field, Caldwell Field, and Carroll Gymnasium. Teams are coached by former national champions. Volunteer coaching assistants are welcomed.

3. Insert WordArt, similar in size and shape and in a position beneath the first WordArt you inserted in step 1. Use a shape similar to the one shown in the illustration, with the words Parks & Recreation; choose the desired font and font size for the text.

4. Insert clip art related to parks; drag and size the clip art so that it looks similar to the one in the illustration.

5. Select a picture style of your choice for the clip art.

6. Apply a color to the text in the WordArt to complement the clip art you have inserted.

7. Insert WordArt, about the same size and in the same position as the one below the WordArt you inserted in step 3. Type the words Youth Sport Activities and apply a font color that complements the overall design.

8. Insert a 3-column, 9-row boxed table. Drag the table to a position immediately below the WordArt inserted in step 7 as shown in the illustration that follows.

9. Use Calibri 16 pt. for all entries in the table. Type the following table entries:

Program/Event	Date	Age Group
Baseball	June 7 to July 12	7 to 14 years old
Gymnastics	June 18 to July 16	4 to 8 years old
Softball	July 13 to August 17	7 to 14 years old
T-Ball	June 7 to July 12	5 and 6 years old
Tumbling	June 9 to July 7	6 to 9 years old
U8 Coed Soccer	June 12 to July 10	6 and 7 years old
U10 Coed Soccer	July 8 to August 5	8 and 9 years old
Wrestling	June 23 to July 28	6 to 14 years old

10. Apply a table style of your choice. In Row 1 and Column A, verify that all text is bolded.

11. Automatically adjust the column widths in the table.

12. Insert a text box, about the same size and in the same position as the one shown in the illustration, using justified alignment.

13. Use Calibri 16 pt, and type the following words in the text box:

All registration fees are $25. Late registration is $50. Registration runs from May 10 to June 1. All sporting events are scheduled at Bonner Field, Caldwell Field, and Carroll Gymnasium. Teams are coached by former national champions. Volunteer coaching assistants are welcomed.

14. Apply a border and a texture of your choice to the text box that coordinate with the color used in the WordArt.

15. Apply a page color that complements the overall design.

Report 107-82
Announcement

1. Insert WordArt, about the same size and in the same position as the one at the top of the illustration that follows.

2. Use a shape similar to the one shown in the illustration, with the words Breckenridge Rentals; choose the desired font and font size for the text.

3. Insert clip art related to skiing; drag and size the clip art so that it looks similar to the one in the illustration.

4. Apply a color to the text in the WordArt to complement the clip art you have inserted.

5. Insert a text box, about the same size and in the same position as the one below the clip art.

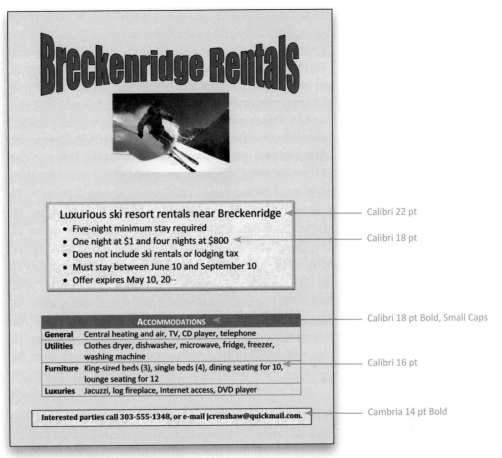

Callouts on the flyer image:
- Calibri 22 pt
- Calibri 18 pt
- Calibri 18 pt Bold, Small Caps
- Calibri 16 pt
- Cambria 14 pt Bold

Luxurious ski resort rentals near Breckenridge
- Five-night minimum stay required
- One night at $1 and four nights at $800
- Does not include ski rentals or lodging tax
- Must stay between June 10 and September 10
- Offer expires May 10, 20--

ACCOMMODATIONS	
General	Central heating and air, TV, CD player, telephone
Utilities	Clothes dryer, dishwasher, microwave, fridge, freezer, washing machine
Furniture	King-sized beds (3), single beds (4), dining seating for 10, lounge seating for 12
Luxuries	Jacuzzi, log fireplace, Internet access, DVD player

Interested parties call 303-555-1348, or e-mail jcrenshaw@quickmail.com.

6. Type the following information in the text box. Use Calibri 22 pt. for the centered heading; then change to Calibri 18 pt. to format the remaining lines as a bulleted list:

```
Luxurious ski resort rentals
near Breckenridge
```
- Five-night minimum stay required
- One night at $1 and four nights at $800
- Does not include ski rentals or lodging tax
- Must stay between June 10 and September 10
- Offer expires May 10, 20--

7. Apply a border and texture of your choice to the text box that coordinates with the colors used in the WordArt and clip art.

8. Insert a table with 2 columns and 5 rows. Drag the table to a position immediately below the text box created in step 5.

9. Merge the cells in Row 1.

10. Use Calibri 18 pt. Bold, Small Caps for Row 1; use Calibri 16 pt. for Rows 2 through 5. Type the following table entries:

ACCOMMODATIONS	
General	Central heating and air, TV, CD player, telephone
Utilities	Clothes dryer, dishwasher, microwave, fridge, freezer, washing machine
Furniture	King-sized beds (3), single beds (4), dining seating for 10, lounge seating for 12
Luxuries	Jacuzzi, log fireplace, Internet access, DVD player

11. Manually adjust the cell widths; then apply a table style of your choice. After applying the style, make sure that the text in Row 1 and Column A appears in bold.

12. Insert a text box, about the same size and in the same position as the one shown below the table.

13. Use Cambria 14 pt. Bold to type the following words centered in the text box:

Interested parties call 303-555-1348, or e-mail jcrenshaw@quickmail.com.

14. Apply a border and a texture fill to the text box that match those used in the text box created in step 5.

15. Apply a page color that complements the colors used in the WordArt and clip art.

Report
107-83
Announcement or Flyer

1. Create an announcement or flyer design of your own for an upcoming event at work or on campus.

2. Insert at least one picture related to the topic of the announcement or flyer.

3. Insert at least one text box with a fill and a border.

4. Insert some WordArt.

5. Use a font color to coordinate with the clip art or WordArt.

6. Insert a table that contains information related to the topic of the flyer or announcement.

7. Apply a complementary page color to the page.

Strategies for Career Success

What to Exclude From Your Resume

What items should you omit from your resume? Don't list salary demands. If the job posting requires a salary history, create a separate page listing the salaries for each position you've held. If the job posting wants your salary requirements, in the application letter state, "Salary expectation is in the range . . . ," and provide a range (usually a $5,000 range).

Exclude personal information such as race, gender, health status, age, marital status, religious preference, political preference, national origin, and physical characteristics (for example, height and weight). Do not provide your Social Security number or your photograph.

Exceptions to listing personal information do exist. For example, if you are applying for a job at a political party's headquarters and you are a member of that party, listing your party affiliation might be important to your potential employer.

Your Turn: Review your resume. Have you included any personal information? If your answer is yes, does it serve a purpose for being in your resume?

Designing Newsletters—A

Goals

- Type at least 49wpm/5'/5e.
- Correctly format a newsletter masthead.

A. WARMUP

alphabet

practice: *w* and *e*

easy

1 In the North, quick waxy bugs jumped over the frozen veldt.
2 wet were where we elbow wed dew wide ewe wee wade web endow
3 Jane can buy fuel for the antique auto at the downtown lot.

Skillbuilding

B. PACED PRACTICE

Follow the GDP software directions for this exercise to improve keystroking speed and accuracy.

C. 5-MINUTE TIMED WRITING

Take two 5-minute timed writings.

Goal: At least 49wpm/5'/5e

```
 4        Purchasing a home is probably one of the most major    11
 5   financial decisions you will make in your lifetime. Dozens  22
 6   of questions need to be answered when buying a home. For    34
 7   example, how much of a down payment will you make and how   45
 8   much of a monthly payment on your mortgage will you be able 57
 9   to afford?                                                  60
10        In addition to your mortgage payment, there are other  71
11   costs associated with buying a new home. The mortgage will  82
12   cover the principal and interest for your loan, but you     94
13   will also have homeowner's insurance and utilities to pay,  105
14   such as water, sewer, electricity, or gas.                  114
15        You may want to purchase a home through a real estate  125
16   agent, and it is important that you find out how much of a  137
17   commission will be charged for that service.                146
18        When working with a real estate agent, you need to let 157
19   that person know about the kind of community in which you   169
20   would prefer to live. Do you want to be close to schools,   180
21   shopping centers, and restaurants, or would you rather      191
22   purchase a home in a secluded neighborhood away from the    203
23   noise and congestion of a metropolitan city?                212
24        When you find the home that you like, look at it very  223
25   carefully to see if it is structurally well built, if you   234
26   like the floor plan, and if it is big enough for you.       245
      1 | 2 | 3 | 4 | 5 | 6 | 7 | 8 | 9 | 10 | 11 | 12
```

Formatting

D. NEWSLETTER DESIGN

Newsletters are an excellent forum for communicating information on a wide range of subjects. A well-planned newsletter will employ all the basic principles of good design. However, because newsletters usually include information on a wide variety of topics, they are generally complex in their layouts.

Most newsletters have the following elements in common: mastheads, main headings and subheadings, text arranged in flowing newspaper-column format using various column widths to add interest, text boxes to emphasize and summarize, pictures to draw readers' attention and interest to a topic, and a variety of borders and fills.

The design of a multipage newsletter must look consistent from one page to the next. This consistency provides unity to the newsletter design and is often achieved through the use of headers and footers.

Document Processing

Report
108-84
Newsletter

Follow these steps to create the masthead and footer for the first page of the newsletter shown on the next page.

1. Set all margins to 0.75 inch.
2. Create an open table with 2 columns and 2 rows. Drag the middle column border to the left so that Column A is about 2.0 inches wide.
3. Right-align Column B, Row 1.
4. In Column B, Row 1, change to Calibri 36 pt. Bold and type Planning Today for a Fire Emergency on two lines.
5. Press ENTER 1 time, change to Calibri 14 pt. Bold, and type A Newsletter From HLS Security Systems; then press ENTER 1 time.
6. Move to Column A, Row 2, change to Calibri 12 pt. Bold Italic, and type Volume 5, Issue No. 2
7. Move to Column B, Row 2, and change to right alignment; then change to Calibri 12 pt. Bold Italic and type this:

February 20--

8. Apply a left, right, and bottom border to Row 2.
9. In Column A, Row 1, insert clip art associated with security. Drag and size the clip art so that it looks similar to the one shown in the illustration that follows.
10. Select the newsletter title, and change the font color to coordinate with the picture in Column A.
11. Apply a double-line border to Row 1 using a color that complements the color in the newsletter title.
12. Insert a blank footer, and center and type Page followed by 1 space.
13. Insert a page number and close the footer.
14. Apply a page color to coordinate with the picture and newsletter title.

Planning Today for a Fire Emergency — Calibri 36 pt Bold

A Newsletter From HLS Security Systems — Calibri 14 pt Bold

Volume 5, Issue No. 2 *February 20--* — Calibri 12 pt Bold Italic

Page 1

Report
108-85
Newsletter

1. Create a newsletter masthead of your own related to home safety.

2. Use any picture that enhances the purpose of your newsletter.

Designing Newsletters—B

109

Goals

- Demonstrate improved speed and accuracy while typing.
- Demonstrate acceptable language arts skills in spelling.
- Correctly format a newsletter.

A. WARMUP

alphabet   1 The quizzes for the TV shows were explained by Mick Jagger.

frequent digraphs   2 ed edge wed Eddy bed eyed cede lied fed edited led axed red

easy   3 The neurotic iguana may disorient the neighbor and her dog.

Skillbuilding

B. MAP+: SYMBOL

Follow the GDP software directions for this exercise to improve keystroking accuracy.

PPP

PRETEST » PRACTICE » POSTTEST

PRETEST
Take a 1-minute timed writing.

C. PRETEST: Alternate- and One-Hand Words

```
4        In their opinion, the ornamental bicycle from Honolulu   11
5  may be regarded as an authentic antique. It deserves to be     23
6  treated well because it may attract many new visitors from     35
7  Texas and Ohio to most downtown streets in July and August.    47
     1 |  2 |  3 |  4 |  5 |  6 |  7 |  8 |  9 | 10 | 11 | 12
```

PRACTICE
Speed Emphasis:
If you made no more than 1 error on the Pretest, type each *individual* line 2 times.
Accuracy Emphasis:
If you made 2 or more errors, type each *group* of lines (as though it were a paragraph) 2 times.

D. PRACTICE: Alternate-Hand Words

```
8  maps visual suspend amendment turndown visible height signs
9  form profit penalty shamrocks blandish problem thrown chair
10 snap emblem dormant authentic clemency figment island usual
11 half signal auditor endowment ornament element handle amend
```

E. PRACTICE: One-Hand Words

```
12 serve uphill exceeds killjoy carefree homonym terrace onion
13 trade poplin greater pumpkin eastward plumply barrage holly
14 defer unhook reserve minimum attracts million scatter plump
15 exact kimono created phonily cassette opinion seaweed union
```

F. POSTTEST: Alternate- and One-Hand Words

Language Arts

G. SPELLING

16 operations health individual considered expenditures vendor
17 beginning internal pursuant president union written develop
18 hours enclosing situation function including standard shown
19 engineering payable suggested participants providing orders
20 toward nays total without paragraph meetings different vice

21 The participents in the different meetings voted for hours.

22 The presdent of the union is working toward a resolution.

23 The health of each individal must be seriously considered.

24 Engineering has suggested providing orders for the vendor.

25 One expanditure has been written off as part of oparations.

26 He is inclosing the accounts payible record as shown today.

Document Processing

Open the file for Report 108-84. Follow these steps to continue the newsletter as shown below:

1. Move your insertion point to the end of the document; then press ENTER 1 time.
2. Insert File 109, and turn on automatic hyphenation.
3. Carefully place your insertion point in front of the first character of the text you inserted from File 109.
4. Select all the newly inserted text, including 1 blank line below the last line of text.
5. With the text still selected, create a 3-column page layout.
6. Select the following side headings in the newsletter, and change the font to Calibri 20 pt. Bold:

   Plan Ahead
   Make a Diagram
   Plan Your Escape
   Avoid Smoke

7. Insert clip art in the space below the first two side headings. The clip art should be related to the topic of each of the paragraphs (*plan* and *drawing*).
8. Set text wrapping to place text above and below the image, but not beside the image.
9. Set the clip art height to 1.8 inches; let the width adjust proportionally to the height.
10. Drag the clip art into a position similar to the clip art shown in the illustration.
11. Compare the placement of the columnar text to see if it's similar to that shown in the illustration. Check to see if the side heading "Plan Your Escape" appears at the top of Column C. If not, adjust the size and placement of the clip art.

Planning Today for a Fire Emergency

A Newsletter From HLS Security Systems

Volume 5, Issue No. 2   *February 20—*

All family members must know what to do in case of a fire emergency in the home. Fighting a fire should be left to professional firefighters; family members should exit a burning home without delay.

There are several individual steps that must be taken to initiate a fire-evacuation plan.

Plan Ahead

One of the first steps at the beginning of your plan is to install smoke detectors and be sure they are operating. Also, close bedroom doors while sleeping. It takes 10 to 15 minutes for a fire to burn through a wooden door. Those few minutes could mean the difference between escaping or being trapped by the fire.

Make a Diagram

Develop a drawing of the floor plan in your home. Mark all exits, windows, doors, stairs, halls, and the locations of all fire alarms. Be sure that the children know how to identify an alarm sound when it is activated.

Plan Your Escape

Each family member must know how to exit the home by at least two different routes. The first route will most likely be the door normally used to exit; the second route might be through a window. Make sure that all windows open freely without restriction.

If a door is going to be used as an emergency exit, be sure that it is checked carefully before it is opened. If the door is hot, it means that the fire is immediately outside the door and that another exit should be chosen.

Avoid Smoke

If you are caught in a room filling with smoke, be sure to stay as low as

Page 1

possible to the floor and crawl toward the nearest exit. Smoke and heat rise, so the cleanest air will always be at the floor level.

If the door is closed between you and the fire and it is not possible for you to exit, stuff the cracks and cover vents to keep the smoke out.

Page 2

1. Open the file for Report 108-85 with the newsletter masthead you created.
2. Follow the steps for Report 109-86, and then delete the "Avoid Smoke" section at the bottom of Column C.
3. Insert a picture after the side heading "Plan Your Escape."
4. Drag and size the picture so that it is similar to the ones previously inserted on the page. Make certain that all of the text remains on that page and does not wrap to a second page.

Keyboarding Connection

E-Mail Privacy

How private are your e-mail messages? Although there has been a lot of discussion about hacking and Internet security, e-mail may be more secure than your phone or postal mail. In fact, most new-generation e-mail programs have some kind of encryption built in.

It is not hackers who are most likely to read your e-mail. It is anyone with access to your incoming mail server or your computer. If your computer and incoming server are at work, then you can assume your supervisor can read your e-mail. In some companies, it is normal practice to monitor employees' e-mail. Therefore, you should not send e-mail from work that you don't want anyone there to read.

If you are serious about e-mail privacy, you may want to examine other encryption methods. Different products are available to ensure that your e-mail is read only by the intended recipient(s). However, some companies don't allow employees to add software to their computers for legal reasons, so check your company's computer policies. It may be wiser to send personal e-mail from your own computer outside of work.

Your Turn: Perform a keyword search using a search engine for information on different products that are available to protect your e-mail privacy.

Designing Newsletters—C

Goals

- Type at least 49wpm/5'/5e.
- Correctly format a newsletter.
- Successfully complete a Progress and Proofreading Check with zero errors on the first scored attempt.

A. WARMUP

alphabet
number/symbol
easy

1 The glum, wavy-haired ex-cons bequeathed fake topaz jewels.
2 gilp@comcast.net (11%) Ng & Ma 4/5 No! $13.86 *Est. #20-972
3 Nancy and Blanche cut six bushels of corn in the cornfield.

Skillbuilding

B. 12-SECOND SPEED SPRINTS

Take three 12-second timed writings on each line.

4 He may go with us to the giant dock down by the handy lake.
5 The old chapel at the end of the big lake has an odd shape.
6 His body of work may charm the guests who visit the chapel.
7 His civic goal for the city is for them to endow the chair.
   ' ' ' '5' ' '10' ' '15' ' '20' ' '25' ' '30' ' '35' ' '40' ' '45' ' '50' ' '55' ' '60

C. TECHNIQUE PRACTICE: ENTER KEY

Type each line 2 times. Type each sentence on a separate line by pressing ENTER after each sentence.

8 Don't! We are. Give. Speak. Type it. Beg. Be there. We did?
9 Step on it. See to it. Wait. Find it? Says who? We do. Sit.
10 Who knows? See me. Get up. Eat! Where? Who is he? Finished?
11 When? Today. Do it now. We are up. Al saw her. Do not. All?

Take two 5-minute timed writings.

Goal: At least 49wpm/5'/5e

D. 5-MINUTE TIMED WRITING

```
12      When the rate of unemployment is very low, jobs are      11
13  easier to find. Although you may find a job easily, what     22
14  can you do to make sure your job is one you will enjoy?       33
15  Here are some suggestions to assist you.                      41
16      First, be certain you receive a job description when     52
17  you are hired. The job description should list all of the    64
18  requirements of the job and the details of what you will be  78
19  expected to do.                                               79
20      Second, you should receive some type of orientation to  90
21  your job and the company. During orientation, you will fill 102
22  out various tax forms, benefit forms, and insurance papers. 114
23  You may view a video that will help you learn more about     126
24  the company and available benefits.                          133
25      Third, when you start your training, you should take    144
26  notes, pay attention, and ask questions. You should also     155
27  have your trainer check your work for a period of time to    167
28  be sure you are performing your duties correctly. If your    178
29  tasks are complex, you can break them down into smaller      189
30  parts so you can remember all aspects of your job.           200
31      Finally, when you know your job requirements, chart     210
32  your work each day. Concentrate on being part of the team.  222
33  Be zealous in striving to work beyond the expectations of   234
34  your supervisor. Then, you will achieve job satisfaction.   245
     1  |  2  |  3  |  4  |  5  |  6  |  7  |  8  |  9  | 10 | 11 | 12
```

Document Processing

Report 110-88
Newsletter (Continued)

Open the file for Report 109-86. Follow these steps to finish creating the newsletter shown below.

1. Verify that automatic hyphenation is on.
2. Place your insertion point directly after the final period at the end of the sentence in Column A. Then press ENTER 2 times.
3. Change to Calibri 20 pt. Bold, and type Practice the Plan as a side heading. Then press ENTER 1 time.
4. Change to Calibri 14 pt., press ENTER 1 time, and then type the following paragraph:

Effective fire evacuation is only as good as family members are aware of how it is supposed to function. Have them practice the plan, and be certain all family members are aware of all escape routes. Practice the escape plan at different hours.

5. With your insertion point after the final period you typed in step 3, press ENTER 2 times; then insert File 110.
6. Select the following side headings in the text that was inserted, and change the font to Calibri 20 pt. Bold:

Exit Safely
Plan to Meet
Assist Others

7. Insert clip art in the space below the side heading "Exit Safely." The clip art should be associated with the topic of the paragraph (*exit*).

8. Set the clip art with a height of 1.55 inches; let the width adjust proportionally to the height.

9. Apply the same picture style to the clip art that was used for the clip art on page 1 of the newsletter.

10. Drag the clip art into a position similar to the clip art shown in the illustration below. Set text wrapping to place text above and below the image, but not beside the image.

11. Move your insertion point to the end of the newsletter.

12. Insert a text box at the bottom of Column C, about the same size and shape and in the same position as the one shown in the illustration.

13. Change to Calibri 16 pt. Bold; then center and type this in the text box:

Future Issues

14. Press ENTER 1 time, change to Calibri 11 pt. Bold, and then center and type this:

```
March: Homeland Security
April: Updating Your System
May: Emergency Supplies
June: Safety Seminars
```

15. Apply a textured fill to the text box that complements the page color of the newsletter.

16. Change the shape of the text box to complement the shape used for the clip art in the newsletter.

17. Make whatever adjustments are needed to make your newsletter look attractive.

18. The newsletter should look similar to the illustrations that follow.

nominative pronoun
Column A (*"they"*)

possible to the floor and crawl toward the nearest exit. Smoke and heat rise, so the cleanest air will always be at the floor level.

If the door is closed between you and the fire and it is not possible for you to exit, stuff the cracks and cover vents to keep the smoke out.

Practice the Plan

Effective fire evacuation is only as good as family members are aware of how it is supposed to function. Have them practice the plan, and be certain all family members are aware of all escape routes. Practice the escape plan at different hours.

Exit Safely

Exiting safely through a ground-floor window or

door is usually uneventful. However, if you are on the second floor or higher, exiting will require you to take some precautions. If you attempt to jump from an upper floor, you might injure an ankle or leg. One suggested solution would be to purchase a ladder for the upstairs bedrooms to use for emergency exits. Make sure to inspect the ladders annually to be sure they operate properly.

If living in an apartment, never use an elevator in case of fire. An elevator may cease operating during a fire and stop between floors or at a floor where the fire is located. As an alternative, use a fire escape or stairwell to escape.

Teach your family that, once they are outside a burning building, they should never go back into the building.

Plan to Meet

A special meeting place should be considered that is always located a

safe distance from the house. Knowing where this meeting place is will assist all family members in determining where to meet to see if everyone is safe and has exited the home.

Assist Others

You may have to provide some special assistance to young children.

If children are afraid, they may choose to hide under a bed or in the closet. Encourage them to exit outside the home, a safe distance away from the fire. Make certain that your children can operate all windows, open all doors, descend a ladder, or lower themselves to the ground.

You may also need to consider assistance for the elderly, who may have difficulty in exiting the premises.

Future Issues

March: Homeland Security
April: Updating Your System
May: Emergency Supplies
June: Safety Seminars

Page 2

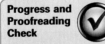

1. Insert WordArt about the same size as the one in the illustration that follows. Center the WordArt horizontally, and apply a color of your choice for the text. Use the following text for the WordArt:

   `Premier Real Estate`

2. Insert clip art related to homes; drag and size the clip art so that it looks similar to the one in the illustration.

3. Select an attractive visual style of your choice for the clip art.

4. Apply a font color to the text in the WordArt to complement the clip art you have inserted.

5. Create a text box, about the same size and in the same position as the one in the illustration. Use Calibri 20 pt. Bold Italic to type and center the words "`Serving the Canton area for 55 years`" in the text box. Use a shape fill that complements the color of the WordArt.

6. Create a boxed table with 3 columns and 9 rows. Drag the table to a position immediately below the text box created in step 5.

7. Use Calibri 16 pt. for Row 1; use Calibri 14 pt. for Rows 2 through 9. Type the table entries as follows:

Weekly Specials: April 10 Through April 16		
Address	Price	Agent
224 Birchfield Run, Green Bay	$242,000	Angie Summers
4134 Diamond Court, DePere	$257,000	Doug McClure
812 Eagles Nest Circle, Allouez	$263,000	Angie Summers
427 Matthews Avenue, Green Bay	$269,000	Connie McCormack
1280 Timbermill Circle, Allouez	$283,000	Doug McClure
628 Clifton Terrace, DePere	$297,000	Chad Burnett
829 Cypress Court, Green Bay	$323,000	Angie Summers

8. Apply a style of your choice to the table. After applying the style, make sure that the text in Row 1, Row 2, and Column A appear in bold.

9. Apply a page color that complements the colors used in the WordArt and clip art.

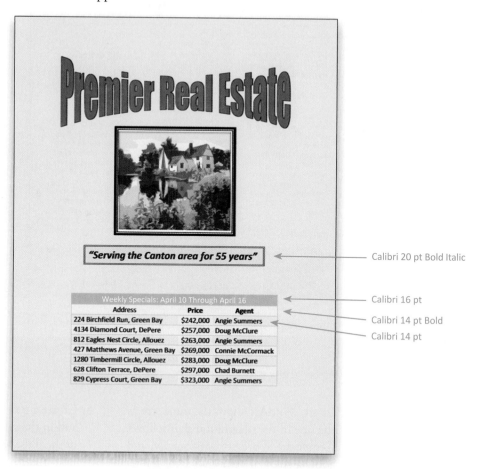

Premier Real Estate

"Serving the Canton area for 55 years" ← Calibri 20 pt Bold Italic

Weekly Specials: April 10 Through April 16		
Address	Price	Agent
224 Birchfield Run, Green Bay	$242,000	Angie Summers
4134 Diamond Court, DePere	$257,000	Doug McClure
812 Eagles Nest Circle, Allouez	$263,000	Angie Summers
427 Matthews Avenue, Green Bay	$269,000	Connie McCormack
1280 Timbermill Circle, Allouez	$283,000	Doug McClure
628 Clifton Terrace, DePere	$297,000	Chad Burnett
829 Cypress Court, Green Bay	$323,000	Angie Summers

Calibri 16 pt
Calibri 14 pt Bold
Calibri 14 pt

Mail Merge—A

Goals

- Type at least 50wpm/5′/5e.
- Correctly use Word's mail merge feature to create merged letters.
- Correctly format a form letter in block style.

A. WARMUP

alphabet   1   Dr. Jekyll vowed to finish zapping the quixotic bumblebees.

one hand   2   secret hominy dew hip beasts nonunion edge monk staff nylon

easy   3   Susie's sorority is proficient in their work with the city.

Skillbuilding

Take a 1-minute timed writing on the boxed paragraph to establish your base speed. Then take a 1-minute timed writing on the following paragraph. As soon as you equal or exceed your base speed on this paragraph, move to the next, more difficult paragraph.

B. SUSTAINED PRACTICE: CAPITALS

4	Even though he was only about thirty years old, Jason	11
5	knew that it was not too soon to begin thinking about his	23
6	retirement. He soon found out that there were many things	34
7	involved in his plans for an early and long retirement.	45

8   Even without considering the uncertainty of social   10
9   security, Jason knew that he should plan his career moves   22
10   so that he would have a strong company retirement plan. He   33
11   realized that he should have an Individual Retirement Plan.   45

12   When he became aware that The Longman Company, the   10
13   firm that employed him, would match his contributions to a   22
14   supplemental retirement account, he began saving even more.   34
15   He used the Payroll Department funds from the Goplin Group.   46

16   He also learned that The Longman Company retirement   11
17   plan, his Individual Retirement Plan, and his supplemental   22
18   retirement account are all deferred savings. With those   34
19   tax-dollar savings, Jason bought New Venture Group funds.   45

  1 | 2 | 3 | 4 | 5 | 6 | 7 | 8 | 9 | 10 | 11 | 12

C. 5-MINUTE TIMED WRITING

```
20        Employers want the people who work for them to have    11
21  many qualities of good character. Character is defined as a  23
22  distinctive feature of a person or thing. Character may be   34
23  what you are known for and may be why you remember someone   46
24  else. What are some of the traits you think of that are      57
25  linked with good character? A few traits might be respect,   69
26  honesty, trust, caring, leadership, attitude, tolerance,     81
27  fairness, and patience.                                      85
28        All people should have respect for themselves and for  96
29  others. If you respect people, you have a high regard for   108
30  the way they conduct themselves in all aspects of life.     119
31  However, before you can respect others, you need to have    131
32  respect for yourself.                                       135
33        Honesty and trustworthiness are similar traits. In    145
34  business dealings, people expect honesty and will admire    157
35  people who have this quality. They like to build business   168
36  relationships with companies whose employees are honest,    180
37  just, and trustworthy.                                      184
38        Your attitude is reflected in the way you act toward   195
39  other people or in the way you speak to them. You can make  207
40  great strides in advancing your career by taking a look at  219
41  the way you interact with people. You may want to take a    230
42  closer look at some character traits you want to improve.   242
43  Such improvements in life will amaze you.                   250
        1 | 2 | 3 | 4 | 5 | 6 | 7 | 8 | 9 | 10 | 11 | 12
```

Formatting

D. FORM LETTERS

A form letter is a letter that combines standard and variable information for a number of different recipients to create a set of merged documents. Mail merge is also very useful when creating corresponding envelopes and labels for a form letter. The same variable information used to create the address block in the form letter may be used to create the address block in envelopes or labels.

Two files must be created before a merge can occur. The main document (in this example, a form letter) contains generic content that doesn't change. The data source file contains variable information specific to the recipient (the person receiving the finalized merged document), such as the inside address block and the first and last name in the salutation.

After these two files are created, placeholder fields (codes that will be replaced with actual text after the files are merged) are inserted into the main document. These fields link the variable content from the data source file to the generic text in the main document. Finally, the main document file is merged with the data source file to create a number of finished documents that combine generic text from the main document with variable text from the data source file into a single file.

When the main document or data source is updated, all changes will be reflected in each new merged document. The following illustration shows a letter created as a main document with corresponding placeholder fields inserted.

December 12, 20--

«AddressBlock»

«GreetingLine»

Thank you so much for signing up to work as a volunteer at Henry Mayo Memorial. Generous individuals like you are the reason HMM is able to offer so many outstanding services to our patients during their hospital stay.

Physicians, staff, and patients all appreciate each and every service you provide. Pet visitation, patient ambassador visits, and many other services will be discussed at the orientation for new volunteers in January. I have enclosed a brochure with all pertinent details.

Thank you once again for your generosity and kindness.

Sincerely,

Darlene Shaw
Director of Volunteer Services

urs
Enclosure

Placeholder field codes for the inside address and salutation in the main document

E. WORD PROCESSING: MAIL MERGE—LETTERS

GO TO
Word Manual

Study Lesson 112 in your Word Manual. Complete all of the shaded steps while at your computer. Then format the documents that follow.

Document Processing

Correspondence
112-95
Business Letter in Block Style

1. Create the main document without any placeholder fields, and save the main document file as *Correspondence 112-95-main.*
2. Create a data source file for each recipient listed, and save the data source file as *Correspondence 112-95-data.*
3. Insert the appropriate placeholder fields in the form letter; select a colon as the punctuation mark for the salutation.

4. Adjust the blank lines above or below the placeholder fields as needed to format the inside address and salutation correctly.
5. Preview your results and make any adjustments as needed.
6. Merge the main document and the data source file to create one file with the four merged letters, and save the file as *Correspondence 112-95.*

Main Document

February 14, 20--
«AddressBlock»
«GreetingLine»
¶ Welcome to Lakeshore Terrace! I hope you are enjoying the stunning vistas of nearby Lake Tahoe, the golf course, and the recreation center that are all part of the amenities available to every homeowner in our planned community.
¶ Be assured that the Lakeshore Terrace Residential Community Association is committed to maintaining the guidelines set forth by our association so that our

(continued on next page)

residents will continue to enjoy all the amenities of this community for many years to come.

¶ If you have any questions at all, please feel free to e-mail me at cbrown@ltrca.com or call me at 530-555-2992. Also, check our Web site at http://ltrca.org for upcoming community events and other items of interest.

¶ Once again, welcome to the neighborhood!

Sincerely, | Carly Brown | Assistant Association Manager | urs

Data Source

Type the data shown in the table in the appropriate fields in the dialog box.

Title	First Name	Last Name	Address Line 1	City	State	ZIP Code
Dr.	Karen	Simpson	4309 Pine Bouquet Road	Lake Tahoe	CA	96150
Ms.	Gloria	Freeman	4135 Zephyr Road	Lake Tahoe	CA	96150
Mr.	Justin	Frazier	1900 Jansen Beach Road	Lake Tahoe	CA	96150
Mrs.	Lillian	Hunt	1135 Pioneer Trail Road	Lake Tahoe	CA	96150

Mail Merge—C

Goals

- Type at least 50wpm/5'/5e.
- Correctly format a form letter in block style.

A. WARMUP

alphabet	1	Why did Max become eloquent over a zany gift like jodhpurs?
frequent digraphs	2	te tee ate byte tell tea termite ten Ute tent teed teen Ted
easy	3	The auditor's panel had the right to risk a firm's profits.

Skillbuilding

B. PROGRESSIVE PRACTICE: NUMBERS

Follow the GDP software directions for this exercise to improve keystroking speed.

C. TECHNIQUE PRACTICE: SHIFT KEY

Type each line 2 times. After striking the capitalized letter, return the SHIFT KEY finger immediately to home-row position.

4 Alex Bly and Clara Dye wed. Ella Fochs and Gil Hall talked.
5 Ida Jackson met Kay Lang for a fast lunch at Mamma Nancy's.
6 Otis Pike should call Quint Richards about Sophia Townsend.
7 Urich Volte will take Winona Xie to visit Yadkin in Zurich.

Goal: At least 50wpm/5'/5e

D. 5-MINUTE TIMED WRITING

8   Before you apply for a job, you will want to do some   11
9 detective work. First, choose a company where you want to   23
10 work, and then use the Internet to find out about the firm.   34
11 If you find a site for the business, then you can learn all   46
12 about the company, its hiring policies, the job listings,   58
13 or ways to apply for a job there.   65
14   When you are researching a business, you want to   75
15 learn about the history of the company. You may be able   86
16 to find out how stock analysts expect the company stock   97
17 to perform in the coming months if the firm is publicly   108
18 traded. When you find a job opening for which you know that   120
19 you want to apply, read carefully to see what type of work   132
20 experience and education the business requires for the job.   144
21   When you prepare your resume, emphasize your major   155
22 qualifications based on the requirements listed for the   166
23 job. If the person who will receive the job inquiries is   177
24 not listed, contact the company by phone or e-mail to learn   189
25 his or her name. You should personalize the cover letter   201
26 and resume to stress what the firm needs.   209
27   The information you find in your research will be   219
28 very helpful during the interview with a manager at the   230
29 company. Ask good questions and speak confidently about   242
30 the job. Emphasize how your skills fit in.   250

1 | 2 | 3 | 4 | 5 | 6 | 7 | 8 | 9 | 10 | 11 | 12

Document Processing

**Correspondence
114-97**
Business Letter in
Block Style

1. Create the main document without any placeholder fields, and save the main document file as *Correspondence 114-97-main.*
2. Create a data source file for each recipient listed, and save the data source file as *Correspondence 114-97-data.*
3. Insert the appropriate placeholder fields in the form letter; select a colon as the punctuation mark for the salutation.
4. Adjust the blank lines above or below the placeholder fields as needed to format the inside address and salutation correctly.
5. Preview your results and make any adjustments as needed.
6. Merge the main document and the data source file to create one file with the four merged letters, and save the file as *Correspondence 114-97.*

Nov. 1, 20--

<<GreetingLine>>

<<AddressBlock>>

¶ Welcome to Movie Flix! As a new member, you're entitled to 6 months of free dvds by mail. Because we have over 150 shipping points across the Nation, you can count on receiving ~~your~~ *a* DVD in about one business day. Due dates and late fees are a thing of the past. For every new member you refer, you will receive an additional 2 months of free premium membership. You have a wide array of DVDs to choose ~~from~~ *from which*. Many new-release movies ~~and~~ and current-season TV episodes are available. If you prefer, we can stream all your entertainment to you via a Movieflix device or directly/online to your personal computer at *no* extra charge. Please visit our *Web* site at www.mflix.com for complete listings. *and details*

¶ If you have any questions or concerns whatsoever, don't hesitate to contact me at 800-555-7662 or e-mail me at rphillips@mflix.com. I'm at your service.

Sincerely, | Roy Phillips | Subscriber Relations Specialist | urs

Mr. | Estrada | Andres | 123 N. Thomas Road | Phoenix | AZ | 85400

Ms. Joyce | Evans | 1172 Yellowstone High way | Cody | WY | 82414

Mr. | Ken | Newwton | 459 South Meridian | Oklahoma City | OK | 73108

~~Mr.~~ *Mrs.* | Brandy | Burgess | 29 Riverside Dr. | Corning | NY | 14830

Skillbuilding and In-Basket Review

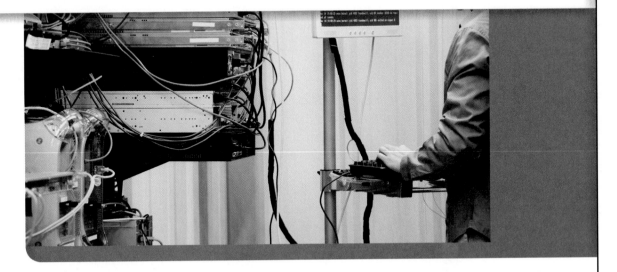

Skillbuilding and In-Basket Review—Banking

Goals

- Type at least 50wpm/5'/5e.
- Correctly format a memo template, boxed table, and letterhead form.

A. WARMUP

alphabet
1 We promptly judge antique ivory buckles for the next prize.

concentration
2 gastroenterologists interdenominational individualistically

easy
3 Dirk may visit the island by the oaks with his tan bicycle.

Skillbuilding

B. SUSTAINED PRACTICE: PUNCTUATION

Take a 1-minute timed writing on the boxed paragraph to establish your base speed. Then take a 1-minute timed writing on the following paragraph. As soon as you equal or exceed your base speed on this paragraph, move to the next, more difficult paragraph.

4	Have you ever noticed that a good laugh every now and	11
5	then really makes you feel better? Research has shown that	22
6	laughter can have a very healing effect on our bodies. It	33
7	is an excellent way to relieve tension and stress all over.	46

8	When you laugh, your heart beats faster, you breathe	11
9	deeper, and you exercise your lungs. When you laugh, your	22
10	body produces endorphins--a natural painkiller that gives	34
11	you a sense of euphoria that is very powerful and pleasant.	46

12	Someone said, "Laugh in the face of adversity." As it	11
13	happens, this is first-rate advice. It's a great way to	22
14	cope with life's trials and tribulations; it's also a good	34
15	way to raise other people's spirits and relieve tension.	45

16	Finding "humor" in any situation takes practice--try	11
17	to make it a full-time habit. We're all looking for ways	22
18	to relieve stress. Any exercise--jogging, tennis, biking,	34
19	swimming, or golfing--is a proven remedy for "the blues."	45

1 | 2 | 3 | 4 | 5 | 6 | 7 | 8 | 9 | 10 | 11 | 12

C. 5-MINUTE TIMED WRITING

20   A few factors should be considered before you buy a   11
21 new printer for your computer. First, decide how you will   22
22 use your new printer. If you plan to use the printer for   34
23 typing letters and reports, you may decide you want a laser   45
24 printer at a reasonable price and that is capable of doing   57
25 general tasks you will need.   63
26   If you are buying the printer for office use, you may   74
27 decide to shop for a printer that prints documents more   85
28 quickly and is of exceptional value. Then, if you plan to   97
29 use a digital camera with the printer, you will want to get   109
30 a printer that is made to print documents of photo quality.   121
31   Resolution, speed, and paper handling are some other   132
32 factors you should consider when you buy a new printer.   143
33 Resolution refers to how sharp the image appears on the   154
34 paper. With printers that have a higher resolution, the   165
35 image gives you output of higher quality. You will see an   177
36 amazing difference when you compare some samples of print   188
37 from the other kinds of printers.   195
38   If you expect to print long documents, then you will   206
39 want to search for a reliable printer with a feed tray that   218
40 holds a large amount of paper. The more expensive printers   230
41 are usually faster printers. After assessing your printer   241
42 needs, you are ready to make your purchase.   250

1 | 2 | 3 | 4 | 5 | 6 | 7 | 8 | 9 | 10 | 11 | 12

Document Processing

Situation: Today is October 10. You are employed in the office of First National Savings in Del Mar, California. Ms. Sabrina Talavaro, vice president, has written the memo shown next. Type it using a memo template; send it to all bank employees with a copy to T. J. Hurley, president. Ms. Talavaro prefers to use her name and title in the From field. The subject of the memo is "Revision to Online Access Agreement."

Form 116-15   Memo Template

¶ The revised OAA (Online-Access Agreement) becomes effective on October 20. Our customers have been notified of the new agreement via e-mail and letters. However, we do anticipate customer inquiries for specific details and individual account questions. Below is a recap of significant changes made to the OAA.

(continued on next page)

¶ The agreement was simplified and includes two important changes. First, the rights and responsibilities of account owners and delegates have been amended to add an option for an account owner to delegate account-management authority to another person. Second, online banking terms and conditions have been incorporated into the OAA for the convenience of our customers.

¶ The revised OAA also specifically clarifies details regarding the "Payment-Send-on Date" for Automatic Bill Pay that has historically been a source of confusion. Also, the sections related to online banking were revised to better describe the enrollment process.

¶ Please visit www.fns.com/oaa/about to review all changes in depth. I have also attached a table that can be used as a quick reference to relevant sections in the OAA. Contact me at stalavaro@fns.com if you have any questions.

When the memo is distributed, the table below should be attached. Ms. Talavaro asks you to use attractive borders and shading to give this table a desktop-published appearance.

Table
116-55
Boxed Table

Your completed table may look different from the one shown.

ONLINE ACCESS AGREEMENT* First National Savings	
Topic	**Section**
Online banking terms and conditions	1, 3, 4, and 29
Guest users and authorized users defined	2A, 2B, and 5D
Bill Pay Account name change	7A
Bill Pay Account number changes	10A
Online billing provider definition	6A
Enrollment process for eligible accounts	10
Legal disclosures	20A and 20B
*Update effective October 20, 20--.	

Ms. Talavaro has sketched out a letterhead form and wants you to design the finished letterhead for First National Savings. The top of the letterhead should include the company name, address, phone number, and Web site address with each element separated by a diamond-shaped symbol. The main office address is 1701 Coast Boulevard, Del Mar, CA 92014; the phone number is 800-555-2447, and the Web site address is www.fns.com. Type the company slogan First National Savings: the key to your financial future at the bottom of the letterhead form.

To begin the form, change all margins to 0.6 inch.

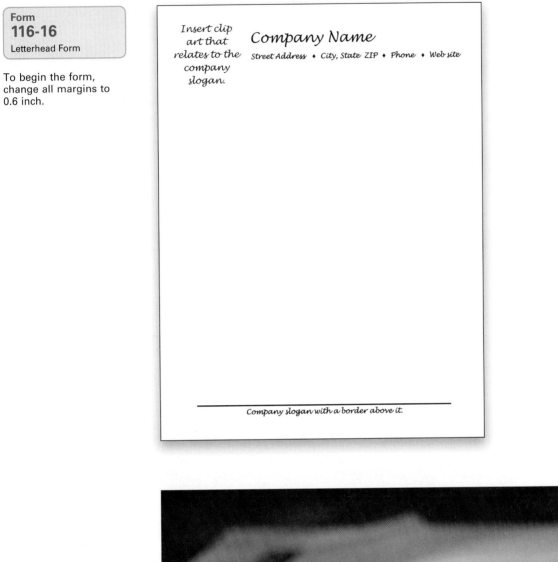

Insert clip art that relates to the company slogan.

Company Name

Street Address ♦ City, State ZIP ♦ Phone ♦ Web site

Company slogan with a border above it.

Skillbuilding and In-Basket Review—Education

Goals

- Demonstrate improved speed and accuracy while typing.
- Demonstrate acceptable language arts skills in word usage.
- Correctly format an academic report, a flyer, and a left-bound business report.

A. WARMUP

alphabet   1 Jackie quietly gave the dog owner most of his prize boxers.

one hand   2 stages phylum wet pop affect jumpily tact junky beard pinky

easy   3 Duane's handy bicycle is to be thrown in the dormant field.

Skillbuilding

B. MAP+: ALPHABET

Follow the GDP software directions for this exercise to improve keystroking accuracy.

C. PROGRESSIVE PRACTICE: ALPHABET

Follow the GDP software directions for this exercise to improve keystroking speed.

Language Arts

Study the rules at the right.

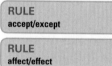

RULE
accept/except

RULE
affect/effect

RULE
farther/further

RULE
personal/personnel

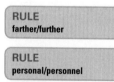

RULE
principal/principle

D. WORD USAGE

Accept **means "to agree to";** ***except*** **means "to leave out."**

All employees <u>except</u> the maintenance staff should <u>accept</u> the agreement.

Affect **is most often used as a verb meaning "to influence";** ***effect*** **is most often used as a noun meaning "result."**

The ruling will <u>affect</u> our domestic operations but will have no <u>effect</u> on Asian operations.

Farther **refers to distance;** ***further*** **refers to extent or degree.**

The <u>farther</u> we drove, the <u>further</u> agitated he became.

Personal **means "private";** ***personnel*** **means "employees."**

All <u>personnel</u> agreed not to use <u>personal</u> e-mail for business.

Principal **means "primary";** ***principle*** **means "rule."**

The <u>principle</u> of fairness is our <u>principal</u> means of dealing with customers.

Edit each sentence to correct any errors.

4 The company cannot accept any collect calls, except for his.

5 The affect of the speech was dramatic; everyone was affected.

6 Further discussion by office personal was not appropriate.

7 Comments made during any meeting should never be personal.

8 If the meeting is held any further away, no one will attend.

9 The principle reason for the decision was to save money.

10 Office ethics are basic principles that should be practiced.

11 He cannot except the fact that the job was delegated to Jack.

12 Any further effects on office personnel will be evaluated.

Document Processing

Situation: Today is September 25. You are employed in the office of Dr. Daniel Lopez, dean of online education, at Arizona Technical College in Phoenix. Dr. Lopez has written the report shown next and left it in your in-basket for you to type and format. The title of the report is "PREPARING TO TEACH ONLINE." In his reports, he uses "Dr. Daniel V. Lopez, Dean" as the byline followed by the complete date.

Report 117-92
Academic Report

affect/effect

principal/principle

affect/effect

principal/principle

affect/effect

There are many strategies for becoming a successful online instructor. Adapting class management strategies and developing related course management systems will affect the outcome and success of any online course. A few basic principles are discussed here.

CLASS MANAGEMENT STRATEGIES

To make a successful transition from a traditional class setting to an online class setting, you must be very cognizant that class management strategies must be adapted. In particular, course policies related to due dates and timelines as well as the effects of late work on student success must be spelled out and strictly enforced.

Dr. Bill Maedke, a principal expert in online teaching, says that if students are not held accountable for delivering assignments on time, student success is greatly affected.

(continued on next page)

farther/further

accept/except

Attrition increases as they procrastinate beyond the point of no return. When they finally realize they are getting further and further behind, many will drop out rather than accept a failing grade.[1]

COURSE MANAGEMENT SYSTEMS

accept/except

A course management system that supports the course requirements and facilitates the exchange of work between instructor and student is critical. Take time to research the various courseware management systems and compare their features. For a comprehensive list of accepted course management systems at ATC, visit www.atc.edu/online/courseware. The article "The Fine Art of Teaching at a Distance" by Dana Evans is another excellent resource.[2]

STAFF-DEVELOPMENT TRAINING SESSIONS

personal/personnel

farther/further

The best way to prepare to teach online at Arizona Tech is to attend a series of upcoming staff-development training sessions entitled "Teaching Online @ ATC" that will be available to all interested instructional personnel. Look for a flyer in your mailbox and in your school e-mail soon that will provide further details on these training sessions.

Italicize publication titles.

[1]Bill Maedke, "Class Management Strategies for Teaching at a Distance," The Collegian Journal, February 1, 2010, p. 29.
[2]Dana Evans, "The Fine Art of Teaching Online," Education Today, April 17, 2010, pp. 85-91.

Dr. Lopez has left a sketch of a flyer for the staff-development workshop entitled "Teaching Online @ ATC" that he would like you to design. He has asked you to use WordArt for the title, a rounded text box for the announcement, a predesigned table format for the workshop schedule, and landscape orientation for the page layout.

personal/personnel

Teaching Online @ ATC

Insert a picture that relates to the @ symbol.

Dr. Daniel V. Lopez, dean of online education, would like to extend a personal invitation to all instructional personnel to attend a series of staff-development workshops that will focus on strategies for teaching at a distance.

- *The workshops will be held at the Faculty Conference Center at Arizona Technical College beginning November 2.*
- *The schedule and topics are listed below.*

Date, Time, and Location	Topic
Monday, November 2, Room 1A	Online Pedagogy
Tuesday, November 10, Room 1B	Course Design
Wednesday, November 18, Room 2A	Learning Objects
Monday, November 30, Room 2C	Online Resources
For further details, visit www.atc.edu/online/workshops.	

farther/further

Open the file for Report 117-92, and make the following changes:

1. Change the format from an academic report to a left-bound business report.
2. Change the report title to this: ONLINE TEACHING AND LEARNING RESOURCES.
3. Change the date to September 30, 20--.
4. Delete the second sentence in the first paragraph.
5. Insert this side heading and the paragraph that follows it into the report just above the "COURSE MANAGE-MENT SYSTEMS" heading:

INSTRUCTIONAL TECHNOLOGY
A learning object is an online instructional resource that supports learning via the use and reuse of digital instructional components designed to deliver small amounts of information in different contexts. For example, a set of digital flash cards might include a course concept on one side of the card and the corresponding definition on the other side. The flash card content could be written by an instructor or purchased as part of a digital instructional package.

Skillbuilding and In-Basket Review—Nursing Facility

Goals

- Type at least 50wpm/5'/5e.
- Correctly format a business letter in block style, an itinerary, and a newsletter.

A. WARMUP

alphabet

practice: *o* and *i*

easy

1 Jacqueline was vexed by the folks who got the money prizes.
2 oil boil folio polio Rio coin icon into Ohio olio silo void
3 Her ruby handiwork is fine, and she is so proficient at it.

Skillbuilding

B. PACED PRACTICE

Follow the GDP software directions for this exercise to improve keystroking speed and accuracy.

C. 5-MINUTE TIMED WRITING

Take two 5-minute timed writings.

Goal: At least 50wpm/5'/5e

4	Job sharing is a current concept that many places are	11
5	using to keep valued workers. People are finding a wide	22
6	range of reasons for not wanting to work full time. Here	34
7	are some tips on how to approach your boss if you would	45
8	like to attempt job sharing.	51
9	First, check your company handbook for an authorized	61
10	policy regarding this concept. If there is no rule that	73
11	prohibits the concept, then try to enlist a coworker who	84
12	would like to job-share and help you in writing a proposal	96
13	for job sharing where you work.	102
14	Next, define your needs and your goals. Develop a work	113
15	schedule that will meet all of your personal and monetary	125
16	needs. Be sure that you include enough time to get the work	137
17	done. If you want to work at your home on occasion, be sure	149
18	to state your desires.	154
19	You might find it is often quite helpful to maintain a	165
20	journal of your job duties, noting how much time is devoted	177
21	to each task. Your plan must also include details about the	189
22	logistics of the proposal. Decide how to handle unexpected	201
23	crisis situations.	205
24	Finally, time your presentation so there will be no	215
25	unnecessary interruptions. Be organized, persistent, and	227
26	professional in your presentation. Prepare to be successful	239
27	by compiling clearly defined ideas to support your plans.	250

1 | 2 | 3 | 4 | 5 | 6 | 7 | 8 | 9 | 10 | 11 | 12

Situation: Today is February 10. You work at The Meadows at Ivy Glen, an assisted-living residence in Connecticut, for Ms. Angelica Casillas, director. Ms. Casillas has written the letter shown next. It should be sent to Mrs. Sandra Elliott, 1122 King Street, Greenwich, CT 06831. Ms. Casillas uses "Sincerely yours" as her standard complimentary closing, uses "Ms. Angelica Casillas" as her writer's identification, and prefers her business title typed under her name in the closing lines.

Correspondence
118-101
Business Letter in Block Style

¶ Thank you for your inquiry regarding the assisted-living facilities here at The Meadows at Ivy Glen. We know that you, like so many of our residents, wish to live as independently as possible for as long as possible. We're here to help bridge the gap between independent living and living with assistance.

¶ I've spoken with Molly Fitzgerald, your dear friend who has been a resident for the past six months. She speaks fondly of you and believes that you would be very happy living here. I would like to meet with you in person to evaluate which level of assistance would best meet your needs. Based on the information in your application, I believe that you would benefit from basic assistance with laundry, housekeeping, and medications.

¶ Please call me at your earliest convenience at 203-555-2435 to set up an appointment. I will be happy to give you a personal tour of our lovely grounds and review our range of services and facilities at that time. I will also arrange for Molly to join us for a leisurely lunch.

¶ Thank you again for your interest in The Meadows at Ivy Glen, and I look forward to meeting you very soon.

Report
118-95
Itinerary

Ms. Casillas will be attending the Assisted-Living Federation of America Conference in Philadelphia in June and has asked you to prepare an itinerary with the title ASSISTED-LIVING FEDERATION OF AMERICA CONFERENCE. Type Itinerary for Angelica Casillas as the subtitle. The inclusive trip dates are June 12–14.

THURSDAY, JUNE 12

7:09 a.m. - 8:28 a.m. Flight from New York city, La Guardia Airport, to Philadelphia; Continental 1282 (800-555-3668); eticket; Seat 24C; nonstop.

¶ Roz Jorgensen (Cell: 215-555-7635; Office: 215-555-2121) will meet your flight on Thursday, provide transportation during your visit, and arrange for transportation back on *to the airport* Saturday morning.

SS ¶ Philadelphia Courtyard Suites (215-555-1200)

King-sized bed, *non*smoking room; late arrival guaranteed; Reservation No. 35762-M1.

Friday, MARCH 13 ALFA Conference and Expo

Philadelphia Royale Hotel

1239 Market St.

Philadelphia, PA 19107

(215-555-1876)

8 p.m. Dinner at the Amalfi Eatery next door to the Philadelphia *Hotel* Royale

SAT., MARCH 14

6:30 a.m. Meet ~~Tom Clinton~~ *Roz Jorgensen* in the ~~hotel restaurant~~ *lobby* of the Philadelphia Courtyard Suites for transportation to the airport.

9:30 a.m.-10:40 *a*p.m. Flight from New York City to Philadelphia LaGuardia Airport; Continental 1541; e-ticket; Seat 11A; nonstop.

Report 118-96 Newsletter

Ms. Casillas has written the spring newsletter and has sketched out a masthead. She would like you to design the newsletter using these guidelines:

1. Set all margins at 0.75 inch.
2. For the masthead table, use clip art that is inspired by the spring season, and set the height to 2 inches.
3. Press ENTER 2 times outside the masthead table to begin typing the body.
4. Select a page color and font colors for titles and headings that complement the clip art.
5. Add or remove borders to enhance the design.
6. For the 2-column body, use automatic hyphenation, full justification, and Calibri 16 pt. so the residents will be able to read the newsletter more easily.
7. After you type the body, format the headings in bold and change the font to Cambria 24 pt.

Insert clip art that relates to spring. Set the height to 2 inches.

The Meadows at Ivy Glen

Spring 20--

With summer just around the corner, it's time to pull out your social calendars and reserve time for the great activities we have planned. Read on, and let Joyce Fontana know if you plan to participate.

Healthy Sleep

Are you getting enough sleep? Sleep debt might be keeping you from having the energy you need to participate in our fitness fun. Try this to improve your sleep time:

- Exercise early in the day to help you relax at night.
- Avoid coffee and nicotine as they can both disturb the quality of your sleep.
- Take a warm bath or shower just before bed.
- Establish a sleep pattern by going to bed and getting up at the same time each day.

Spring Fitness Fun

With the warmer months approaching, many folks are thinking about stepping up their exercise regimen. Join Ray Kirk in the rose garden for an energizing fitness walk beginning March 20 at 9 a.m.

Tee Time

Beginning April 1, join Alex Taylor on the putting green each day at 10-11 a.m. for two weeks for some golf instruction. At that time, you can sign up for excursions to our fabulous local golf courses.

Fat Burners

We've added new items to our menu that are low in calories but high in taste and are nutritious! Give them a try.

Skillbuilding and In-Basket Review — Government

119

Goals

- Demonstrate improved speed and accuracy while typing.
- Demonstrate acceptable language arts skills in spelling.
- Correctly format a business letter in block style, a ruled table, and an e-mail message.

A. WARMUP

alphabet	1	My grandfathers picked up quartz and a valuable onyx jewel.
frequent digraphs	2	at ate bat cat eat tat fat hat mat oat pat rat sat vat beat
easy	3	The girls may fish for cod in the lake or buy them in town.

Skillbuilding

B. MAP+: SYMBOL

Follow the GDP software directions for this exercise to improve keystroking accuracy.

PPP   PRETEST » PRACTICE » POSTTEST

PRETEST
Take a 1-minute timed writing.

C. PRETEST: Close Reaches

4	Casey hoped that we were not wasting good grub. After	11
5	the sun went down, he swiftly put the oleo and plums in the	23
6	cart. Bart opened a copy of an old book, Grant had a swim,	35
7	and Curt unearthed a sword in a hole in that grassy dune.	46

   1 | 2 | 3 | 4 | 5 | 6 | 7 | 8 | 9 | 10 | 11 | 12

PRACTICE
Speed Emphasis:
If you made no more than 1 error on the Pretest, type each *individual* line 2 times.
Accuracy Emphasis:
If you made 2 or more errors, type each *group* of lines (as though it were a paragraph) 2 times.

D. PRACTICE: Adjacent Keys

8	as mask last past easy vase beast waste toast reason castle
9	op hope flop open mops rope opera droop scope copier trophy
10	we west owed went weld weep weigh weary wedge wealth plowed
11	rt hurt port cart dirt fort court party start hearty parted

E. PRACTICE: Consecutive Fingers

12	sw swat swim swan swig swap swift sweet sword switch swirly
13	un tune spun unit dune punt under prune sunny hunter uneasy
14	gr grow grim grab grub grew great graze gripe greasy grassy
15	ol role oleo pool sold hole troll folly polka stolen oldest

POSTTEST
Repeat the Pretest timed
writing and compare
performance.

F. POSTTEST: Close Reaches

Language Arts

G. SPELLING

Type these frequently
misspelled words,
paying special attention
to any spelling problems
in each word.

16 practice continue regular entitled course resolution assist
17 weeks preparation purposes referred communication potential
18 environmental specifications original contractor associated
19 principal systems client excellent estimated administration
20 responsibility mentioned utilized materials criteria campus

21 It is the responsability of the administration to assist.

22 The principle client prepared the excellent specifications.

23 He mentioned that the critiria for the decision were clear.

24 The contractor associated with the project referred them.

25 He estamated that the potential for resolution was great.

26 I was told that weeks of reguler practice were required.

Document Processing

Situation: Today is April 25. You work as an administrative assistant at the Centers for Disease Control and Prevention for Ms. Tina Min, traveler health specialist. Ms. Min has written the letter shown next. The letter should be sent to Mr. Carlos De Leon, 539 Locust Street, Des Moines, IA 50309. Ms. Min uses "Sincerely" as her standard complimentary closing, uses "Ms. Tina Min" as her writer's identification, and prefers her title typed under her name in the closing lines.

**Correspondence
119-102**

Business Letter in
Block Style

¶ Your inquiry regarding vaccinations required for international travel was referred to me, and I am happy to answer your excellent questions. Preparation for a trip abroad does require a few weeks of planning to avoid potential problems associated with the timing of vaccinations.

¶ You mentioned that you are leaving in three months. Have you scheduled a visit to your doctor? Ideally, you should

(continued on next page)

set up a visit at least four to six weeks before your trip. Because so many environmental factors are at play when international travel is involved, you would be wise to go to a travel medicine provider specialist who can assist you with all details related to vaccinations. A principal responsibility of a provider of this type is to inform patients about the latest specifications for all health-related aspects of international travel.

¶ Please visit http://www.cdc.gov/travel.aspx for more helpful details and informative travel podcasts, or call CDC at 1-800-CDC-INFO. Enjoy your vacation, and I wish you continued good health.

Table
119-56
Ruled Table

HEALTH INFORMATION FOR TRAVELERS TO AUSTRALIA

Vaccination or Disease	Recommendations or Requirements for Vaccine-Preventable Disease
Routine	Recommended if you are not up to date with routine shots, such as measles/mumps/rubella (MMR) vaccine and the diphtheria/pertussis/tetanus (DPT) vaccine.
Hepatitis B	Recommended for all unvaccinated persons who might be exposed to blood or body fluids, have sexual contact with the local population, or be exposed through medical treatment, such as for an accident, even in developed countries, and for all adults for the purpose of protection from HBV infection.
Japanese encephalitis	Recommended if you visit Torres Strait and any zones associated with far Northern Australia.

This e-mail message should be sent to Regina Crawford, a close associate of Ms. Min. They address each other on a first-name basis. Ms. Min's e-mail address is tmin@cdc.gov. Her office phone number is 323-555-1876.

Correspondence
119-103
E-Mail Message

Hi, Regina:

¶ I mentioned to you yesterday that I am researching an inquiry related to health information for travelers to Australia. Please review the attached table, and let me know if it is complete or requires further information. I utilized the CDC Web site as my principal resource.

¶ Thank you, Regina, for your excellent assistance.

Skillbuilding and In-Basket Review—Software Development

Goals

- Type at least 50wpm/5'/5e.
- Correctly format a business report and a business letter in modified-block style.
- Successfully complete a Progress and Proofreading check with zero errors on the first scored attempt.

A. WARMUP

alphabet	1	Brown jars prevented the mixture from freezing too quickly.
number/symbol	2	coy20@cox.net 70% Hsu & Van 5/7 Win! ($4.93) *op. cit #16-8
easy	3	Jay may ask if my own neighbor is proficient in such a job.

Skillbuilding

B. 12-SECOND SPEED SPRINTS

Take three 12-second timed writings on each line.

4   Leo may visit the island by the giant oaks on his tan bike.
5   Nan may sign over the title to her car when she is in town.
6   She is so good at her work and likes what she does as well.
7   The old men may have a duel down by the lake at noon today.

    ' ' ' '5' ' ' '10' ' ' '15' ' ' '20' ' ' '25' ' ' '30' ' ' '35' ' ' '40' ' ' '45' ' ' '50' ' ' '55' ' ' '60

C. TECHNIQUE PRACTICE: BACKSPACE KEY

Type each line 2 times, using your Sem finger to strike the BACKSPACE key when you see the ← symbol. For example, type *kid*, backspace, and type *n*, thus changing *kid* to *kin*.

8   kid←n jag←m law←y oaf←k pat←y tag←m hid←m ice←y inn←k
9   fro←y mud←m rat←p sue←m flu←y bog←o gym←p big←n hug←m
10   dug←n and←y zag←p hex←y mow←p art←m tow←y age←o her←n
11   dad←m fur←n sin←p elf←k bar←n bud←m spa←y log←o fad←n

Goal: At least 50wpm/5'/5e

D. 5-MINUTE TIMED WRITING

```
12      With modern technology, it is possible to work at a    11
13 job full time and never leave your house. You can set up a   22
14 home office with a phone line, a facsimile, and a computer   34
15 system. Before choosing to work at home, however, you will   46
16 want to examine carefully your reasons for working at home.  58
17      Some people think about working at home so they can     69
18 have more time to spend with their families. Other people    80
19 like to have more flexibility in their work schedule. They   92
20 are looking for the opportunity to enjoy a better quality   104
21 of life or to participate in other activities.              113
22      There are some factors to consider before you make    123
23 the decision to work at home. You will want to consider the 135
24 ultimate cost of benefits that you could give up if you     147
25 change your place of work. You will want to check with your 159
26 employer to see if you are entitled to paid vacation days   170
27 and health insurance or if you can make contributions to    182
28 your retirement plan. Another factor to consider is the     193
29 limited contact with peers.                                 198
30      Before making the ultimate decision to work at home,  209
31 develop some realistic expectations of how you will spend   221
32 each day. Although you can organize your work to fit your   232
33 schedule, you will find the real challenge is to determine  244
34 a routine that works for you.                               250
```
```
  1 | 2 | 3 | 4 | 5 | 6 | 7 | 8 | 9 | 10 | 11 | 12
```

Document Processing

Situation: Today is September 1. You work for Software Solutions, a software development company in Washington. Your boss is Mr. Jeffrey Hill, software development manager. Mr. Hill has written the business report shown next and left it in your in-basket for you to type and format. The title of the report is "NEW PROJECT-DEVELOPMENT STRATEGIES." He prefers to use "Jeffrey Hill, Software Development Manager" as the report byline followed by the above date and the current year.

Report
120-97
Business Report

¶ In january our company was given the Bantam and Jones Project. As you know, this project was critical from a monetary stand point. We also knew that Bantam and Jones was carefully scrutinizing the quality of this project. Because this was a fixed-price project, and we had to deliver the work by the end of July in order to avoid huge customer fees. The problem was that the project was out sourced to a different project team in a different location, and the quality of the end product that was turned over to us for final review was questionable. As we later found out, the

(continued on next page)

project remote team had slowly disintegrated, and our home-based Seattle team had to come in at the last moment to rescue this project. In order to avoid this type of situation in the future, we will be implementing some new project-development ~~project~~ strategies.

TEAM COMMUNICATION

¶ The design phase of any project is always exciting and energizing. Our analysts are talking to our clients, software architects are meeting with developers and managers are coordinating the flow of communication. As the project progresses, communication breaks down. The analysts have ~~has~~ moved on to the next project, the architects have finished their design, and the manager is reviewing status reports only ~~occasionally~~ on occasion. The developers are working at a feverish pace to get the project out on time, and the team is no longer working in unison. The following changes are going to be implemented to avoid this type of communication breakdown:

¶ Pair Programming. Studies show that 2 programmers work harder on a given task than they would if they were working independently and produce 15 % fewer bugs. On all future projects, programmers will work in pairs to keep each other in check. One person will type in code while the other reviews each line of code as it is being typed at the same keyboard. We will provide programmers with "people-skills" training, since issues related to personal interaction are the biggest drawback to successful pair programming.

¶ **Customer Status Reports.** Our customer is going to become ~~be~~ an integral part of this team approach. A weekly status report will keep our customer in the loop and hold our teams accountable for both content and deadlines. The project manager will oversee and coordinate communication between all parties.

CONCLUSION

¶ Our company has earned a reputation for exceptional quality control in this industry. We are making a renewed commitment to maintain that reputation and hopefully surpass our own impressive standards. Another Status Report will be issued in 2 weeks regarding how these measures will be implemented and ~~on~~ what the effects will be for specific projects currently underway.

Correspondence
120-104
Business Letter in
Modified-Block Style

Mr. Hill has written the letter shown next. The letter should be sent to Ms. Patty Chang, Project Director, Silicon Valley Consulting Services, 15125 South Market Street, San Jose, CA 95113. Mr. Hill uses "Sincerely" as his standard complimentary closing and prefers his title typed under his name in the writer's identification. Add this postscript to the letter: Our president is very impressed with all your recommendations to date. Send a blind copy to Hong Chan Cho.

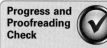
¶ Thank you for your prompt input as we have worked through ideas on the Bantam and Jones project. Your recommendations are sure to have a very powerful and positive impact on future projects.

¶ I have enclosed a copy of the report that was distributed to all Software Solutions employees involved in project development. Please review it and let me have your reactions. I feel confident that once our teams are comfortable with the new strategies and see the positive outcomes, they will embrace the recommendations.

¶ Please let me have your recommendations regarding training for our programmers as we implement our new pair-programming strategy. Here is a table with the proposed training schedule:

PROPOSED TRAINING SCHEDULE Pair Programming, Phase I	
Date	Workshop Topic
September 30	Communication Techniques
October 10	Tools for Pair Programming
October 20	Refactoring to Patterns
October 30	Design Patterns

¶ I need your final recommendations no later than September 15. I would assume that it makes more sense to begin with a workshop on communications techniques since the typical reaction to change by most employees is resistance. Perhaps if our programmers realize that the transition to pair programming will take place in phases, they will be more likely to accept the new approach and react positively.

(continued on next page)

¶ We need to arrange a face-to-face meeting for in-depth discussions on this very important transition. The following individuals will be invited to attend as they will play key roles during this transitional period:

- Hong Chan Cho
- Alicia King
- Barry Kidd
- Steven Cozell
- Colleen Cunningham

¶ Please call me when you receive this letter so that we can make the proper arrangements and coordinate schedules.

5-Minute Timed Writing

1	The potential to reach your career goals has never	10
2	been better. The person who will move forward in a career	22
3	is the one who will make the bold moves to follow his or	33
4	her dreams. He or she will have the required attributes of	45
5	initiative and motivation to put forth maximum efforts in	57
6	order to realize a fulfilling position.	65
7	If you want to get ahead in the highly competitive	75
8	business world today, you need a personal coach or mentor	87
9	who is experienced in motivating people who want to reach	98
10	their potential. You may be afraid to go after your dream	110
11	career because you are afraid of failure. Your personal	121
12	mentor will help you to minimize any problems you incur. He	132
13	or she will encourage you to strive for more.	142
14	When you decide to work with a qualified coach, you	153
15	are investing in yourself. You can trust your coach to help	165
16	you through this joyful process of expanding your horizons	177
17	until you reach your goals.	182
18	When you think you have reached your limit, your coach	194
19	will make suggestions for additional improvement. He or she	206
20	will present the strategies you can use to be successful.	217
21	Your coach will guide you in making the critical decisions	229
22	for advancing your career. The final decision to improve	240
23	your skills and be successful is yours, however.	250

1 | 2 | 3 | 4 | 5 | 6 | 7 | 8 | 9 | 10 | 11 | 12

Form Test
6-17
Memo Template

Type this memo using the preselected blank memo template that opens automatically.

To: Brian Collins, Director of human resources

CC: Vincent Alvarez, President

From: April Mendoza, Chair Committee

Date: May 15, 20--

Re: Sierra Madre Health Run

The Sierra Madre Health Run is being scheduled again this year on June 17, 20--. As you may recall, last year we were able to raise $12,000 for the Sierra Madre home for youth. Since its inception 5 years ago, we have raised over $75,00 that has gone directly to the building fund at the home.

(continued on next page)

We ^Thank you for participating in this annual event and a special thanks goes to all those who donated ~~there~~ *their* time and effort to make this event such a ~~tremendous~~ success over the years.

As ^Human ^Resources ^Director, ~~we~~ hope (you'll) again encourage all your employe*e*s to participate in the Health Run. We hope *we will be able* to exceed last year's donations by 10%. With Crosby ̲international's participation, we know that will be a *very* ^reasonable goal to reach.

urs

Your completed resume may look different from the one shown. This table is shown with "View Gridlines" active.

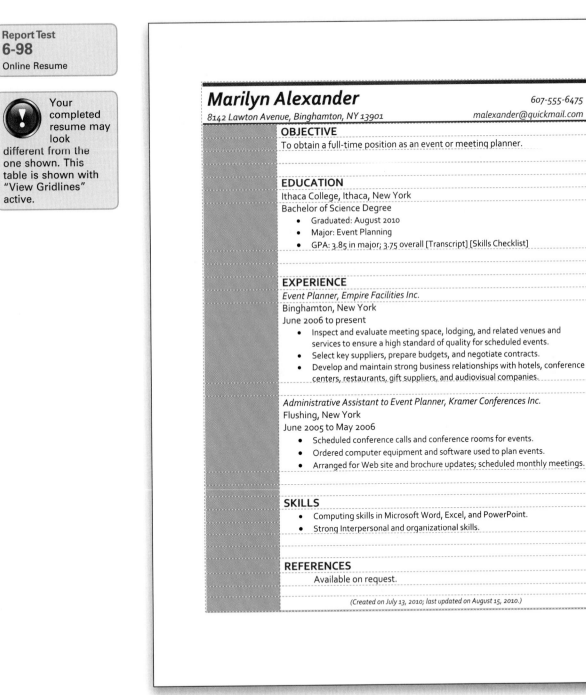

Marilyn Alexander

8142 Lawton Avenue, Binghamton, NY 13901

607-555-6475
malexander@quickmail.com

OBJECTIVE

To obtain a full-time position as an event or meeting planner.

EDUCATION

Ithaca College, Ithaca, New York
Bachelor of Science Degree
- Graduated: August 2010
- Major: Event Planning
- GPA: 3.85 in major; 3.75 overall [Transcript] [Skills Checklist]

EXPERIENCE

Event Planner, Empire Facilities Inc.
Binghamton, New York
June 2006 to present
- Inspect and evaluate meeting space, lodging, and related venues and services to ensure a high standard of quality for scheduled events.
- Select key suppliers, prepare budgets, and negotiate contracts.
- Develop and maintain strong business relationships with hotels, conference centers, restaurants, gift suppliers, and audiovisual companies.

Administrative Assistant to Event Planner, Kramer Conferences Inc.
Flushing, New York
June 2005 to May 2006
- Scheduled conference calls and conference rooms for events.
- Ordered computer equipment and software used to plan events.
- Arranged for Web site and brochure updates; scheduled monthly meetings.

SKILLS

- Computing skills in Microsoft Word, Excel, and PowerPoint.
- Strong Interpersonal and organizational skills.

REFERENCES

Available on request.

(Created on July 13, 2010; last updated on August 15, 2010.)

Use a predesigned table style of your choice.

WordArt

Page color

Calibri 24 pt Bold

Calibri 20 pt

Calibri 16 pt Bold

Calibri 14 pt

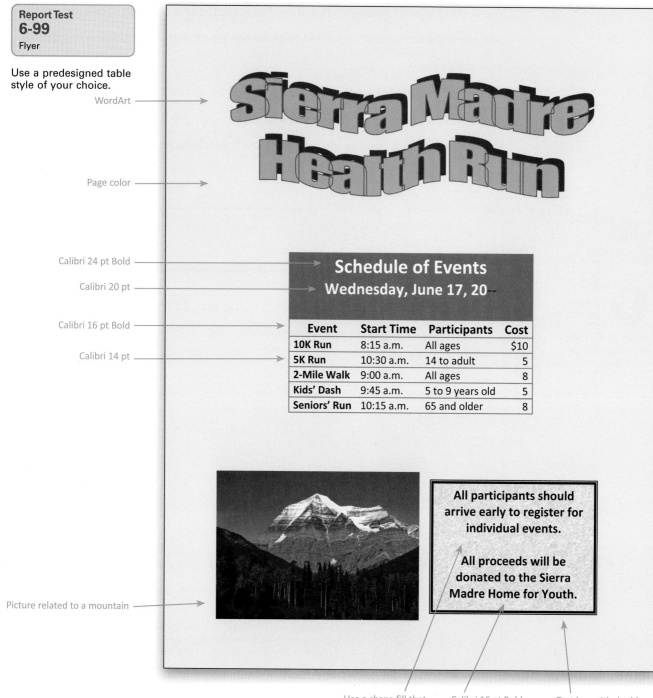

Sierra Madre Health Run

Schedule of Events
Wednesday, June 17, 20--

Event	Start Time	Participants	Cost
10K Run	8:15 a.m.	All ages	$10
5K Run	10:30 a.m.	14 to adult	5
2-Mile Walk	9:00 a.m.	All ages	8
Kids' Dash	9:45 a.m.	5 to 9 years old	5
Seniors' Run	10:15 a.m.	65 and older	8

Picture related to a mountain

All participants should arrive early to register for individual events.

All proceeds will be donated to the Sierra Madre Home for Youth.

Use a shape fill that complements the page color

Calibri 16 pt Bold

Text box with double line border

Skillbuilding

Skillbuilding

Progressive Practice: Alphabet

This skillbuilding routine contains a series of 30-second timed writings that range from 16 wpm to 104 wpm. The first time you use these timed writings, take a 1-minute timed writing with 3 or fewer errors on the Entry Timed Writing paragraph. Push moderately for speed.

Select a passage that is 1 to 2 wpm *higher* than your Entry Timed Writing speed. Then take up to six 30-second timed writings on the passage.

Your goal each time is to complete the passage within 30 seconds with no errors. When you have achieved your goal, move on to the next passage and repeat the procedure.

Entry Timed Writing

```
      Bev was very lucky when she found extra quality in the   11
home she was buying. She quietly told the builder that she     23
was extremely satisfied with the work done on her new home.    35
The builder said she can move into her new house next month.   47
     1 | 2 | 3 | 4 | 5 | 6 | 7 | 8 | 9 | 10 | 11 | 12
```

16 wpm

```
The author is the creator of a document.
```

18 wpm

```
Open means to access a previously saved file.
```

20 wpm

```
A byte represents one character to every computer.
```

22 wpm

```
Hard copy is usually text that is printed out on paper.
```

24 wpm

```
Soft copy is text that is displayed on your computer
screen.
```

26 wpm

```
Memory is that part of your word processor that stores your
data.
```

28 wpm

```
The menu is a list of choices used to guide a user through
a function.
```

30 wpm

```
A sheet feeder is a device that will insert sheets of paper
into a printer.
```

32 wpm

```
An icon is a small picture that illustrates a function or
an object in software.
```

34 wpm

```
Active icons on your desktop represent the programs that
can be run on your computer.
```

Skillbuilding

36 wpm
To execute means to perform an action specified by the user or also by a computer program.

38 wpm
Output is the result of a word processing operation. It can be either printed or magnetic form.

40 wpm
Format refers to the physical features which affect the appearance and arrangement of your document.

42 wpm
A font is a type style of a particular size or kind that includes letters, numbers, or punctuation marks.

44 wpm
Ergonomics is the science of adapting working conditions or equipment to meet the physical needs of employees.

46 wpm
Home position is the starting position of a document; it is typically the upper left corner of the display monitor.

48 wpm
The purpose of a virus checker is to find those programs that may cause your computer to stop working as you want it to.

50 wpm
An optical scanner is a device that can read text and enter it into a word processor without the need to type the data again.

52 wpm
Hardware refers to all the physical equipment you use while computing, such as the display screen, keyboard, printer, and scanner.

54 wpm
A peripheral device is any piece of equipment that will extend the capabilities of a computer system but is not required for operation.

56 wpm
A split screen displays two or more different images at the same time; it can, for example, display two different pages of a legal document.

58 wpm
To defrag the computer means that you are reorganizing the files so that related files will be located in the same general place on a hard drive.

60 wpm
With the click of a mouse, one can use a button bar or a toolbar for fast access to features that are frequently applied when using a Windows program.

Skillbuilding

62 wpm

Gadgets are typically controls which are placed on your desktop to allow you to have immediate access to frequently used information such as time and date.

64 wpm

Turnaround time is the length of time needed for a document to be keyboarded, edited, proofread, corrected if required, printed, and returned to the originator.

66 wpm

A local area network is a system that uses cable or another means to allow high-speed communication among many kinds of electronic equipment within particular areas.

68 wpm

To search and replace means to direct the word processor to locate a character, word, or group of words wherever it occurs in the document and replace it with newer text.

70 wpm

Indexing is the ability of a word processor to accumulate a list of words that appear in a document, including page numbers, and then print a revised list in alphabetic order.

72 wpm

When a program needs information from you, a dialog box will appear on the desktop. Once the dialog box appears, you must identify the option you desire and then choose the option.

74 wpm

A facsimile is an exact copy of a document, and it is also a process by which images, such as typed letters, graphs, and signatures, are scanned, transmitted, and then printed on paper.

76 wpm

Compatibility refers to when a computer is able to share information with other computers or also to communicate with different hardware. It could be accomplished by other methods.

78 wpm

Some operators like to personalize their desktops when they use Windows by making various changes. For example, they can change their screen colors or the pointer so that they will have more fun.

80 wpm

Wraparound is the ability of a word processor to move words from one line to another line and from one page to the next page as a result of inserting and deleting text or changing the size of margins.

82 wpm

It is possible when using Windows to evaluate the contents of different directories on the screen at the very same time. You can then choose to copy or move a particular file from one directory to another.

Skillbuilding

84 wpm

List processing is a capability of a word processor to keep lists of data that can be updated and sorted in alphabetic or numeric order. A list can also be added to any document that is stored in your computer.

86 wpm

A computer is a device that accepts data that are input and then processes those data to produce the output. A computer performs its work by using various stored programs that provide all the necessary instructions.

88 wpm

A word processor is more than a program that can process words. Word processors have many other capabilities such as merging documents; executing some mathematical equations; and inserting clip art, shapes, and pictures.

90 wpm

Help and support in Windows are available to assist you in finding answers to questions you may have about just how the computer functions. You can find help on topics like security, files, folders, printing, and maintenance.

92 wpm

When you want to look at the contents of two windows when using Windows, you might want to reduce the window size. Do this by pointing to a border or a corner of a window and dragging it until the window is the size that you want.

94 wpm

Scrolling means to display a very large quantity of text by rolling it horizontally or vertically past your display screen. As text disappears from the top section of your screen, new text will appear in the bottom area of your screen.

96 wpm

You have several options available to you when you print a document. For example, you can determine which printer to use, the pages you desire to print, the number of copies to be printed, the print quality desired, and the paper size used.

98 wpm

An ink-jet printer and a laser printer are popular printers used in a home office. Many users prefer an ink-jet printer because it is not as expensive to buy. But a laser printer provides a higher-quality print and is often the preferred choice.

Skillbuilding

100 wpm

E-mail, text messaging, cell phones, and chat rooms have enabled us to communicate quickly with people all around the globe. We can transmit a call or a message on the spur of the moment and receive a response to our call or message almost instantly.

102 wpm

Many different graphics software programs have been brought on the market in past years. These programs can be very powerful in helping with a business presentation. If there is a requirement to share data, using programs like these could be very helpful.

104 wpm

Voice mail is an essential service used by many people in the business world. This technology enables anyone placing a call to your phone to leave you a message if you cannot answer it at that time. This unique feature can help many workers be more productive.

Progressive Practice: Numbers

This skillbuilding routine contains a series of 30-second timed writings that range from 16 wpm to 80 wpm. The first time you use these timed writings, take a 1-minute timed writing with 3 or fewer errors on the Entry Timed Writing paragraph. Push moderately for speed.

Select a passage that is 1 to 2 wpm *higher* than your Entry Timed Writing speed. Then take up to six 30-second timed writings on the passage.

Your goal each time is to complete the passage within 30 seconds with no errors. When you have achieved your goal, move on to the next passage and repeat the procedure.

Entry Timed Writing

```
        Their bags were filled with 10 sets of jars, 23 cookie   11
cutters, 4 baking pans, 6 coffee mugs, 25 plates, 9 dessert   23
plates, 7 soup bowls, 125 recipe cards, and 8 recipe boxes.   35
David delivered these 217 items to 20487 Mountain Boulevard.  47
   1  |  2  |  3  |  4  |  5  |  6  |  7  |  8  |  9  |  10  |  11  |  12
```

16 wpm

There are 37 chairs in Rooms 24 and 156.

18 wpm

About 10 of the 39 boxes were torn on June 8.

20 wpm

Only 3 papers had errors on pages 28, 40, and 197.

22 wpm

My 46 letters were sent on May 10, June 3, and June 27.

24 wpm

The 79 freshmen, 86 juniors, and 54 seniors arrived at home.

26 wpm

The school needs 150 pens, 38 reams of paper, and 42 new folders.

28 wpm

Only 1 or 2 of the 305 new books had errors on pages 46, 178, and 192.

30 wpm

They met 10 of the 23 tennis players who received 4 awards from 5 trainers.

32 wpm

Those 8 vans carried 75 passengers on the first trip and 64 on the next 3 trips.

34 wpm

I saw 2 eagles on Route 86 and then 4 eagles on Route 53 at 9 a.m. on Monday, May 10.

Skillbuilding

36 wpm

The 17 firms produced 50 of the 62 records that received awards for 3 of the 4 categories.

38 wpm

The 12 trucks hauled 87 cows, 65 horses, and 49 pigs to the farm, which was 30 miles northeast.

40 wpm

She moved from 87 Bayview Drive to 659 Bay Street and then 3 blocks south to 4012 Gulbranson Avenue.

42 wpm

My 2 or 3 buyers ordered 5 dozen in sizes 6, 7, 8, and 9 after the 10 to 14 percent discounts were added.

44 wpm

There were 134 men and 121 women waiting in line at Gate 206 for the 58 to 79 tickets to the Cape Cod concert.

46 wpm

Steve had listed 5, 6, or 7 items on Purchase Order 243 when he saw that Purchase Requisition 89 contained 10 more.

48 wpm

Your items numbered 278 will sell for about 90 percent of the value of the 16 items that have code numbers shown as 435.

50 wpm

The managers stated that 98 of those 750 randomly selected new valves had about 264 defects, far exceeding the usual 31 norm.

52 wpm

Half of the 625 volunteers received over 90 percent of the charity pledges. Approximately 38 of the 147 agencies might enjoy this.

54 wpm

Merico hired 94 part-time workers to help the 378 full-time employees during the 62-day period when sales go up by 150 percent or more.

56 wpm

Kaye only hit 1 for 4 in the first 29 games after an 8-game streak in which she batted 3 for 4. She then hit at a .570 average for 16 games.

58 wpm

The mail carrier delivered 98 letters during the week to 734 Oak Street and also took 52 letters to 610 Faulkner Road as he returned on Route 58.

60 wpm

Pat said that about 1 in 5 of the 379 swimmers had a chance of being among the top 20. The best 6 of these 48 divers will receive special recognition.

Skillbuilding

62 wpm

It rained from 3 to 6 inches, and 18 of those 20 farmers were fearful that 4 to 7 inches more would flood about 95 acres along 3 miles of the new Route 79.

64 wpm

Those 17 sacks weighed 48 pounds, more than the 30 pounds that I had thought. All 24 believe the 92-pound bag is at least 15 or 16 pounds above its true weight.

66 wpm

They bought 7 of the 8 options for 54 of the 63 vehicles last month. They now have over 120 dump trucks for use in 9 of the 15 new regions in the big 20-county area.

68 wpm

Andy was 8 or 9 years old when they moved to 612 Glendale Street and away from the 700 block of Henry Lane, which is about 45 miles directly west of Boca Raton, FL 33434.

70 wpm

Doug had read 575 pages in the 760-page book by August 30; Darlene had read only 468 pages. Darlene has read 29 of those optional books since October 19, and Doug has read 18.

72 wpm

The school district has 985 elementary students, 507 middle school students, and 463 high school students. This total represents the greatest increase in total enrollment for us.

74 wpm

Attendance at last year's meeting was 10,835. Your goal for this year is to have 11,764 people. This might enable us to plan for an increase of 929 participants, a rise of 8.57 percent.

76 wpm

David's firm has 158 stores, located in 109 cities in the South. The company employs 3,540 males and 2,624 females, a total of 6,164 employees. About 4,750 of those employees work part-time.

78 wpm

Memberships were as follows: 98 members in the Drama Guild, 90 members in Zeta Tau, 82 members in Theta Phi, 75 in the Bowling Club, and 136 in the Ski Club. This meant that 481 joined the group.

80 wpm

The association had 684 members from the South, 830 members from the North, 1,023 members from the East, and 751 from the West. This total membership was 3,288; these numbers increased by 9.8 percent.

Skillbuilding

Paced Practice

The Paced Practice skillbuilding routine builds speed and accuracy in short, easy steps by using individualized goals and immediate feedback. You may use this program at any time after completing Lesson 9.

This section contains a series of 2-minute timed writings for speeds ranging from 16 wpm to 96 wpm. The first time you use these timed writings, take the 1-minute Entry Timed Writing with 2 or fewer uncorrected errors to establish your base speed.

Select a passage that is 2 wpm higher than your Entry Timed Writing speed. Then use this two-stage practice pattern to achieve each speed goal: (1) concentrate on speed and (2) work on accuracy.

Speed Goal. To determine your speed goal, take three 2-minute timed writings in total. Your goal each time is to complete the passage in 2 minutes without regard to errors. When you have achieved your speed goal, work on accuracy.

Accuracy Goal. To type accurately, you need to slow down—just a bit. Therefore, to reach your accuracy goal, drop back 2 wpm from the previous passage. Take consecutive timed writings on this passage until you can complete the passage in 2 minutes with no more than 2 errors.

For example, if you achieved a speed goal of 54 wpm, you should then work on an accuracy goal of 52 wpm. When you have achieved 52 wpm for accuracy, move up 4 wpm (for example, to the 56-wpm passage) and work for speed again.

Entry Timed Writing

If you can dream it, you can live it. Just follow your heart. There are many careers, which range from the mundane to the exotic to the sublime.

Start your career planning now by quizzing yourself about your talents, skills, and personal interests.

1 | 2 | 3 | 4 | 5 | 6 | 7 | 8 | 9 | 10 | 11 | 12

16 wpm

Your future is now, so you must seize every day.

After exploring your interests, quickly check the sixteen career clusters for a wide range of potential jobs.

18 wpm

When exploring various career options, think about what a job means for you.

Recognize that it can mean what you do just to earn money or what you find quite challenging overall.

20 wpm

If you acquire a job that you enjoy, then it means even more than simply earning an excellent wage.

It also means making a contribution, taking pride in your work, and utilizing all of your talents.

Skillbuilding

22 wpm

What is the difference between a job and a career? Think carefully. A job is work that you have to do for money.

A career is a sequence of related jobs that optimize your interests, experience, knowledge, and training.

24 wpm

Learn all about the world of work by looking at the sixteen career clusters. Most jobs are included in one of the clusters that have been organized by the government.

When exploring careers, list all the unique clusters that interest you.

26 wpm

Once you identify the career clusters that interest you, look at the jobs that are within each cluster.

Analyze exactly what skills and aptitudes are needed, what training is required, what the work setting is like, and what your chances for advancement are.

28 wpm

Use your career center and your school or a public library to research your career choice. Go on the Internet, and ask experts for their unique views of certain careers.

As you gather data about your job options, you might learn about new career options that are on the horizon.

30 wpm

You must gain insight into a career. You can become a volunteer, sign up for an internship, or even work in a part-time job in the field.

You will become more familiar with a specific job while you develop your skills. You will quickly gain prized experience, whether you choose that career or not.

Skillbuilding

32 wpm

No matter which path you choose, strive for a high level of pride in yourself and in your job. Your image is affected by what other people think of you as well as by what you think of yourself.

Next, analyze your level of confidence. If you have any self-doubts, strive to acquire more self-confidence and self-esteem.

34 wpm

Confidence is required for a positive attitude, and a positive attitude is required for success at work. While you may not control all that happens at work, recognize that you must control how you react to what happens.

Become more confident and cultivate positive thoughts, which will provide you with extra power in life and on the job.

36 wpm

Quite a few factors lead to success on the job. People who have analyzed these factors say that it is the personal traits one exhibits that determine who is promoted and who is not.

One of the best traits a person can have is the trait of being likable. That means that you are honest, loyal, courteous, thoughtful, pleasant, kind, considerate, and positive.

38 wpm

If you are likable, you will relate well with most people. If you have excellent social contact with others, it will humanize the workplace and make your work there more enjoyable. Think of all the hours you are required to spend with one another each day.

If you show that you are willing to collaborate with your coworkers, most likely you will also receive their cooperation.

Skillbuilding

40 wpm

Cooperation begins on the first day of your new job. When you work for a firm, you quickly become a part of that team. Meeting people and learning new skills can be quite exciting.

For some people, though, a new situation can trigger some anxiety. The best advice is to remain calm, do your job with zeal, learn the workplace policies, be flexible, avoid being too critical, and always be positive.

42 wpm

When you begin a new job, even if you have recently received your college degree, chances are you will start at the bottom of the organizational chart. Each of us has to start somewhere. Do not despair or become lazy.

With hard work, you should start your climb up the corporate ladder. If you are smart, you will quietly take on even the most tedious task, take everything in stride, and exercise any chance to learn.

44 wpm

If you think learning is restricted to an academic setting, think again. You have much to learn on the job, even if it is a position for which you have been trained.

As a new employee, you will not be expected to know everything. When necessary, do not hesitate to ask your employer questions. Learn all you can about your job and the company. Capitalize on the new information to enhance your job performance and to build toward success.

46 wpm

Begin every valuable workday by prioritizing all of your tasks. Decide which tasks must be done immediately and which can wait. List the most important items first; then determine the order in which each item must be done.

After you complete a task, then quickly cross it off your priority list. Maximize your time; that is, do not put off work you should do. If a job must be done, just do it. You will stay on top of your list when you utilize time wisely.

Skillbuilding

48 wpm

Do not let the phone control your time. Learn how to manage all your phone calls. Phone calls can be extremely distracting from other duties, so be jealous of your quiet time. When making a phone call, organize the topics you want to discuss. Gather needed supplies such as pencils, papers, and files.

Set a time limit and stick to the topic. Give concise answers, summarize the points discussed, and end your talk politely. Efficient phone usage will help you manage your time.

50 wpm

As with everything, practice makes perfect, but along the way, we have all made some mistakes. Realize that the difference between successful people and those who are less successful is not that the successful people make fewer mistakes. It is just that they will never quit.

Instead of letting mistakes bring you down, use your mistakes as opportunities to grow. If you make a mistake, be patient with yourself. You might be able to fix your mistake. Look for success to be just around the corner.

52 wpm

Be patient as you learn how to take care of problems and accept criticism. Accepting criticism may be quite a test for you. Still, it is vital to many of us at work. Criticism that is given in a way to help you learn, expand, or grow is called constructive criticism.

If you look at criticism as being helpful, it will be easier to deal with. You might be amazed to learn that some people welcome it since it teaches them the best way to succeed on the job. Try to improve how you accept helpful criticism from others.

Skillbuilding

54 wpm

People experience continuous growth during a career. Goal setting is a key tool to acquire for any job. Some people believe that goals provide the motivation we need to get to the place we want to be. Setting goals encourages greater achievements. The higher that we set our goals, the greater the effort we need to reach them.

Each time we reach a target or come closer to a goal, we should realize an increase in our confidence and in our performance, which leads to greater accomplishments. And the cycle continues to spiral for years.

56 wpm

One goal we must all strive for is punctuality. When employees are absent or just tardy, it costs the company money. If you are frequently tardy or absent, others have to do extra work to cover for you. If you are absent often, your peers may begin to resent you, which causes everyone stress in the department.

Being late and missing work might penalize your own relationship with your manager and have a negative effect on your career. To avoid such potential problems, develop a personal plan to ensure that you arrive every day on time and ready to work.

58 wpm

To hold a job is a chief part of being an adult. Some people start their work careers as teens. From the start, a range of work habits are developed that are as crucial to success as the actual job skills and knowledge that someone brings to his or her job.

What traits are expected of workers? What do employers look for when they rate their own workers? Vital personal traits would include being confident, helpful, positive, and loyal. If you are also kind, passionate, and organized, you may now have many of these qualities that employers value most of all in their staffs.

Skillbuilding

60 wpm

Being dependable is a required work trait. If a job must be done by a special time, the manager will be pleased to learn that his or her workers are going to meet that deadline. Those who are dependable learn to utilize their time to attain maximum results. Loyal workers can also be counted on, they have good attendance records, they are well prepared, and they get to work on time and ready to start.

If the firm wants to meet its goals, it must have a team of loyal and dependable workers. You, your peers, your supervisors, and your managers are all team members who work to reach their goals.

62 wpm

The ability to organize is an important quality for the worker who would like to display good work habits. The worker should have the ability to plan the work that needs to be done and then to be able to execute that plan in a timely manner.

An employer requires a competent worker to be well organized. If the office worker is efficient, he or she handles requests swiftly and deals with messages without delay. The organized worker does not allow his or her work to accumulate on the desk. Also, the organized worker will return all phone calls quickly and make lists of the jobs that still need to be done each day.

Skillbuilding

64 wpm

Efficiency is one work habit that is important. The efficient worker does each task quickly and starts work on the next task eagerly. He or she thinks about ways to save steps or time. For example, an efficient worker may plan just one trip to the copier with a number of copying jobs rather than take many trips to do each separate job.

Being efficient also means that you have all of the required supplies to finish each job. An efficient worker zips along on each project, uses his or her time wisely, and then stays focused on that one task. With careful and detailed planning, a worker who is efficient can finish tasks in less time.

66 wpm

Cooperation is another ideal work habit. It begins on the first day of the job and means that you quietly think of all team members when you make a decision. A person who cooperates is willing to do what is needed for the good of the whole group. For you to be a team player, you must take the extra steps to cooperate.

Cooperation may mean that you need to be a good sport if you are asked to do something you would rather not do. It may mean that you have to correct some mistakes made by another person in the office. When each employee has the interests of the company at heart and works well with other workers, then everyone is a good corporate citizen.

Skillbuilding

68 wpm

Enthusiasm is still another work trait that is eagerly sought after by employers. If you are enthusiastic, then you have lots of positive energy. This is reflected in your actions toward your work, coworkers, and employer. It has been noted that eagerness can be catching. If you show you are excited to try any project, then you may quickly not only achieve the highest praise but also will be considered for career advancement.

How much enthusiasm do you show at the workplace? Do you encourage people or complain to people? There should always be lots of good jobs for workers who are known to have a wealth of zeal and a positive approach to the jobs that they are assigned.

70 wpm

Acceptance is a work trait required of all of us. In the work world of today, each business includes both men and women of different religions, races, cultures, skills, and beliefs. You will interact with many types of people as customers, coworkers, and owners. Treat each one fairly, openly, and honestly.

All types of prejudice are hurtful, hateful, and, in short, unacceptable. Prejudice is not allowed at work. Each of us must learn to accept and even prize the many kinds of differences that are exhibited by all of us. Since so many diverse groups work side by side in the work world, it is vital that all workers maintain a high degree of shared insights. Embrace each of us for who we are.

Skillbuilding

72 wpm

It can be concluded that certain work habits or traits should play the major role in deciding the success of all workers. Most managers would be quick to agree on the high importance of these traits. It is most likely that these habits would be analyzed on performance appraisal forms. Promotions, pay increases, new duties, and your future with the company may be based on these yearly job assessments.

You should request regular job performance assessments even if your company does not conduct them. This feedback might then expand your job skills and career development by helping you grow. If you always look for ways to improve your work habits and skills, you will enjoy success in the world of work and beyond.

74 wpm

You can be sure that no matter where you work, you will use some form of technology. Almost every business depends on computers. Firms use such devices as voice mail, fax machines, cell phones, and personal digital assistants. These tools help us to do our work quickly and efficiently. They also take some of the drudgery out of our lives.

One result of the use of these tools is globalization, which means worldwide communication links between people. Our world has turned into one global village. We should expand our thinking beyond the office walls. We must become aware of what happens in other parts of the world. These events may directly affect you and your job. The more you know, the more valuable you will become to a company.

Skillbuilding

76 wpm

Each advance in technology has had an effect on all aspects of our lives. For example, the dawn of the age of the Internet has changed how people get and send data. It is the largest data network in the world. It is called the information superhighway since it is a vast network of big computers that can link people and resources around the world. It is an exciting medium to help you access current data and be more useful on the job and at home.

Without a doubt, we are all globally linked, and data technology services can support those links. The industry offers different job opportunities in dozens of fields. Keep in mind that keyboarding skills are required in this field as well as in most others. Touch-typing skills are just assumed in most jobs.

78 wpm

It is amazing to learn about the many jobs in which keyboarding skill is needed today. The use of a computer keyboard by executive chefs is a prime example. The chefs in large restaurants must prepare parts or all of the meals served while they direct the work of their staff of chefs, cooks, and others in and near the kitchens.

The computer has become a prime tool for a wide range of tasks, including tracking stocks of their food supplies. By seeing which items are favorites and which items are not requested, the chef can work out the food requirements, order food, and supervise the purchase of foods. Also, the computer has proved to be a very practical tool for such tasks as helping to plan budgets, prepare purchase orders for vendors, write menus, and print reports.

Skillbuilding

80 wpm

Advanced technology has opened the doors to a wide variety of amazing new products and services to sell. It seems that the more complex the products get, the higher the price of the products is and that the larger the sales commission is, the stiffer the competition is. To sell a technical product requires detailed product knowledge, good verbal skills, smooth sales rapport, and also expert typing skills.

Business favors those who have special training. For example, a pharmacy company may choose a person who has a strong knowledge of chemistry to sell its products. Sales is for those who enjoy using their command of persuasion to make the sales. The potential for good pay and commissions is quite high for the salesperson who is trained well. You should perhaps think about a job in sales.

82 wpm

As you travel about in your sales job or type a report at the office or create the Friday night pizza special for your new diner, you should always plan to put safety first. Accidents happen, but they do not have to happen regularly or to have such severe results. Accidents cost businesses billions of dollars each year in medical expenses, lost wages, and insurance claims.

Part of your job is to make certain that you are not one of the millions of people injured on the job each year. You may believe you work in a safe place, but accidents occur in all types of businesses. A few careless people cause most accidents, so ensure your safety on the job. Safety does not just happen. It is the result of the very careful awareness of those people who plan and put into action a safety program that benefits everyone.

Skillbuilding

84 wpm

In the world of today, you need more than the needed skills or the personal qualities to succeed on the job. Managers also expect all workers to have ethics. Ethics are the codes of conduct that tell a person or a group how to act. Workers who act ethically do not lie, cheat, or steal. They are honest and fair in all their dealings with others. In short, they are good citizens.

Workers who act ethically gain a good reputation for themselves and for their companies. They are known to be dependable. Unethical behavior can have a spiraling effect. A single act can do a lot of damage. Even if you have not held a job yet, you have had some experience with ethical problems. Life is full of a range of occasions to behave ethically. Do the right thing when faced with decisions. The ethics you follow will carry over into the workplace.

86 wpm

Now that you know what will be expected of you on the job, how do you make sure you will get the job in the first place? Almost everyone has at least once gone through the interview process for a job. For some, the interview is a traumatic event, but it does not have to be so stressful. Research is the key. Learn about the firm with whom you are seeking a job. Form a list of questions to ask. Interviews also provide you the chance to interview the organization.

Take a folder of items with you. Include copies of your data sheet with a list of three or more professional references, your academic transcript, and your certificates and licenses. Be sure to wear appropriate business attire. The outcome of the interview will be positive if you have enthusiasm for the job, match your skills to the needs of the company, ask relevant questions, and listen.

Skillbuilding

88 wpm

How can you be the strongest candidate for the job? Be sure that your skills in reading, writing, math, speaking, and listening are strong. These skills should enable you to listen well and communicate clearly, not only during the job interview but also at your place of work. This exchange of information between a sender and a receiver is known as communication.

It does not matter which career you choose; you will still spend most of your time using these basic skills to communicate with others. You should use the skills as tools to gain information, solve problems, and share ideas. You can also use these skills to help you meet the needs of your customers. Most of the new jobs in the next few years will be in industries that will require direct customer contact. Do not jeopardize your chances for success; make sure that you are able to communicate well with others.

90 wpm

Writing well can help you gain a competitive edge in your job search and throughout your career. Most of us have had occasion to write business letters whether to apply for a job, to comment on a product or service, or to place an order. Often it seems easy to sit back and let our thoughts flow freely. At other times, we seem to struggle to find the best words to use to express our thoughts in precisely the correct way. We all sometimes have these issues.

Writing skills can improve with practice. Use these principles to develop your writing skills. Try to use words that you would be comfortable using in person. Use words that are simple, direct, kind, and confident. When it is possible, use words that emphasize only the positive side. Remember to proofread your work. Well-organized thoughts and proper grammar, spelling, and punctuation will show your reader that you care about quality.

Skillbuilding

92 wpm

Listening is such a vital part of the communication process. It is the key for learning, getting along, and forming rapport. Do you think that you are an active or a passive listener? Listening should not be just a passive process. To listen actively means to analyze what is being said and to interpret what it means. Active listening makes you a more effective worker because you react to what you have heard as well as to what you have not heard.

Study these steps to expand your listening skills: Do not cut people off; let them finish their remarks before you speak. If what they said is unclear, write down your questions, and wait for the discussion to be finished until you ask them. Reduce personal and environmental noise so you can focus on the message. Keep an open mind. Remain attentive and maintain eye contact when possible. By using these skills, you can become even more confident and more effective.

94 wpm

Speaking is also a form of communication. In the world of work, speaking is an important way in which to share information. Regardless of whether you are speaking to an audience of one or one hundred, you will want to be sure that your listeners hear your message. Be clear about your purpose, your audience, and your subject. A purpose is the overall goal or reason for speaking. An audience is anyone who receives information. The subject is the main topic or key idea that you wish to analyze.

Research your subject. Use specific facts and examples to give you credibility. As you speak, be brief and direct. Progress logically from point to point. Speak slowly and pronounce clearly all your words. Is the quality of your voice friendly and pleasant or is it shrill and offensive? These factors influence how your message is received. A good idea is worthless if you cannot present it well, so take all the time you need to get ready.

Skillbuilding

96 wpm

Building a career is a process. You have looked at all your interests, values, skills, talents, and feelings. Your look into the world of work has begun, but the journey does not stop here, for the present is the perfect place to start thinking about the future. It is where you start to take steps toward your goals. It is where you can really make a difference.

As you set personal and career goals, remember the importance of small steps. Each step toward a personal goal or a career goal is a small victory. The feeling of success encourages you to take other small steps. Each step builds onto the next. Continue analyzing your personal world as well as the world you share with others. Expect the best as you go forward. Expect a happy life, loving relationships, success in life, and fulfilling and satisfying work in a job that you really love. Last but not least, expect that you have something unique and special to offer the world, because you do.

Skillbuilding

Supplementary Timed Writings

All problem solving, whether or not it is personal or   11
academic, involves decision making. You make decisions in   23
order to solve problems. On occasion, a problem occurs as a   35
result of a decision you have made. For example, you may   46
decide to smoke, but later in life, you might then face the   58
problem of nicotine addiction. You may decide not to study   70
math and science because you think that they are difficult.   82

Because of this choice, some career options may be   93
closed to you. There is a consequence for each action. Do   108
you see that events in your life do not just happen, but   116
that they are the result of your choices and decisions?   127

How can you best prepare your mind to help you solve   138
problems? A positive attitude is a great start. Indeed,   149
your attitude will determine the way in which you may solve   161
a problem or make a decision. Approach your studies, such   173
as science and math courses, with a positive attitude. Try   185
to think of academic problems as puzzles to be solved and   195
not just as work to be avoided.   203

Critical thinking is a type of problem solving that   213
allows you to decode, analyze, reason, assess, and process   224
data. Since it is basic for all successful problem solving,   235
you should try to explore, probe, question, and search for   248
all the right answers.   253

A problem may not always be solved on the first try,   263
so do not give up. Try, try again. To find a solution may   275
take a real effort. Use your critical thinking skills to   286
achieve success in a world that is highly competitive and   298
demanding.   300

1 | 2 | 3 | 4 | 5 | 6 | 7 | 8 | 9 | 10 | 11 | 12

Skillbuilding

For many of us, the Internet is an important resource 11
in our private and public lives. The Internet provides us 23
with quick access to countless Web sites that may contain 34
news, products, games, and other types of data. The Web 45
pages on these sites can be designed, authored, and posted 57
by anyone from anywhere around the world, so you must use 69
critical thinking skills when reviewing these Web sites. 80

Just because something is said on the radio, printed 91
in the newspaper, or shown on television does not mean that 103
it is true. This applies to data found on the Internet as 115
well. Do not fall into the trap of believing that if it is 126
on the Net, it must be true. A wise user of the Internet 138
thinks critically about data found on the Net and evaluates 150
this material before he or she decides to use it. 160

When you assess a new Web site, think about who, what, 171
how, when, and where. Who refers to the author of the Web 183
site. The author may be a business firm, an organization, 194
or a person. What refers to the validity of the data. Can 206
this data be verified by a reputable source? 215

How refers to the viewpoint of the author. Are your 225
data presented without prejudice? When refers to the time 237
frame of your data. Do you have recent data? Where refers 249
to your data source. Are the data from a trusted source? 260

By answering these critical questions, you will learn 271
more about the accuracy and dependability of a Web site. 283
When you surf the Net next time, be quite cautious. Anyone 294
can publish on the Internet. 300

1 | 2 | 3 | 4 | 5 | 6 | 7 | 8 | 9 | 10 | 11 | 12

Skillbuilding

Most office workers perform a wide range of tasks in	11
their workday. These tasks may require them to handle phone	23
calls or forward personal messages, to send short e-mail	34
notes or compile complex office reports, or to write simple	46
letters or assemble detailed letters with tables, graphics,	58
and imported data. Office workers are thus a basic part of	70
the structure of the firm.	75
The office worker must use critical thinking in order	86
to carry out a wide array of daily tasks. Some of the tasks	98
are more urgent than other tasks and should be done first.	110
Some tasks take only a short time, while others take a lot	122
more time. Some tasks demand a quick response, while others	134
may be taken up as time permits or even postponed until the	146
future. Some of these tasks might require input from other	158
people.	159
Whether a job is simple or complex or big or small,	170
the office worker must decide what is to be done first by	182
setting the priority for each task.	189
When setting priorities, critical thinking skills are	200
essential. The office worker must assess each aspect of the	212
task. It is a good idea to identify the size of the task,	223
learn about its complexity, estimate the effort needed,	235
judge its importance, and set its deadline.	243
Once the office worker assesses a task that is to be	254
done within a certain span of time, then the priority for	266
completing all those tasks can be set. Critical thinking	277
skills, if applied well, can save the employer money, but	289
if they are applied poorly, they might cost an employer.	300

1 | 2 | 3 | 4 | 5 | 6 | 7 | 8 | 9 | 10 | 11 | 12

Skillbuilding

Supplementary Timed Writing 4

Each day business managers must make choices that keep 11
their firms running in a smooth, skillful, and gainful way. 23
Every decision needs to be quick and sure. 32

To make good decisions, all managers must use critical 43
thinking. They must gather all the needed facts so that 54
they can make sound, well-informed choices. Over time, they 66
can refine their skills. Then, when they face a similar 77
problem, they can use their knowledge to help them solve 89
new problems with ease and in less time. 97

What types of decisions do you think managers make 107
that involve critical thinking? Human resource managers 119
need to decide whom to hire, what to pay the new worker, 130
and where to place him or her. In addition, human resource 142
managers should be able to help resolve conflicts between 153
workers. 155

Office managers must purchase copy machines, software, 166
computers, and supplies. Top executives must make business 178
policies, appoint other managers, and assess the success of 190
the firm. Plant supervisors must set schedules, gauge work 202
quality, and assess workers. Sales managers must study all 214
of the new sales trends, as well as provide sales training. 226

Most managers use critical thinking to make wise and 237
well-thought-out decisions. They carefully check all the 248
facts, analyze these facts, and then make a final judgment 259
based upon these facts. They should also be able to clearly 271
discern fact from fiction. Through trial and error, most 283
managers learn their own ways to solve problems and find a 294
solution for their firms. 300

1 | 2 | 3 | 4 | 5 | 6 | 7 | 8 | 9 | 10 | 11 | 12

Skillbuilding

Supplementary Timed Writing 5

In most classes, teachers just want the students to 11
analyze situations, draw conclusions, and solve problems. 22
Each of these tasks requires students to use good thinking 34
skills. How do students acquire these skills? What process 46
do students follow to develop these skills? 55

During early years of life, children learn words and 65
then combine these words into sentences. From there, they 77
learn to declare ideas, share thoughts, and express their 89
feelings. Students learn numbers and math concepts. They 100
may learn to read musical notes, to keep rhythm, to sing 111
songs, and to recognize popular and classical pieces of 123
music. Students learn colors and shapes and start to draw. 134

During their early years, students learn the basic 145
models of problem solving. One way for students to solve 156
problems and apply thinking skills is to use the scientific 168
approach. This approach requires a student to state the 179
problem to be solved, collect the known facts about that 191
problem, analyze the problem, and pose viable solutions. 202
Throughout this process, teachers ask questions that force 214
students to expand their thinking skills. 222

Teachers may want to ask questions such as these: Did 233
you clearly state the problem? Did you get all the facts? 245
Did you get the facts from the right place? Did you assume 257
anything? Did you pose other possible answers? Did you keep 269
an open mind to all solutions? Did you let your bias come 280
into play? Did you take the time to listen to other people? 292
Finally, does the solution make sense? 300

1 | 2 | 3 | 4 | 5 | 6 | 7 | 8 | 9 | 10 | 11 | 12

Skillbuilding

Supplementary Timed Writing 6

A major goal for all instructors in school is to teach 11
critical thinking skills to their class. This skill is the 23
process of deciding in a logical way what we should do or 35
believe, and it also involves an ability to compare and 46
contrast, solve problems, make decisions, analyze results, 58
and combine and use knowledge. Can you see that these are 69
important skills you can use all your life? 78

These skills help the student who later becomes a part 89
of the workforce. Whether someone is in a small business, 101
is in a corporate setting, or is self-employed, the world 112
of today is a competitive one, and skilled employees are 124
always in demand. 127

One part of gaining success in the workforce is having 139
the skill to deal with the mixed demands of the fast-paced 150
business world. A few of the required skills are insightful 162
decision making, creative problem solving, and productive 174
contact among diverse groups. 180

In school, we learn the basics of critical thinking. 191
This skill extends far beyond the borders of the classroom 203
and lasts a lifetime. We use critical thinking in all of 214
our daily lives. We constantly analyze and assess pursuits 226
such as music, movies, speech, fashion, magazine articles, 238
and television shows. 242

We all had experience using critical thinking skills 253
well before we even knew what they were. So you should keep 265
on learning and growing. The classroom can be the perfect 276
place for your exploration, so use that time to learn how 288
others solve problems. There are always new goals to reach. 300

1 | 2 | 3 | 4 | 5 | 6 | 7 | 8 | 9 | 10 | 11 | 12

Skillbuilding

One of the first steps you should take to unlock your 11
creativity is to realize that you have control over your 22
mind; your mind does not control you. Creativity is just 34
using a new or different way to solve a problem. 44

Many of our inventions have involved breakthroughs in 55
traditional ways of thinking, and the result has often been 67
amazing. For example, Einstein broke with the old ways and 78
tried obscure formulas that have changed all scientific 90
thought. Your attitude can form a mental block that may 101
keep you from exercising creativity. When you free up your 113
mind, the rest will follow. 118

Do your best to unleash your mind's innate creativity 129
by turning problems into puzzles. When you think of the 140
task as a puzzle, a challenge, or a game instead of as a 152
difficult problem, you will open up your mind and free your 164
creative side to operate. Creative ideas come when you are 176
enjoying yourself and are involved in unrelated tasks. 187

Old habits often restrict you from trying new ways of 198
solving problems. There is often more than one solution, so 210
strive to see each situation in a fresh, new light. How 221
many times have you told yourself that you must follow the 233
rules and perform tasks only in a certain way? 242

If you want to be creative, then look at situations in 253
a new light, break the pattern, explore new opportunities, 265
and challenge old rules. If you are facing a hard problem 277
and cannot find an answer, take a quick walk or relax for a 289
few minutes; you can then go back to the problem renewed. 300

1 | 2 | 3 | 4 | 5 | 6 | 7 | 8 | 9 | 10 | 11 | 12

Skillbuilding

Keyboarding is a very popular business course that 10
most students take. The major goals of a keyboarding course 22
are to develop touch control of the keyboard, to use proper 34
typing techniques, to build basic speed and accuracy, and 46
to receive considerable practice in applying those basic 57
skills to format letters, reports, tables, memos, and other 69
kinds of personal and business documents. 78

In the first part of a keyboarding course, you must 88
learn to stroke the keys by touch, using proven techniques. 100
You learn to strike the keys in a quick and accurate way. 112
After the keys are learned, you then focus your attention 123
on producing documents of many sizes and types. 133

When you first learn to keyboard, there may be certain 144
steps, guidelines, and exercises that should be followed. 156
There are rules to help you learn and in due time to master 168
the keyboard. To create each document requires that you 179
apply critical thinking. What format or layout should be 190
used? What font and font size would be best? Are all the 202
words spelled correctly? Does the document look neat on the 214
page? Are the figures accurate? Are the punctuation and 225
grammar correct? 228

Being creative also has a lot to do with risk taking 239
and courage. It takes courage to explore new ways to think 251
and to risk looking different and even to risk being wrong. 263
Your path to creativity is such a vital component of your 274
critical thinking skills. Allow your creative thoughts to 286
flow freely when you produce each keyboarding task. Enjoy 298
the journey. 300

1 | 2 | 3 | 4 | 5 | 6 | 7 | 8 | 9 | 10 | 11 | 12

Skillbuilding

**Supplementary
Timed Writing 9**

More employees are injured using the computer keyboard 11
in the United States than using any other equipment in the 23
workplace. Therefore, you should find the most comfortable 35
and ergonomic position when you are keyboarding. 45

Your chair should be on rollers, be adjustable to fit 56
your individual height, and have substantial support for 67
your lower back. You should sit with your hips pushed as 78
far back in the chair as possible, and your thighs should 90
not touch the underside of the workstation. 99

Your monitor should be aligned with your keyboard and 110
centered opposite you. The display should be just slightly 122
below eye level and tilted away from you slightly. When you 134
sit back in the chair and hold your arm out horizontally, 145
your middle finger should touch the middle of the monitor. 157
That way you won't need to make excessive head movements to 169
see the viewing area of your screen. 176

A document holder should be positioned at the same 187
height and distance as the screen in order to minimize any 199
head movements and at the same angle as the screen. Place 210
the document holder to the side of the screen opposite the 222
mouse. Position the mouse at the identical height as the 233
keyboard, and you should move the mouse with your whole arm 245
and not just with your wrist. 251

There's no research to show that an ergonomic keyboard 263
is any more beneficial than the standard keyboard layout. 274
If your keyboard has pop-up legs, these should not be used 286
because a negative slope to the keyboard is by far the most 298
healthful. 300

1 | 2 | 3 | 4 | 5 | 6 | 7 | 8 | 9 | 10 | 11 | 12

Skillbuilding

One of the most important decisions we all have to face is choosing a career. Your options can appear to be a bit overwhelming at first. But you should not worry because your critical thinking skills will help.

Start with a self-assessment. What are your interests? Would you prefer to work inside or outdoors? Would you like to work with numbers or with words? Are you an independent type or would you rather work within a group? What are your preferred courses? Think about each of these questions, and then make a list of your interests, skills, aptitudes, and values. What you learn about yourself might help you find the career that is just right for you.

After you have explored your own interests, look at the sixteen career clusters for a wide range of possible jobs. Most jobs are included in one of these clusters that have been organized by the government. During your search, make a note of the clusters that interest you and look into all the clusters.

Get as much information as you can by making use of all available resources. Scan the employment section in the major Sunday newspapers for job descriptions and salaries. Search the Internet, which provides access to job listings around the world. If you want to evaluate closely a certain company, access its home page and look around.

Sign up for interviews with companies that visit your campus. Talk with people in your field of interest to ask questions and get advice. Taking the initiative in your job search will pay off.

1 | 2 | 3 | 4 | 5 | 6 | 7 | 8 | 9 | 10 | 11 | 12

Index

H

Half-page stationery, R-4B
Hanging indent, in report, R-10D
Heading(s)
 braced column, R-13A
 in report, R-8A–C, R-8C, R-9A, R-9D, R-10A, R-10C
 2-line, R-13B
Heading block, in tables, R-5, R-8B, R-13A–D
Holidays, capitalization of, R-21
Horizontal reaches, 267–268, 402–403
Hyperlinks, 361, 431
Hyphen (-)
 automatic, 243
 columns and, 294
 in compound adjectives, 256, R-17
 in compound numbers, R-17
 in U.S. telephone numbers, 336

I

IDD. *See* International Direct Dialing (IDD)
In-basket review
 banking documents, 479–481
 education documents, 483–485
 government documents, 491–492
 nursing facility documents, 486–489
 software development documents, 494–497
Indented display
 in business reports, 356
 in correspondence, R-3A
 in report, R-8B, R-8C
Independent clause, R-15
Information technology (IT) services, careers in, 323
In reaches, 267, 402
Inside address, in correspondence, R-3A
International address, 327, R-3D, R-5A
International Direct Dialing (IDD), 336
International formatting of addresses and dates
 Canada, 326–329
 China, 345–346
 France, 336–338
 Germany, 340–343
 Mexico, 331–334, 336–338
 URLs, 331–334
International telephone access codes, 336–337
Internet
 business information on, 247
 copy image or graphic from, 372
 e-mail (*See* E-mail)
 hyperlinks, 431

international URLs, 331
 transferring text from Web page, 393
 Yellow Pages on, 401
Interviewing techniques, 279
Introductory expression, R-15, R-18
Italics, for titles of published works, 243, 484, R-18. *See also* Underline
Italy, telephone dialing code, 337
Itinerary
 document processing, 278–279
 formatting, 277–278
 in report, 487–488, R-11C

J

Japan, telephone dialing code, 337
Journal article reference, R-9B
Judgment, 391, 410

K

Keyboard, computer, R-2A–B
Keyboarding Connection (feature)
 antivirus programs, 359
 copy image or graphic from Internet, 372
 e-mail
  management of, 427
  privacy, 453
  signature file, 266
 home page, choosing different, 435
 hyperlinks, 431
 netiquette, 290
 search
  for people, 329
  Yellow Pages, 401
 spam, 383
 teleconferencing for meetings, 346
 transferring text from Web page, 393
 Yellow Pages, searching, 401
Keys. *See* INDIVIDUAL KEYS (punctuation, functions, and symbols)

L

Labels, formatting, 474
Language arts
 abbreviations, 257, 353–354, R-22
 adjectives and adverbs, 415–416, R-20
 agreement, 257, 325–326, 415–416, R-19
 apostrophes ('), R-17
 capitalization, 460–461, R-21
 colons, 369–370, R-18